General Edwin
Vose Sumner, USA

D0905315

General Edwin Vose Sumner, USA

A Civil War Biography

THOMAS K. TATE

McFarland & Company, Inc., Publishers
Jefferson, North Carolina, and London

Library of Congress Cataloguing-in-Publication Data

Tate, Thomas K., 1936–
General Edwin Vose Sumner, USA : a Civil War biography /
Thomas K. Tate.
        p.   cm.
Includes bibliographical references and index.

ISBN 978-0-7864-7258-1
softcover : acid free paper

    1. Sumner, Edwin V. (Edwin Vose), 1797–1863.   2. Generals—
United States—Biography.   3. United States—History—Civil
War, 1861–1865.   I. Title.
E467.1.S96T38 2013
355.0092—dc23
[B]   2013026678

British Library cataloguing data are available

Front cover: Major General Edwin Vose Sumner, "Old Bull of the
Woods." Massachusetts Commandery Military Order of the Loyal
Legion and the U.S. Army Military History Institute; border and
bulls © 2013 Clipart.com

Manufactured in the United States of America

McFarland & Company, Inc., Publishers
  Box 611, Jefferson, North Carolina 28640
  www.mcfarlandpub.com

To my six grandchildren in the order of their births:
Emily, Jack, Graham, Christina, Hannah and Tyler,
the one most likely to follow in the footsteps and hoofprints
of General Edwin Vose Sumner.

Table of Contents

Acknowledgments

This biography rests on a foundation of research made possible by certain individuals and institutions. Many thanks are due to Ms. Barbara Hoffman and Ms. Lona Beitler of the library at Lehigh/Carbon Community College, Schnecksville, Pennsylvania. Ms. Hoffman provided many basic library services and Ms. Beitler handled interlibrary loan requests.

I want to thank the staffs of the following institutions for providing photocopies of their holdings on General Edwin V. Sumner and his family: the Milton Historical Society, Milton, Massachusetts; the Massachusetts Historical Society, Boston; the U.S. Army Military History Institute, Carlisle, Pennsylvania; the Kutztown University Library, Kutztown, Pennsylvania; and the Tennessee State Library and Archives, Nashville.

I particularly want to thank Mr. Graham T. Dozier at the Virginia Historical Society, Richmond, for making it possible to get photocopies of letters of James E.B. Stuart. I am indebted to Ms. Sarah Kozma of the Onondaga Historical Association, Syracuse, New York, for information on General Sumner particularly during the 1850s and 1860s. Two other individuals deserving thanks are retired colonel Robert J. Dalessandro and Mr. James A. Tobias of the U.S. Army Center of Military History, Fort McNair, Washington, D.C. Thanks also to Mr. W.C. Smith at the U.S. Army Heritage and Education Center, Carlisle, Pennsylvania. They provided material on the criteria for granting officer commissions to qualified civilians.

I am very appreciative of the map made by Ms. Julie Krick, Glen Allen, Virginia. Both her husband Robert E.L. Krick and her father-in-law Robert K. Krick were helpful in providing background information regarding locations on the Peninsula and men who served with General Sumner prior to the Civil War.

I want to acknowledge the conversation I had with retired professor

Charles P. Roland at Sarasota, Florida, in January 2012 concerning Albert Sidney Johnston. He was very gracious and free with his time.

Particularly deserving of my thanks is Dr. Michael P. Gabriel, professor of history, at Kutztown University. Professor Gabriel made some university facilities available to me and read parts of the manuscript, making valuable suggestions. He interrupted his work on his history of the Revolutionary War Battle of Bennington, Vermont, to be of assistance.

Undoubtedly this work would benefit from more maps. But I refer to a paragraph in Jennings Cropper Wise's *The Long Arm of Lee*. In concluding his preface Wise wrote, "The author is conscious of the fact that maps ... would add greatly to the value of the book, but it has been found impractical to include them." A road atlas can help the reader locate many of the sites mentioned.

Introduction

In the opening chapter of his eminent biography of Jefferson Davis, William C. Davis wrote, "Childhood is all too often the lost chapter of biography." Unless one is writing a biography of Mozart, the biographer will find few exciting and still fewer noteworthy accomplishments of his subject during his early years. While General Sumner's early years are covered in this biography it is not until Sumner's late teens that his life became eventful.

One of Abraham Lincoln's biographers quoted him as having written, "Biographies, as generally written, are not only misleading but false." Lincoln believed the biographer magnified his subject's perfections and minimized his shortcomings. Having been alerted by Lincoln's judgment I have tried to follow a course between these two extremes.

Following his death on March 21, 1863, Sumner was remembered and his qualities lauded. Writing of the battle of Chancellorsville, artillery captain Thomas W. Osborn remembered Sumner's successful tactics at Savage Station: "The tactics General Sumner adopted at Savage Station would have won this fight." After Gettysburg Osborn wrote that despite Sumner being excited to the last degree at Savage Station, "his command of troops on the field was perfect. With a smaller force that [John B.] Magruder commanded in that battle, he whipped him in an hour." In his battlefield report following Gettysburg General Winfield Scott Hancock, who had served under General Sumner before and during the Civil War wrote of the performance of his Second Corps of the Army of the Potomac, "This corps sustained its well-earned reputation on many fields, and ... the boast of its gallant first commander, the late Maj. Gen. E.V. Sumner, that the Second Corps had 'never given to the enemy a gun or color,' holds good now as it did under the command of my predecessor, Major-General Couch."[1]

On January 14, 1865, Colonel John V. Du Bois, inspector general, Department of the Missouri, wrote of Sumner as a worthy example of an officer: "I remember the good old days when such men as the late General Sumner, then colonel commanding a department, would attend nearly every roll and other call, visit every sentinel post, and bring every delinquent up for correction and punishment."[2] However, Sumner had his critics. Not everyone was as positive in his opinion of General Sumner as was Colonel Du Bois.

Francis W. Palfrey in his work *The Antietam and Fredericksburg* stated, "He seems to have possessed no judgment as a tactician." But historian Joseph L. Harsh found Palfrey's book, written before operational reports had been published, "shallow and frequently confused."[3]

Francis A. O'Reilly in his monumental work, *The Fredericksburg Campaign: Winter War on the Rappahannock*, wrote, "Sumner had limited mental capacity." Stephen W. Sears, author of *Landscape Turned Red: The Battle of Antietam*, stated, "Sumner was ... afflicted with the narrowest of military minds."

However, two Union generals whose mental capacities have never seriously been questioned by historians were George B. McClellan and Henry W. Halleck. During the Second Manassas Campaign, Halleck, at the end of a day when bad news from General John Pope was followed by worse news from General Pope, implored McClellan, "I beg you to assist me in this crisis with your ability and experience. I am utterly tired out." At one point he replied to a request from General John Pope, "Just think of the immense amount of telegraphing I have to do, and then say whether I can be expected to give you any details as to movements of others, even when I know them."[4]

For all of McClellan's intelligence, and it was impressive, he could never understand nor free his mind from his fixation that General Robert E. Lee's forces outnumbered his own. The poet James Russell Lowell accurately observed that one had to go back to Cervantes's *Don Quixote* to find a self-deception comparable to General McClellan's.[5]

Some criticism of General Sumner seems excessive if not mean-spirited. What real basis did Stephen Sears have for his claim, "At sixty-five Sumner was the oldest of the army's corps commanders, and any military imagination he once possessed had ossified after decades of frontier service in the old army"?[6] Sears was fond of McClellan's line from a letter to his wife after the battle of Williamsburg on the peninsula in 1862: "Sumner has proved he was even a greater fool than I supposed & had come within an ace of having us defeated."[7] This quote comes from a self-serving, boastful and highly inaccurate letter to his wife that only goes to prove the poet Lowell's remark as to McClellan's penchant for self-deception. Though the battle of Williamsburg may not have been well commanded by General Sumner, and McClellan's faults and failures do not excuse those of General Sumner, the battle was far from being "within an ace of having us defeated."

Colonel Charles S. Wainwright, an artillery officer, claimed to have learned some things from a conversation with General Philip Kearny that to Wainwright partially explained why Sumner did not reinforce General Joseph Hooker. This idea of a failure to support General Hooker was a commonly-held belief, particularly among the officers of the Third Corps. His explanation notwithstanding, still Wainwright did not want to serve under Sumner if his conduct at Williamsburg was an example of his generalship.[8]

In 1862, when nearly every officer was learning how to fight and command troops on the scale involved during the American Civil War, General Edwin V. Sumner commanded Union soldiers in three major Civil War campaigns, namely the Peninsula Campaign, the Maryland Campaign of 1862 (Antietam) and Fredericksburg. If he did not display great generalship, he displayed great personal courage and leadership, the kind that is inspirational to the men who served under him. Even Stephen Sears begrudgingly acknowledged his brave and timely crossing of the rain-swollen Chickahominy River to come to the aid of his comrades. Perhaps this is Sumner's best known and most heralded action. Sumner made a second though less well known decision resulting in saving lives when he convinced General Ambrose E. Burnside not to renew his planned attack at Fredericksburg after the Union repulse on December 13, 1862.[9]

Edwin V. Sumner's military career spanned the years from 1819 to 1863. During those years the U.S. Army changed, and Sumner was responsible for some of those changes. He established the Cavalry School of Practice at Carlisle Barracks, Pennsylvania, in the late 1830s. He was not a West Point graduate but that seemed not to have been a handicap. Although a soldier through and through in whom "Duty, Honor, Country" was as ingrained as in any academy graduate, Sumner was also a teacher, a diplomat and a peacekeeper. He could be abrasive and as such was unpopular during his tour in the Southwest during the early 1850s. But Sumner knew men and how to motivate them. He had a practical frame of mind and knew how to get things done. He was protective of his military prerogatives and impatient to the point of thwarting at times what he considered civilian interference.

By 1860, Sumner, the old dragoon, no longer took an active part in campaigning in the field and was in command of the Department of the West, headquartered in Saint Louis, Missouri. Although a Democrat he was an early supporter of President Abraham Lincoln and escorted Lincoln from Springfield, Illinois, to Washington, D.C. He was probably too old to have taken an active part in the Civil War, particularly after he suffered a fall when his horse stumbled in late 1861. However, his long years of service and the experiences he could draw from them seemed too valuable to be dispensed with by the Lincoln administration, which was coping with a war no one really knew how to organize and prepare for. Sumner was too old and too loyal to deny his president his total support.

By the end of the battle at Antietam and the Maryland Campaign, Sumner realized he should withdraw from field service and asked to command a military district. But with the selection of General Ambrose Burnside to replace General George B. McClellan as commander of the Army of the Potomac, Sumner was asked to stay on. Burnside, unsure of himself, needed the old general as someone he could trust and rely upon. Following the Union defeat at Fredericksburg in December 1862, Sumner asked to be relieved and got his wish. He was once again to go to Saint Louis and command the Department of the West. He died while on leave and on his way to his new post.

I have drawn heavily upon letters, reports and statements of those who knew him to show Sumner's character, personality, attitudes and positions on the questions of his day as well as his approach to the challenges that faced him. Many of his fellow soldiers occupy space in his biography. Winfield Scott, Robert E. Lee, Stephen Watts Kearny, Phil Kearny, Philip St. George Cooke, Albert Sidney Johnston, Joseph E. Johnston and John Sedgwick were all Sumner's contemporaries and, at least until the Civil War, his friends. He also soldiered with Winfield Scott Hancock, Richard S. Ewell, Samuel D. Sturgis, James E.B. Stuart, Ambrose E. Burnside and certainly George B. McClellan. Sumner however was frequently at odds with General William S. Harney. Personally, his greatest sorrow, other than the deaths of several of his children, may have been his separation from two of his daughters who married men who served the Confederacy.

While two biographies of General Sumner have been written, they were printed privately and are not widely available. He deserves a new biography. I have been able to draw upon some sources either overlooked or unavailable to General Sumner's earlier biographers. I have been fortunate in being able to draw upon contemporary newspaper stories reporting on the general's activities and to correct some accounts that were printed in error. This biography strives to show Edwin V. Sumner from his boyhood to his deathbed.

The battle of Antietam was the last battle in which General Sumner took an active part on the field and was exposed to shot and shell. His conduct on the field has been the source of much of the criticism leveled at him. Because of this, Antietam and the 1862 Maryland Campaign receives much attention in this biography. At Antietam both General Sumner and his long-time friend but now antagonist General Robert E. Lee had sons they had to order into harm's way. As fathers they may have shared this common anguish.

No matter how one may judge Sumner's generalship at Antietam, no one can deny that he was physically vigorous and active on that day of September 17, 1862. One may then justifiably question the accuracy of Colonel Charles S. Wainwright's observation made on August 12, 1862: "General Sumner is said to be very feeble, and failing fast; he has never got over the severe fall from his horse he had last winter."[10]

To take the true measure of a man, his conduct through life, his growth, his maturing, and his relations with others need to be taken into account. General Edwin V. Sumner's life and legacy as well as his personal courage, loyalty, fidelity to the service, concern for the men who served under him and general appreciation of fair play assure him his proper place in the ranks of the military pantheon.

1

The Road Not Taken

"God help my country, the United States of America." With his last spoken words General Edwin Vose Sumner fell back onto his bed and died, on March 21, 1863. Evidence for his dying words is confirmed in an unusual source. Confederate Major General James Ewell Brown Stuart, writing to his wife on Good Friday, 1863, included in his letter: "Gen'l Sumner died the other day in Syracuse N.Y. after illness from cold. He rose up in bed exclaimed 'God help my country the United States of America' & fell back dead. Col [Armistead Lindsay] Long received these particulars from the family by flag of truce." Colonel Long had been General Sumner's aide and was one of two sons-in-law to serve the Confederacy.[1]

Perhaps Stuart felt some sympathy for the old general under whom he had served on the plains in the 1850s. Both Sumner and his old comrade-in-arms, Philip St. George Cooke, Stuart's own father-in-law, knew the bitter pangs of families separated by conflicting loyalties. While Stuart and his wife Flora never forgave Cooke, a Virginian, for remaining with the Union, Stuart may not have harbored such resentment for Sumner, who was of Massachusetts birth and a resident of New York State.

The announcement that came through the lines under a flag of truce reached Colonel Long with less trouble than his wife had when she tried to return home after traveling north to attend her father's funeral. Mrs. Long made no attempt to hide her Confederate sympathies. Mary Heron Sumner Long needed the express permission of the Federal secretary of war to return to her home in the South. She was reported to have been "open-mouthed and shameless (even to the disgust of her own family) in proclaiming secession doctrines." Mrs. Long made purchases in the amount of two thousand dollars to take back to Richmond with her "and probably will bear dispatches to the South from Northern traitors."[2]

Armistead Lindsay Long ranked 17th in the West Point class of 1850, and served in the Second and Third U.S. Artillery. He resigned from Federal service on June 10, 1861. Long met General Robert E. Lee shortly after First Manassas, July 1861. Lee invited Long to be his military secretary on April 19, 1862.[3]

Mrs. Long missed the funeral. The *Syracuse Journal* reported in its Monday, April 6, 1863, edition that Mrs. Long, daughter of the late Gen. Sumner, and wife of Col. Long of the rebel army, reached this city from the South, on Saturday evening. That would have been April 4. The *Journal* in its March 26 edition printed a column reporting on General Sumner's funeral the day before.

The two Sumner sisters who married Confederate officers were Mary Heron Sumner, Mrs. Armistead L. Long, and her older sister, Margaret Foster Sumner, Mrs. Eugene E. McLean. Mary Chestnut wrote diary entries concerning the two sisters. Of Mrs. McLean, eleven years older than her sister Mary, Mrs. Chestnut wrote that she was a clever woman. She visited Mrs. Chestnut bringing along her nephew, her sister Mary's baby. Mrs. Chestnut said of Mrs. Long, referring to a comment made by William Porcher Miles, that Mrs. Long was fascinating and a new beauty. Miles, a known flirt, had been a U.S. congressman from South Carolina between the years of 1857 and 1860. He was a former professor of mathematics at the College of Charleston and had been the mayor of that city. Miles served as an aide to General P.G.T. Beauregard early in the war. There is evidence in Mary Chestnut's diary that Mrs. Hannah Sumner, Mrs. Long's mother, received some letters from her daughter during the war years.[4]

At the time of General Sumner's death the *Syracuse Journal* on March 30, 1863, printed an account of the general's attitude towards his daughter, Mrs. Long. She had written to her mother requesting some small items and some children's shoes. Sumner refused his daughter's request, not wanting to encourage contraband trade.

It is unknown how many of the Massachusetts Sumners followed the motto on the family coat of arms, *In medio tutissimus ibis* (You will be safest in the middle course). However, Edwin Vose Sumner, frequently under orders and more concerned with carrying them out than with safety, often took an alternate path. In 1819, at the age of twenty-two, he abandoned the safer career of a merchant to become an officer in the United States Army. Neither was it the safest course for Mrs. Long to come north to be with her family following her father's death.

Ordered by Union general George B. McClellan to be ready to move at a moment's notice, General Edwin V. Sumner, at sixty-five the oldest general in the Army of the Potomac, advanced the two divisions of his Second Corps to the bridges they built over the rain-swollen Chickahominy River on the Virginia Peninsula, formed by the York and the James rivers.[5]

According to Colonel Wesley Brainerd of the 50th New York Volunteer Engineers, who entertained himself on the peninsula by shooting black snakes out of the trees with his revolver, the bridges were built in a rude and unsubstantial manner. One of them was sometimes called "the Grapevine Bridge," Brainerd related, because it bore a resemblance to a grape vine in the crooked, winding way it crossed the Chickahominy. General Sumner put the men of the First Minnesota Regiment under division commander General Israel B. Richardson to work building the lower bridge while men of the Fifth New Hampshire Regiment in General John Sedgwick's division worked to build the upper or Grapevine Bridge about a mile and a half upstream.[6]

At 2:30 on the afternoon of May 31, 1862, Sumner received McClellan's order to cross the Chickahominy and come to the aid of the Fourth Corps. To the warnings of his engineers not to cross on the reputedly dangerously frail, sagging, swaying, partially submerged bridge of logs lashed together with ropes, General Sumner paid no heed. Brigade Commander General Oliver O. Howard, although part of General Richardson's division, was re-routed to cross on the Grapevine Bridge and overheard the exchange between General Sumner and his engineers. Howard recorded the scene. When General Sumner along with General John Sedgwick came up to the Grapevine Bridge it rose and began to float with the current. General Howard could see great cracks and separations between the logs. An engineer officer met General Sumner and strongly recommended he not cross.

"General Sumner, you cannot cross this bridge!" the officer was quoted as saying.

"Can't cross this bridge! I can sir; I will, sir!"

"Don't you see the approaches are breaking up and the logs displaced? It is impossible!"

"Impossible! Sir, I tell you I can cross. I am ordered."

The orders had come and that ended the matter with Sumner.[7]

To a man like General Sumner, who had led 270 dragoons against 4,000 lancers during the Mexican War, twice crossed the quicksand bottom of the South Platte River with his column, and charged an array of Cheyenne Indians with sabers, a swollen Virginia river and a rickety bridge of logs were no deterrent. Yet this bold river crossing may be the thing for which General Sumner is most remembered. Upon his death the artillerist Colonel Charles S. Wainwright, often a critic of Sumner, wrote:

> But the old soldier was as honest as the day, and as simple as a child. The fault was not so much his, as of those who put him and kept him in such a place, while the glorious way in which he pushed across the half-gone bridges to the relief of [General Erasmus] Keyes at Fair Oaks suffices to cover all his faults. He was one of those whom every one must hate to find fault with; yet whose removal from command of a corps was generally looked on as a relief.[8]

Edwin Vose Sumner, the fifth child of merchant Elisha Sumner and his wife Nancy, née Vose, first saw the light of a wintry Boston day on January 30, 1797. His paternal ancestors went back to William and Mary Sumner, who having come from Dorchester, England, settled in Dorchester, Massachusetts, in 1636. Edwin was a second cousin to future senator Charles Sumner. Charles Sumner's great-grandfather was the half-brother of Seth Sumner, Edwin Sumner's grandfather. The distance between the two was increased by Charles' father being the illegitimate son of Major Job Sumner and Esther Holmes. Major Sumner fought along with George Washington in the American Revolution. Edwin's maternal grandfather, Joseph Vose, (1738–1815) was a Continental Army officer who fought in the Revolution from May 1775 until the war's conclusion. He joined Washington's army and took part in the battles of the Monmouth Campaign in 1778. His name heads the list on a bronze tablet to the First Massachusetts Infantry at Valley Forge Park. That regiment was part of Brigadier General John Glover's command. Vose commanded a battalion of Massachusetts companies in General John Peter Gabriel Muhlenburg's brigade in Lafayette's division. Vose served with his brothers Lieutenant Bill Vose and Captain Elijah Vose.[9]

Although born in Boston, where his father was engaged in the mercantile trade, Edwin grew up in Milton, Massachusetts, the family returning to Milton where Edwin's parents were born. Accounts differ as to the date of the return, either 1800 or 1803. The latter seems more reliable. Edwin grew up among his five sisters— Betsy, Nancy, Margaret, Eleanor and Mary. He had one brother, Nathaniel Robbins Sumner. Edwin studied under the Reverend Dr. Richmond and later at Billerica and Milton academies. He also studied at the West School in Milton. Milton Academy began in 1808, and young Edwin Sumner was one of its first thirty-five students. His grandfather, Seth Sumner, was a trustee. The purpose of Milton Academy was to prepare young men for college, Harvard in particular. Edwin studied English and Latin grammar, literature, arithmetic, astronomy, navigation, surveying, natural law and rhetoric. Milton Academy took pride in having a part in the education of men such as "Colonel Paul Revere and General Sumner, of Civil War fame." Other scholars educated there were historian and theologian John Gorham Palfrey, William Parsons Lunt, whom Henry Adams considered the best speaker he had ever heard, and Professor Samuel Langley, "who solved the mathematics of flight." Sometime after Sumner's death Milton Academy board president James M. Robbins eulogized Sumner's "death in battle." We hope Mr. Robbins was better acquainted with Sumner's academic record than he was with the nature of his death. Somewhere in his studies Edwin Sumner must have learned French, as later in his military career he spent the better part of a year in France studying and observing French military operations.[10]

On January 19, 1807, a little more than a week before Edwin Sumner turned ten and when he was not yet at a scholar at Milton Academy, a boy was born in tidewater Virginia who would come in contact with Sumner many times during Sumner's life. He was Robert Edward Lee.

Following his schooling Edwin began as a merchant in Troy, New York. The date of his entering into business may have been 1816 at the age of nineteen. That year his parents moved from Milton to a farm in Rutland, Massachusetts, where they lived the rest of their lives. Elisha Sumner died on April 1, 1839; his wife Nancy on March 6, 1848.

Edwin entered the business firm of Storrow and Brown. Thomas Wentworth Storrow was a successful merchant who resided temporarily in Montreal and established his business there, before expanding to Troy, New York. It was very likely Samuel Appleton Storrow interceded with General Jacob Brown to secure a second lieutenancy for Edwin in 1819. Samuel A. Storrow, for whom Edwin Sumner and his wife would name their youngest surviving son, was judge advocate of the army in 1816 and resigned on February 5, 1820.[11]

Two of General Jacob Brown's brothers, John and Samuel, were engaged in business; Samuel took over the family store in 1813 when his father died. Having been quartermaster under his older brother during the War of 1812, Samuel would likely have been chosen for that job based upon his merchant's background. In August 1819, the year Edwin Sumner entered the army, Samuel Brown was arrested over a dispute with the government involving between ten and fifteen thousand dollars in connection with the building of Madison Barracks at Sackets Harbor, New York. John Brown, the other brother involved in business, was reported to have been a poor manager.[12]

A story, most likely untrue, was published in the *Springfield* (Massachusetts) *Republican* and carried in the *Syracuse Daily Journal*, the official paper of the city, its masthead declared. In his youth, the newspaper reported, Sumner drove a stage coach. It overturned on an icy road in the Berkshire hills in western Massachusetts but Sumner, the driver, managed to bring the upset coach to a safe stop. One passenger on board was reputed to have been William J. Worth, an army officer to receive fame as a general in the Mexican War. It was Worth, supposedly, who encouraged Sumner to join the army. This story was contradicted by a short piece carried in the *Syracuse Journal* (not to be confused with the *Syracuse Daily Journal*) on April 6, 1863.

More likely Sumner's own inclination for a military career was hastened by his business setback as a merchant. A business failure was often looked upon by the public, particularly in Massachusetts where Sumner still had family, as a disgrace. Charles Russell Lowell Sr.'s business failure in the panic of 1837 is a tragic example of the humiliation and shame brought on by such a failure. The Lowell family was deeply affected by this business failure.[13]

Edwin Sumner's decision to enter the army in March 1819 may also have been based upon a bad business climate resulting from the Panic of 1819. The causes of the panic were to be found far from our shores. For one, European agriculture, disrupted by the Napoleonic Wars, was recovering, thus reducing the demand in Europe for American foodstuffs. Revolutions in Latin America cut off the supply of precious metals, the base of the international money supply. In the depression that followed hundreds of thousands lost their jobs. In Philadelphia, for instance, unemployment reached 75 percent. One man, commenting on what he had witnessed, wrote that he had seen upwards of 1,500 men looking for work who had been unemployed for nearly a year. Wages, for those fortunate enough to find work, were as low as nineteen cents a day.[14]

There is some evidence that Edwin Sumner was in business in Watertown, New York, before entering the army. The following notice appeared in the Albany, New York, *Argus* on June 18, 1819: "By order of Abel Cole, Esq. first judge of the court of common pleas in and for the county of Jefferson, notice is hereby given to all the creditors of Edwin V. Sumner, in his individual capacity, and as a member of the firm of the firm of E.V. Sumner, & Co. of the town of Watertown, in said county, an insolvent debtor...."

It was not at all uncommon for a young man, especially with connections, to be appointed into the U.S. Army as an officer. According to correspondence with a W.C. Smith at the U.S. Army Heritage and Education Center, Carlisle, Pennsylvania, it was "reasonably feasible for Sumner to enter service directly as a 2d LT." Any combination of such things as level of schooling, business experience, social standing, net worth, and who you knew could lead to a direct commission. Then, too, Sumner knew of his ancestors' military service and may have wanted to continue in that line. Writing in 1833 to his cousin Charles P. Sumner, the father of Charles Sumner, the future senator from Massachusetts, Edwin V. Sumner wrote, "For you know I inherited my propensity for the saddle from our ancestory [sic]."[15]

Sumner may have received his appointment at the ideal time, before 1821. From that date and for the next decade, almost all appointments went to West Point graduates. Just as the army's organization improved under Secretary of War John C. Calhoun, the academy improved under Captain Sylvanus Thayer. Yet not all regular army officers embraced Thayer's system of military education. The great victories of history were not achieved by rule and compass or the measurement of angles, according to Inspector John E. Wool, but by highly cultivated and enlarged minds constantly surveying human events.[16]

The army at the time Sumner entered was in a state of flux that had begun at the close of the War of 1812. That war established the need for a permanent national force that few men would question. However, governmental support for a strong military establishment was short lived. The absence of a viable foreign threat, an economic slump in 1819, plus congressional antimilitarism led to a reduction in 1821 from a force of about 12,000 officers and men to a number of about 6,000.

At the end of the War of 1812, the army's support services were an uncoordinated jumble of offices with no systematic procedures. Neither the Quartermaster Department nor the Medical Department had a central headquarters. These were the problems John C. Calhoun undertook to correct as secretary of war when young Edwin Sumner entered the service.[17]

During the eight years Calhoun held the cabinet position of secretary of war (1817–1825) under President James Monroe, he presided over the reorganization of the army and introduced practices that remained until the early twentieth century. Under pressure from Congress to cut military expenses, Calhoun proposed his idea of an "expansible" army. Major General Jacob J. Brown contributed to the details of this plan. The idea was to retain most of the officers so they could maintain their professional skills and prepare for future wars. In other words they would be a cadre. In time of war privates would be enrolled and quickly trained by the officer corps. Calhoun's plan had support in the Senate but not in the House; Congress rejected the plan. Congress passed a bill that reduced the number of officers from 674 to 540 and the number of enlisted men from 11,709 to 5,586.[18]

Although mostly remembered as a dragoon and cavalry officer, Sumner began his army career in the Second Infantry Regiment at Sackets Harbor, New York. The Second can trace its lineage to 1808. In 1815, it was consolidated with the 16th, 22nd, 23rd and 32nd Infantry. During the War of 1812, it fought in Canada, at the Chippewa, at Lundy's Lane and in the South. In 1814, it was in Florida with Andrew Jackson as part of the Seventh Military District. In 1818, a year before Sumner's assignment to the regiment, the Second Infantry was at Sackets Harbor building Madison Barracks and constructing military roads.[19]

Sackets Harbor had been a fairly bustling community from at least as early as 1807. Farmers in that region looked north for trading partners as there was no easy way to reach markets to their south. Shipping their goods from Sackets Harbor on the eastern shore of Lake Ontario and then into the Saint Lawrence River gave them good access to Montreal. Among the major items of trade was potash the farmers harvested from burning trees after clearing fields for planting. Potash, used for fertilizer, bleaching, and making soap as well as potassium nitrate for gunpowder, brought from $250 to $350 a ton in Montreal.

The Jefferson administration, tired of Britain and France meddling with American trade, enforced the Embargo Act on February 27, 1808. The locals around Sackets Harbor turned to smuggling. During the War of 1812, Sackets Harbor became a major naval base under Captain Isaac Chauncey, former commander of the Brooklyn Navy Yard. Forty ship's carpenters went to Sackets Harbor to construct a fleet of ships. The first ship built, the *Madison,* under direction of Henry Eckford, launched in late November 1812. Nine weeks earlier her timbers had been trees growing in the forest. Secretary of War John Armstrong took the War Department to Sackets Harbor in 1813, to supervise an offensive against Montreal.[20]

Sumner began his service at Madison Barracks at Sackets Harbor in May 1819. On March 31, 1822, he married seventeen-year-old Hannah Wickersham Forster from Erie, Pennsylvania, the daughter of an army officer. They were married in the Presbyterian Church by the Reverend S.S. Snowden. Facts about Mrs. Sumner were reported in her obituary. She was born in Erie, Pennsylvania, on January 31, 1805. Her parents were Thomas Forster and Sarah Petit Montgomery. Thomas Forster was in the American Revolution and served as a colonel during the Whiskey Rebellion of 1794. He was a judge in Dauphin County, Pennsylvania, for five years thereafter. Forster was involved in state affairs and was collector for the port of Erie during the administrations of Thomas Jefferson, James Madison, John Q. Adams and Andrew Jackson. Hannah Sumner's obituary went on to say that she had accompanied her husband to all military posts from the time of her marriage until 1851. She was familiar with military rules and regulations.[21]

Sumner became a first lieutenant in the Second Infantry on January 25, 1823, and served as acting adjutant from January through March of that year. In April 1823, two months after their first child, Nancy, was born, Sumner was transferred to Cantonment Barracks, Sault Ste. Marie, Michigan. There he served as recruiting officer and adjutant until April 1825.

The Sumners' second daughter, Elizabeth Heron Sumner, was born at Sault Ste. Marie on September 30, 1824, but died a year later. From December 1826 through January 1827, Sumner was on recruiting duty in Boston. Then in 1828, he served at Fort Mackinac, Michigan. The couple's third child, Margaret Forster Sumner, was born at Fort Mackinac on June 30, 1828. Next the Sumners came back to Sackets Harbor, where two more children were born. Their first son, Edwin Vose Sumner, was born on July 30, 1830, but died the following September. A fourth daughter, Sarah Montgomery Sumner, was born December 15, 1831.[22]

It would seem very likely that Margaret's middle name would be Forster, her mother's middle name as Sumner's biographer William W. Long recorded on page 5 of his biography. Yet in William Sumner Appleton's book, *Record of the Descendants of William Sumner of Dorchester, Mass., 1636,* Margaret's middle name is spelled Foster. Edwin and Hannah Sumner's family was growing.

2

The Black Hawk War
and Captain of Dragoons

By 1832, the start of the Black Hawk War, First Lieutenant Edwin Sumner had been in the army thirteen years and had served in a variety of locations. Five of his children were born in these far-flung military posts. Sumner's service in the Black Hawk War launched his career by introducing him to several prominent men in the U.S. Army.

T. Harry Williams in his book *The History of American Wars from 1745 to 1918* wrote a succinct account of the sad, bloody and tragic Black Hawk War. The war took its name from the Sac Indian leader Black Hawk. With some justification Black Hawk believed the ceding of Indian lands in what is today Illinois was illegal, and he fought to get them back. Unfortunately for the Indians, Sacs and Foxes mainly, "they were few in numbers and chose to operate in a white-settled area.... Their cause was hopeless, and in the end they were crushed bloodily."[1] The war revealed the deficiencies of the militia system — civilian soldiers unwilling to submit to necessary discipline and led by political officers. Militia from Illinois would not pursue the enemy beyond their state's borders.[2]

Sumner served as one of Colonel Zachary Taylor's four hundred regulars. He most likely was with Taylor at the Battle of the Bad Axe in present day Wisconsin. General Winfield Scott appointed Sumner commissary for the regulars. During this time Sumner closely observed officers such as Henry Atkinson, Zachary Taylor and Winfield Scott. It was during this time that he met Major William S. Harney. Atkinson's influence got Sumner thinking about the dragoons, and he spent his spare time studying cavalry tactics. Sumner began considering cavalry as an independent force. Dragoons up to this time were really mounted infantry.[3]

Captain of Dragoons

By January 1833, Sumner was stationed at Fort Niagara on Lake Ontario outside Youngstown, New York. Seeking to become an officer in what would become the First Dragoons, Sumner wrote on January 11, 1833, to his cousin Charles Pinckney Sumner in Boston, asking for help. There must have been some reserve between the two cousins as Sumner began his letter with "My dear sir." At this time Charles P. Sumner was the sheriff of Suffolk County, Massachusetts, which contained Boston, having been appointed in 1826 by Governor Levi Lincoln. This appointment paid $2,000 a year, about twice what he had made as a lawyer of possibly modest talent, and allowed him to send his son Charles, the future senator from the state, to Harvard.[4] Edwin Sumner reminded his cousin, in case he had not paid much attention to such matters, that there was a bill before Congress to convert the Corps of Rangers into a "Regular Regiment of Horse." Lieutenant Edwin Sumner desperately wished to become Captain Edwin Sumner in this new regiment. He asked his cousin if he would use his influence with members of Congress from Massachusetts in his behalf. Edwin had his hopes that no less a person than Daniel Webster would put in a word for him.

Sumner concluded his letter by asking his cousin what he thought about the Nullifiers in South Carolina. Sumner believed their actions would cause controversy between North and South: "We are ready at this post to move instantly, but we hope and trust that the difficulty will be quietly and happily adjusted without our intervention." Sumner ended his letter by sending along the regards of his wife and sisters.[5]

The series of letters Edwin Sumner wrote to his cousin Charles that are held in the Massachusetts Historical Society span the years 1833 to 1838. In addition to helping place Sumner at various locations during the 1830s, they provide a glimpse into the affairs of the Sumner family and reveal some of Edwin's attitudes and opinions.

The main reason for the correspondence between the two cousins was to transfer money, about twenty dollars annually, to pay Edwin's father's note. From Fort Des Moines, upper Mississippi (near present-day Des Moines, Iowa), Sumner sent a letter to his cousin Charles dated April 2, 1836. Again the salutation was "My dear sir." Another year had passed, Sumner noted to his cousin, and it was time again to pay the sum required on his father's note. Edwin Sumner's letters to his cousin between 1833 and 1836 evidently have not survived. Thinking his request might be a burden to his cousin, Sumner asked if his cousin's son, Charles, could handle this business. "I believe he knows me well enough to feel assured that it will give me pleasure to reciprocate the favor, whenever I have it in my power," Sumner wrote.[6]

This letter makes it clear that General Edwin Sumner and Senator Charles

Sumner were second cousins. The item reported in the *Syracuse Standard* of June 5, 1856, was incorrect. The paper made the claim, "Col Sumner, of the United States Army is not a cousin of Senator Sumner, as stated in several letters from Washington. Col Sumner is a native of Massachusetts and was formerly a merchant in Montreal. Senator Sumner is a son of the late Charles P. Sumner, for many years High Sheriff of Suffolk county [*sic*], Mass."

Edwin Sumner went on to write that he expected to make a long march that summer up the west bank of the Mississippi River to the northern boundary and go cross-country to the Missouri River, then return home. The expedition was to take about four months. The object in making the march, Sumner explained, was "to display our power among the Indian tribes, and thereby keep them quiet, without being obliged to shed blood. It is a humane policy on the part of the Govnt, and ought to have commenced much earlier."

He went on to state that Colonel Henry Dodge of his regiment would be appointed governor of the Wisconsin Territory, creating an opportunity for Sumner to be promoted to major. As a major, he reported, he would be the second member of the family in that grade. In closing Sumner wrote that his wife and children were well and joined him in sending their regards to Charles Sumner and his family. The family included Charles and his brothers Albert, George, Henry and Horace. George, but to a lesser extent than his brother Charles, was a friend and correspondent of Henry W. Longfellow. George spent many years abroad, returning in 1852, after an absence of fourteen years. Horace met his untimely death by drowning off the coast of Fire Island, New York, on July 19, 1850. As the boat that brought him home from Italy floundered in the surf he watched two sailors make it to shore. Young Horace, about twenty-four, threw a plank into the water, jumped in and clung to it. He sank immediately. He did not heed the Sumner motto. Accompanying him to their deaths were the American poet Margaret Fuller Ossoli, her husband and son.[7]

The three years between the dates of Sumner's two letters quoted above were eventful for Sumner. How much good his cousin Charles P. Sumner was in securing his promotion is unknown. However, his commanding officer, Lieutenant Colonel Alexander Cummings, recommended his promotion to captain in the newly-formed First Dragoons. Cummings transferred from the Seventh Infantry to the Second Infantry and served as lieutenant-colonel from August 20, 1828, to December 1, 1839, when he became colonel of the Fourth Infantry.[8]

The First Dragoons grew out of the Mounted Rangers, a six-company unit with a total strength of 685 officers and men. The term troop was not used at this time; it had been dropped and was not reintroduced until after the Civil War. In 1833, Congress increased this mounted unit to a regiment, the First Dragoons. Henry Dodge was promoted to colonel of the First Dragoons with Stephen Watts Kearny as lieutenant colonel and Richard B. Mason as major. Edwin Sumner was made captain of B Company and the captains of ranger companies retained their former commands. Transferred from the Mounted Rangers were lieutenants Jefferson Davis, future president of the Confederacy, and Philip St. George Cooke, destined to become the grand old man of the U.S. Cavalry.

The companies were mounted on horses of the same color — white, black, sorrel, gray, etc. — within the company. This was so the companies could be easier identified in combat. They were armed with a smooth-bore, .64-caliber carbine using the percussion ignition system. The carbine, made by Simeon North of Middletown, Connecticut, was forty-five inches in length and weighed eight pounds four ounces with a rod bayonet, a part of the arm. The mechanism of the carbine was that of the U.S. Rifle Model 1819, Hall, thus the official name "Hall-North." It did, however, use the percussion ignition system. The cone or nipple was set into the top of the breech-block, off center to the right. These percussion arms — the first obtained for U.S. military — came ahead of the adoption of the percussion system by the U.S. Ordnance Department. The cost from the manufacturer was $20.00 each.[9]

Sumner as we have seen was at Fort Niagara, New York, when he received his promotion to captain in the First Dragoons. He began recruiting for his company in New York. In April of 1833, he was in Canandaigua; Watertown in May and Utica in June.

By July 29, 1833, Sumner had seventy-eight men recruited for his Company B, when they left Sackets Harbor for Buffalo, New York. On August 3 the local paper reported that the recruits Sumner had selected were not over twenty-five years of age, about five feet eight inches in height and had a good English education and correct habits. They would earn eight dollars per month. The trip from Sackets Harbor to Jefferson Barracks outside St. Louis, Missouri, took forty days. When they arrived on September 6, 1833, Sumner had picked up a few more recruits along the way. The number climbed to eighty-six. Recruit James Hildreth wrote this of Sumner: "Perhaps no other man in the army could assume the stern dignity of a commander, with a better grace than Captain Sumner." Hildreth wrote the book *Dragoon Campaigns to the Rocky Mountains*, published by Wiley and Long, New York, 1836. Jefferson Barracks became the headquarters for the First Dragoons.[10]

Under Lieutenant Colonel Kearny, companies B, H and I, commanded by Sumner, Nathan Boone (son of Daniel Boone), and Jesse B. Browne, respectively, established Fort Des Moines, Iowa. Sumner got a four-month leave of absence. He was in Harrisburg, Pennsylvania, from December 1834, working to recruit men in Pennsylvania. He traveled to Massachusetts but was back in Harrisburg by January 1835. Later that month Sumner asked permission to use Carlisle Barracks as a recruiting depot because Kearny wanted to bring the regiment up to strength. The improvements he wanted to make for Carlisle, having been denied by the War Department Sumner asked to be relieved from recruiting duty in April and then again in June of 1835.

In late March 1835, Captain Sumner conducted a company of eighty dragoons from Carlisle Barracks to Harrisburg, Pennsylvania, the first step in their journey to St. Louis via Pittsburgh, Pennsylvania. They were to serve in the far west. This was the first company of dragoons ever recruited in Pennsylvania, the *Harrisburg Chronicle* reported; the article claimed Captain Sumner deserved much credit for his men.[11]

While at Carlisle the Sumners' second son and first to reach manhood was born, on August 16, 1835. He too was named Edwin Vose, as his deceased brother had been. Edwin junior would pursue a military career.[12]

By January 1836, Sumner was back at Fort Des Moines. To calm Indian troubles, Sumner and a squadron of horse received orders to visit the Potawatomie, Menominee and Winnebago indians in Illinois and Wisconsin. Indian trouble was also reported in the Green Bay area. Sumner was even-handed with the Indians; he listened to their complaints. Sumner noted that the whites were starving the Indians by rushing into the country and killing the game.

When Colonel Henry Dodge became Wisconsin territorial governor, as Sumner mentioned in his 1836 letter to his cousin Charles P. Sumner, Lieutenant Colonel Stephen W. Kearny succeeded to the command of the First Dragoons in July 1836. Sumner left with Company B for Fort Leavenworth, Kansas, where Kearny relocated his headquarters. From March 26, 1837, to April 26, 1837, Sumner was in temporary command at Fort Leavenworth. Sumner demonstrated his fair dealings with the Indians when he freed five Osage Indian women from a militia detachment. The women had been "married" to Frenchmen for some fifteen to twenty years.[13]

3

Carlisle Barracks

In a letter from Washington, D.C., written to his cousin Charles P. Sumner on May 13, 1838, Edwin's main point once again was the annual payment on his father's note. Edwin sent his cousin twenty dollars plus the dividend he earned from the Bank of Utica. He went on to say that he had arrived in this city a few days before, having arrived from the West. His family, all well, was in Harrisburg, Pennsylvania, the home of Mrs. Sumner's parents. Sumner's business in Washington, which he "accomplished fully," was to establish a "cavalry school of practice" at Carlisle, Pennsylvania. The secretary of war had a deep interest in the idea and assigned Sumner the command of the school. "It will be a very arduous duty," Sumner wrote, "but I am willing to take it, and I am resolved that this school shall equal his expectations." Sumner was appointed to the command on March 19, 1838, and confirmed by General Order 12 dated May 14, 1838.[1]

Captain Edwin Sumner had been selected for the command at Carlisle Barracks after a careful study of officers available for such duty. The army was concerned with solving the problems of cooperative operations between infantry and dragoons, so an officer with infantry background was wanted. In addition to his having served with the Second Infantry, Sumner was a voracious reader who had translated practically every known European work on cavalry tactics.

Some students at the school considered Captain Sumner a martinet. One soldier remembered him as rugged and stern, honest and brave, a man of the old school. He had a good conscience, was devoid of sensibility, detested frivolity and was austerely sober.[2]

A man who truly was a martinet, naval officer Charles Wilkes, visited Carlisle with his family in 1844. Wilkes and his family spent ten days in Carlisle. The population he reported as 3,000, with Dickenson College on the

Top: Dragoon Circle, Carlisle Barracks, Pennsylvania. Dedicated to the Dragoon units stationed at the barracks and those who trained at its Cavalry School of Practice during the school's tenure from 1838 to 1861. *Above:* Close up of plaque at Dragoon Circle, Carlisle Barracks, Pennsylvania. Photographs by the author.

outskirts of Carlisle at that time. "There did not appear any necessity for a police force of this town," Wilkes observed; "a more orderly and quiet one is probably not to be found in the State of Penna."[3]

Colonel Mathew Payne (Wilkes spelled his name "Paine") commanded a regiment of horse artillery stationed at Carlisle Barracks. He staged a full exercise for the benefit of the Wilkes family and other ladies visiting. The well-trained horses galloped at full speed pulling the guns over the fields and went through a variety of maneuvers.[4] Carlisle could not have changed that much when Wilkes visited from the years Sumner spent there. Although Wilkes visited Carlisle Barracks while in Carlisle he failed to visit the U.S. armory while in Harpers Ferry. Two years after Wilkes' visit Francis Parkman came through Carlisle on his way west. After crossing the wide Susquehanna River on a flat boat Parkman traveled the eighteen miles through the Cumberland Valley to Carlisle. He noted how the barracks buildings stood "in the midst of broad meadows."[5]

Sumner wrote to his cousin Charles P. Sumner from Carlisle Barracks on July 9, 1838. This is the last of the several Sumner letters held by the Massachusetts Historical Society. This letter provides some material on the Sumners. Again it begins with a formal "Dear sir." The letter tells of Sumner's own limited finances and his inability to pay off his father's note. His mother received a modest sum from the Society of the Cincinnati to which he added ten dollars a month "devoted exclusively to necessities for the family."[6]

This letter reveals things concerning his family's finances. The remark about his mother's receiving money from the Society of the Cincinnati is a testimony to her family's ties to the American Revolution. His only brother, Nathaniel, was a "ne'er-do-well," having never done anything to support the family. Rather than working to become a respectable farmer, Sumner's brother tried to be "a half fledged gentleman."

His brother it seems never changed. Twenty-four years later he was after money from now-general Sumner, who was on his way to Fredericksburg, Virginia. Nathaniel Robbins Sumner met his brother at Warrenton, Virginia, to ask for money. Nathaniel's mooching must have been well-known throughout the Sumner family. Sam Sumner, the twenty-year-old captain on his father's staff and youngest of Sumner's children, remarked that his Uncle Nathaniel's visit would have his father raving for the rest of the day.[7]

The secretary of war, according to Sumner, took his suggestion and formed a recruiting depot and a cavalry school at Carlisle. Sumner had the secretary's assurance that he would not be relieved of command. "It is however a most laborious station," Sumner wrote. "I am almost constantly engaged from 4 in the morning till 9 at night." He told his cousin that he offered to march to the northern frontier but that move was not required. Sumner noted that his children were all well and attending a fine school.

The reason Sumner offered to march to the northern frontier was the result of constant quarrels between the people of the state of Maine and those of New Brunswick. In 1838–39, the dispute over the boundary almost resulted in a war between the United States and Great Britain. While Winfield Scott prevented hostilities it remained for the Webster-Ashburton Treaty of 1842 to settle the dispute.[8]

Sumner marched a company of eighty dragoons, all mounted on black horses, from Carlisle to Trenton, New Jersey, to bring the number of troops at Camp Washington to about seven hundred. It was on the Delaware River above Philadelphia and near Trenton. Camp Washington had been established by Secretary of War Joel R. Poinsett as a camp of instruction "for the purpose of instructing the troops in the various duties appertaining to their respective arms," General Alexander Macomb wrote to Poinsett. General Macomb went on to write that he had had an opportunity to observe the camp and had witnessed the beneficial results personally, "in September last [1839], just before the breaking up of the camp."[9]

The *Barre Gazette* of Barre, Massachusetts, carried the story that had appeared in the *Newark Advertiser* on page 1 of its June 28, 1839, edition. The paper went on to report that the troops drilled in companies from half past nine to eleven in the morning and from four to half past five in the afternoon. Half an hour before sundown they were on parade.

One of Captain Sumner's students was Richard Stoddard Ewell. He was conspicuous as a dragoon both in the Mexican War and on the western frontier and went on to command of the Second Corps, Army of Northern Virginia. Brevetted a second lieutenant in the First Dragoon Regiment upon his graduation from West Point on July 1, 1840, Ewell went on to Carlisle Barracks. He was at Carlisle about two months. By 1840, there were two regiments of dragoons in the army numbering 750 men in each. Their uniforms were made up of sky blue trousers and navy blue jackets with orange trimmings. One man reported that the dark blue jackets were black. Their weapons were percussion horse pistols, a single shot carbine and a heavy saber.[10]

Sumner impressed young Richard Ewell as "an excellent man" and a capable officer. Ewell also said of him, "Very much pleased with Capt. Sumner, who is strict with himself as well as with us." The daily routine never varied. Between reveille and breakfast was stable call; drill and recitation in tactics went on until dinner; then more drill and stable duty were performed until retreat. But there were diversions. Sumner must have known about all work and no play. He arranged social events for the young officers, inviting many of the local young women.

Ewell's time at Carlisle came to an end on November 20, 1840, when he received orders to report to Company A, First U.S. Dragoons, at Fort Gibson in what is today eastern Oklahoma.[11]

Both Sumner's biographer Stanley and historian Robert M. Utley incorrectly accused Richard S. Ewell of calling Sumner a martinet.[12] They cited a letter in Captain Percy G. Hamlin's book *The Making of a Soldier: Letters of General R.S. Ewell.* Possibly they read the letter too quickly and did not see that it was written by Tom Ewell, Richard's younger brother, to Ben Ewell, their older brother. Writing from Camp Page, Mouth of the Rio Grande, on February 12, 1847, Tom Ewell mentioned "Major Sumner, of the Second Dragoons, the greatest martinet in the service, who for our sins has got command of us." He said, "We are in perfect purgatory here, and Major Sumner would be chief devil anywhere." Tom went on to say that Sumner kept them marching, running, and drilling as skirmishers through knee-deep sand. Tom wrote that the only reason he was able to write that day was that Sumner had given them the day off because the weather was so bad they couldn't drill. "Old Sumner has had one good effect on us," Tom Ewell admitted; "he has taught some of us to pray who never prayed before, for we all put up daily petitions to get rid of him." A first lieutenant in the First Mounted Rifles, Tom Ewell was mortally wounded on April 18, 1847, at the battle of Cerro Gordo. Although he was in the Mounted Rifles, Tom joined the assault on the Telegrafo with the Seventh Infantry. He was shot as he leaped the breastwork on the summit. His brother Richard was at his side when he died.[13]

What was it that kept Captain Sumner so busy from 4:00 A.M. until 9:00 P.M. as he mentioned in his last letter above? Ambitious plans for Carlisle Barracks. Sumner wanted to expand the size of the post. He wrote to the chairman of the Military Committee, House of Representatives, for funds to purchase an additional thirty-one acres of ground adjacent to the barracks for $90.00 an acre. He explained that he did not have sufficient space for cavalry charges nor did the artillery have room for their drill. Additional ground would provide more pasture space for the horses and provide an area for sick and lame horses to recover. When Congress failed to appropriate the money, Sumner went next to Secretary of War Joel Poinsett. Still the money was not granted. Sumner did find money to plant trees, cut brush, put in paths and gravel walkways, and erect stables. He added two one-story wings to the commander's house.[14]

Finding that many of the men recruited were unemployed from New York with no experience with horses, Sumner asked that substations for recruiting be established in areas where men were used to working with horses. Recruiting stations sprang up in Boston; New York; Philadelphia; Albany, New York; and Windsor, Vermont. Recruiting records show that New York City provided the largest number of recruits for the Dragoons. (See appendix Item 8 for a table of the number of recruits from the various cities where recruiting was conducted.) The trainees at the school were not permitted to enter a squadron until they had received at least 250 lessons in the company. At first Sumner thought six weeks long enough to train a dragoon, but he came to believe six months the proper length of time required to make a mounted soldier.

The garrison had about 250 men but only eighty sets of equipment. So the men trained in small groups while the others observed until their time came to use the limited equipment.[15]

Sumner experimented with the ration for his horses. "I find that five quarts of rye," he wrote, "which makes six quarts of meal — and three pounds of straw cut very fine, with a little salt, making a mass of three pecks for a day's ration, keeps my horses in very fine condition, and at the expense of ten cents and eight mills a day against twenty cents with hay and oats ration." In addition the horses received corn on the cob mixed with straw twice a week.

One duty assigned to Sumner while at Carlisle was to test the Jenks carbine and the Colt carbine and pistol for the Ordnance Department. Sumner preferred the Jenks. He reported on August 6, 1841, "I am making experiments with the new carbines but am not yet prepared to make my final report. As far as I have gone, I think favorably of the Jenk's [*sic*] .69 caliber carbine. I found they were 12 rounds quicker than the Colt's carbines."[16]

Later when Captain Sumner made his report he stated that he held no prejudices for or against either of the two arms. Sumner believed the Colt would not do for military purposes, but no specifics were stated in the report as published. Sumner believed the barrel length of the Jenks could be shortened by six inches without detriment to force or accuracy and it would make the arm more convenient for mounted service. Sumner went on to opine that no time of any consequence could be saved by loading from the breech. When the piece became foul from powder residue, Sumner pointed out, it was slower to load than from the muzzle. Sumner's report was cited in a letter dated February 18, 1842, from Ordnance Colonel George Talcott to Secretary of War John C. Spencer. Talcott reported that Sumner's trials with the flintlock version of the Jenks carbine were extensive. Later on Sumner's report was cited in response to Brevet General William S. Harney's 1851 recommendation to replace the musketoon with the Colt carbine for the mounted service.[17]

Sumner's idea that six inches could be cut off of the barrel without any loss of force was probably not based upon any comprehensive tests. A general rule of thumb argues that there is a loss of about one hundred foot-pounds of energy for every inch cut off the barrel. The famous Spencer carbine was quite a bit underpowered in comparison with its big brother the rifle, which had eight more inches of barrel length.

On the other hand, Captain Enoch Steen of E Company, First Dragoons, also tested the Jenks carbines. In his opinion "they were not worth the storeroom they occupy." So Ordnance made further tests of the Jenks carbine in

April of 1842 at Fort Adams. The board fired four Jenks carbines to test their length, force, accuracy and rapidity of fire. Then one of the four fired shots to the number of 4,500. The board reported the Jenks was well adapted to the needs of the service. Evidently still not completely satisfied, the board ordered the carbine to be fired still more. After another 10,313 shots went through it the nipple broke.

The Jenks carbine had been patented on May 25, 1838. It was a backward sliding breech loader operated by a lever. When the piece was to be loaded the stop was removed from behind the plug, and the slide withdrawn; the chamber was then loaded with ball and powder and the slide forced forward. The carbine was made by William Jenks of Columbia, South Carolina. The nipple and therefore the hammer were on the right side of the arm. The hammer, once cocked, swung to the left in an arc to strike the percussion cap. The carbine's 24¼-inch barrel still delivered a muzzle velocity of 1,687 feet per second with energy of 1,381 foot-pounds, the same as the longer barreled Cadet Flintlock Musket. In 1839 the War Department ordered 100 Jenks flintlock carbines, and thirty-five were tested at Carlisle Barracks. The others were converted to the percussion ignition system soon after. One hundred sixty Colt carbines were purchased by the government for field trials held at Carlisle in 1841. The Colt carbine was the model of 1839. Like the Colt revolver, the carbine used a six-shot revolving cylinder. Some of the cylinders were, or became, defective over time. Faulty material as well as corrosion caused pinholes to form in the web between the cylinder chambers. Flame from one discharge could pass through these pinholes, to ignite the powder in the neighboring chamber.[18]

Captain Sumner's Cavalry School of Practice was not the only army unit to occupy Carlisle Barracks. As he stated in his request for funds to purchase additional acreage, the artillery did not have space enough to drill. On November 5, 1838, Secretary of War Poinsett ordered Brevet Major Samuel Ringgold to establish a horse artillery company at Carlisle Barracks. Ringgold had just returned from Europe where he studied briefly at *École Polytechnique* in Paris and the Military Institution in Woolwich, England. Ringgold (1800–1846) was the first West Pointer to be killed in the Mexican War.[19]

Secretary of War Poinsett found "some deficiencies in the dragoon service as to its regulations and details." Three young officers from the First Regiment of Dragoons therefore were sent to France to attend for a year the cavalry school at Saumur, Poinsett wrote in his annual report for 1839. The three were Captain Lloyd J. Beall, Lieutenant William J. Hardee, and Lieutenant Washington Irving Newton. In Poinsett's report for 1840 he was able to write: "The officers sent to the school of cavalry at Saumur have returned, after a twelvemonth's instruction, and are now employed in a manner which I trust will enable the department very much to improve the cavalry service."[20]

When Sumner was due to leave Carlisle in 1842, fifteen members of the Pennsylvania House of Representatives and Senate wrote to President John Tyler to have Sumner stay on. Their request was denied. Citing General Order Number 12 that established the cavalry school in 1838, General Winfield Scott explained the reason Sumner would be transferred. Scott wrote, "Capt. Sumner, who organized the Cavalry School of Practice, has already been nearly 4 years the commander of the same — a *double* tour of duty, & all detached service, in the army is done by *roster* for regular terms, or *tours*. The Captain is an excellent officer & hence has made no application to be continued longer at Carlisle — knowing the rules of service & always ready to conform himself thereto." As Paul E. Zuver wrote, "While loyally applying himself at Carlisle, his heart was set on active service."[21]

According to Sumner's biographer Stanley, Sumner left Carlisle and arrived at Fort Atkinson (Wisconsin) on June 24, 1841, with Company B, First Dragoons, and was there until the start of the Mexican War. His family may have remained in Pennsylvania, because the last of his children to reach maturity, Samuel S. Sumner, was born in Carlisle on February 6, 1842. However, Sumner's biographer William W. Long wrote that the date of Sumner's transfer to Fort Atkinson was April 1842. This later date seems correct in light of Scott's note quoted above and the birth of the Sumner's son Samuel. This is supported by the report mentioned above that Hannah Sumner accompanied her husband to all military posts from the time of her marriage until 1851.

Much of Sumner's time at Fort Atkinson was spent evicting squatters from Indian lands and chasing whiskey peddlers. In the summer of 1845, he went on an expedition against the Sioux. Here he held discussions with Indian chiefs, half-breed traders and Canadian buffalo hunters who were crossing the border into the U.S. illegally. Sumner, who had been fair and understanding in his dealings with Indians, came to the belief that Indians came to parley in order to study ways to steal horses.

4

The Mexican War

"The [Mexican] War," T. Harry Williams wrote, "had its origins in events that occurred years before its inception, events that involved not only the United States and Mexico but also certain European nations." He went on to describe the restless American population, increasing from the influx of European immigrants, pushing the great western movement and occupation of the continent. So large and dynamic was this migration into lands occupied only by beasts and savages that the movement gave rise to a belief that became part of the American creed. That creed came to be called Manifest Destiny, the term coined by John L. O'Sullivan and published in his *Democratic Review* for July and August 1845. The idea had attracted enough people by the mid–1840s to constitute a movement.

The doctrine of Manifest Destiny did not advocate a belligerent United States running roughshod over its neighbors but instead provided an opportunity for our neighbors to join us and receive the benefits of the American Union. All that was required was self-government, no matter how that government was achieved.[1]

Advocates of this belief looked down on Mexico. They saw her failure to improve California, a potential land of Eden, as the result of a slothful population and an incompetent local bureaucracy that had degenerated into a state of anarchy. The same was true, they believed, of the agricultural and mining potential of Mexico proper. If those areas were brought into the American confederation, the people would be taught the value of their blessings and trained to develop them for the good of mankind. Frederick Merk explained how Texas was the perfect example of how Manifest Destiny worked. Before the Americans came to occupy Texas it had been a raw wilderness, its resources untapped. Industrious Americans came, built homes, established communities and applied to the Union for admission. Among the

28

forces that gave rise to the idea of Manifest Destiny, according to Merk, was the concept of expansion and the doctrine of states' rights.[2]

In the presidential election of 1844, neither the Whig candidate Henry Clay nor the Van Buren wing of the Democratic Party understood the strength of the expansionist sentiment. The Democrats rejected Martin Van Buren and nominated the pragmatic expansionist James K. Polk, who was elected the eleventh president of the United States. But Polk's was a narrow victory. He received just 6,332 votes more than Clay in Pennsylvania and 5,000 more than Clay in New York. Had Clay won New York he would have won the election and the map of the United States might have been drawn differently than it is now.[3]

Intending to be but a one-term president, Polk spent his political capital freely to expand the powers of the presidency more than any other president before the Civil War. Polk, as his biographer wrote, welcomed Texas into the Union, "bluffed the British out of half of Oregon, and went to war with Mexico to grab California and the Southwest."[4]

Army of the West

Captain Edwin V. Sumner began his Mexican War service as part of Colonel (later General) Stephen Watts Kearny's Army of the West. President Polk's strategy to achieve New Mexico and California involved, first, a naval blockade of Mexico's main ports. Second, land forces would seize Mexican territory west and south of Texas. Five different American columns were to invade Mexico. The first column, under General Zachary Taylor, entered Mexico by crossing the Rio Grande at Matamoras to capture Monterrey and other northern cities. The second, commanded by General John Wool, moved from San Antonio, Texas, to join Taylor. Third, Colonel Kearny marched from Fort Leavenworth, Kansas, to Santa Fe, New Mexico, and took possession of that vast region. Then he moved on with only a portion of his command to California. Fourth, a portion of Kearny's army under Colonel Alexander Doniphan marched south to Saltillo. Lastly, the fifth column, a large amphibious force under General Winfield Scott, landed at Vera Cruz and moved overland to capture Mexico City.[5]

The acquisition of New Mexico and California was Polk's desire. Taylor's invasion of northern Mexico was to occupy a portion of the country to force Mexico to cede the desired territory. The term New Mexico, as used here, covered the ground now known as the states of New Mexico, Arizona, Utah, and Nevada and parts of Colorado and Wyoming.[6]

Colonel Stephen Watts Kearny led his Army of the West out from Fort Leavenworth, Kansas, for the Pacific by way of Santa Fe. The components of his army had been assembling since late June 1846. His orders from President Polk were "to take the earliest possible possession of, and set up civil governments in the Mexican Provinces of New Mexico and Alta California." At the time of Kearny's departure his army consisted of 2,700 dragoons and Missouri Volunteers. Traveling mainly over the Santa Fe Trail, the army marched 900 miles in fifty-two days, arriving in Santa Fe on August 18, 1846.[7]

Colonel Kearny's army was to grow in size as it went along. General Winfield Scott directed Kearny to recruit as many men as possible from among the caravans at Bent's Fort, a fortified adobe trading post on the Arkansas River in what is now Colorado. General Scott informed Kearny that another thousand Missouri volunteers would be joining his force under Sterling Price. Scott's orders went on to say that when New Mexico was safely garrisoned, Kearny should lead a force and seize Monterey and San Francisco in California.

Because there was little chance of encountering Mexican opposition before reaching Bent's Fort, the Army of the West traveled in small groups in order to conserve the limited grass and water along the way. Colonel Alexander Doniphan's First Missouri Mounted Volunteers, assembling at Fort Leavenworth over a two-week period, departed between June 22 and 28, 1846. Kearny and his staff left on June 30. Kearny's army consisted of 1,458 men, to which 1,000 more would be added later. Despite these efforts to preserve grass and water the trek was a difficult one. As K. Jack Bauer wrote, "The 537-mile march from Fort Leavenworth to Bent's Fort was an exercise in human misery. Most of the men were not yet acclimated to long marches and their discomfort was heightened by the heat, dust, and aridness of the plains."[8]

Kearny preceded his arrival in Santa Fe with a proclamation issued on July 31, 1846. In announcing the impending arrival of the American force it proclaimed the purpose of seeking union with the inhabitants, while promising to ameliorate their condition and protect their civil and religious rights. That same day Sumner, now a major, arrived in camp with two additional companies of dragoons.

When the Mexican War broke out, Sumner and his Company B, First Dragoons, were ordered from Fort Atkinson to join General Zachary Taylor's army in Mexico. Colonel Stephen W. Kearny, about to leave Fort Leavenworth with portions of his Army of the West, wanted both Sumner's Company B and Philip St. George Cooke's Company K, stationed at Fort Crawford, Wisconsin Territory, to join him. Kearny considered companies B and K the two best in the regiment. Kearny's request was granted. Although disappointed to miss seeing action and a probable promotion serving under Taylor, the two company commanders, Sumner and Cooke, friends since the Black Hawk War, met at St. Louis and together went on to Fort Leavenworth. While on the way, Sumner received his promotion to major in the Second Dragoons on June 30, 1846. However, he remained with the First Dragoons for another four months.

Companies B and K, First Dragoons, arrived at Fort Leavenworth on July 3, 1846, after Kearny had departed. Sumner and Cooke left on July 6, hoping to overtake Kearny on the way. But it was the end of July before they joined Kearny, a newly minted brigadier general, at Bent's Fort. At that time General Kearny sent Sumner's friend, Captain Philip St. George Cooke, with twelve dragoons to Santa Fe with agent James W. Magoffin. They carried Kearny's letter to Mexican governor Manuel Armijo.

Kearny departed for California on September 25, 1846. Along the way the column met Kit Carson and nineteen men riding east and carrying Commodore Robert F. Stockton's report of the seizure of California. Hearing this news of a pacified California and a difficult trip ahead with limited forage and water, Kearny decided to send the bulk of his force back to Santa Fe under Major Edwin V. Sumner. Persuading Carson to guide him to California and to allow the other nineteen to carry the message east, Kearny abandoned his wagons and used pack mules for the arduous trip to California. Sumner outfitted Kearny's command, providing them with the best equipment available from what was on hand. Some years later, as we shall see in the pages ahead, Sumner referred to his equipping Kearny's men as an example of how not to undertake an expedition through dry desert country as suggested by General Winfield Scott. In 1861, Scott believed such an expedition would help to secure California to the Union.[9]

One of the more unusual military organizations to form Kearny's Army of the West was the Mormon Battalion, the only unit of the U.S. Army ever designated by religion. President Polk was eager to include these emigrants, who had only recently been driven out of Illinois. Their service with Kearny, Polk believed, would attach them to the United States and keep them from taking part against the nation. Along with Kearny's orders to march on California were those instructing him to organize the Mormon Battalion. Knowing that a large group of Mormons were on their way to California, Secretary of War William Marcy wrote to Kearny that he should muster into service those Mormons who could be induced to serve but that the number was not to exceed one-third of Kearny's entire force. The Polk administration did not want to run a risk of overpopulating California with a questionable religious group.

Brigham Young saw several possible advantages to the Saints in the proposed federal service. Their enlistment would be a public relations victory for the church, demonstrating additional evidence of its loyalty to the United States. As the men were given a uniform allowance at Fort Leavenworth, Kansas, of $42.00 each, paid in advance, for their one-year enlistment and as they were allowed to wear their civilian clothing for the march, the bulk of those funds were immediately donated to a general church fund. These funds were used to purchase wagons, teams, and other necessities for the American exodus (actual wages paid over the next year to the Mormon Battalion totaled nearly $30,000).

On July 16, 1846, some 500 Mormon men assembled at Council Bluffs, Iowa, and took the oath of allegiance. Captain James Allen, a regular army captain appointed to command by Stephen Kearny, administered the oath. However, when Kearny left Santa Fe for California the Mormon Battalion had not yet arrived. What did arrive was a letter from Sterling Price saying that Captain Allen had died. Kearny replaced him with Captain Philip St. George Cooke, who assumed the lieutenant-colonelcy of the battalion.

Some of the Mormon families had been on the trek with the male volunteers. Cooke sent them and the sick to winter quarters near what is today Pueblo, Colorado. The rest marched west on October 19, taking a route far to the south of Kearny's own line of march. Reaching Tucson, Arizona, on December 14, 1846, they had their closest military encounter. But the Mexican garrison fled as they approached, and Cooke was able to replenish his supplies. Finally on January 29 or 30, 1847, they straggled into San Diego, nearly naked but with most of their wagons. The Mormon march, according to K. Jack Bauer, was one of the most notable accomplishments of a war in which American soldiers made some of military history's more illustrious marches. "Cooke's accomplishment," Bauer wrote, "ranks with those of Kearny, Doniphan, and Wool."[10]

When Sumner met Kearny at Bent's Fort he took charge of all the dragoon companies, 420 men and sixteen officers. Later, after Kearny was satisfied with conditions in New Mexico, he left for California on September 25, 1846. Sumner went along with 300 First Dragoons. But he was ordered to return to Albuquerque with 200 dragoons and a major part of the wagon train when Kearny met with Kit Carson.

Sumner next went to New Orleans, where General Winfield Scott put him in command of a newly-formed regiment of mounted riflemen. From there they went to Camp Page near Brazos Santiago at the mouth of the Rio Grande. They trained there, as Tom Ewell recorded in his letter to brother Ben, until they departed for Vera Cruz in March 1847.

At Camp Page, Sumner and Colonel William S. Harney of the Second Dragoons began the feud they would conduct, on and off, for the remainder of their careers. When General Scott arrived at Brazos Santiago in early January 1847, to organize his move on Vera Cruz, two companies of the Second Dragoons were to remain with General Taylor and seven other companies under Harney were to report to Scott. Harney, who disliked Scott and tended to be insubordinate, was not the man Scott wanted. Scott therefore ordered Harney to turn the seven companies over to Sumner, the second in command,

and to then return to General Taylor. Harney refused to obey and was placed under court-martial. To avoid any show of being vindictive and to be as fair as possible, Scott allowed Harney to select the members of the court. Scott, a Whig, and President Polk, a Democrat, were always at odds, so Scott wanted to avoid any appearance that he was "beating up on" the Democrat Harney. Even so the court recommended a severe reprimand for Harney, but Scott reversed the decision. So for a time Sumner was in command of the Second Dragoons.[11]

The Second Dragoons, again under Colonel Harney, left for Vera Cruz on March 5, 1847, and arrived on March 20. Ordnance Lieutenant Theodore T.S. Laidley reported in a letter to his father dated February 26, 1847, that the dragoons were the only troops left to embark and a few days of clear weather would get them off. However, Laidley told his father, about a third of the time nothing could cross the sand bar because of storms. Storms made the trip so hazardous that many of the dragoon's horses were lost at sea. Most dragoons had to fight on foot with the infantry. One storm hit the night of March 10 and lasted until the 14th, during which time nothing could be landed. One company of Second Dragoons under Captain Croghan Ker along with Colonel Harney himself was stranded on an island near Anton Lizardo.[12]

A similar storm struck on December 8, 1846, that sank the brig *Somers,* the scene of the U.S. Navy's so-called mutiny and hanging in 1842. The *Somers'* commander, Raphael Semmes, wrote about the storm fifteen years later on the anniversary of the ship's sinking in the gale. Half of her 120-man crew was drowned when she capsized off Vera Cruz. Flung over by the severity of the storm, the ship's masts and sails were flat upon the sea with water pouring in at every hatchway and scuttle.[13]

Writing his *History of the Mexican War* in his final years, old former Confederate general Cadmus M. Wilcox may have remembered himself as a young brevet second lieutenant just graduated in the West Point class of 1846, and on his way to Mexico to join the Fourth Infantry at Monterrey. He reported for duty on October 23, 1846. His mess mates were first lieutenants Jenks Beaman and Sidney Smith and Second Lieutenant Ulysses S. Grant. Both Beaman, and Smith were killed during the war, and Wilcox was transferred to the Seventh Infantry.[14] Wilcox's *History* narrates some of the earlier exploits of Sumner's new regiment, the Second Dragoons, in action under one of the regiment's more forceful captains, Charles A. May. Wilcox described May as "tall and of soldierly bearing, with long hair and beard, graceful and easy in his seat" on "a superb-looking horse, with arched neck and flowing mane."[15]

According to Wilcox the battle known as Resaca de la Palma was actually fought at Resaca de Guerrero, where Mexican general Mariano Arista, retiring to Matamoros, determined to make a stand. *Resaca* is the Spanish word for ravine, Wilcox explained. Captain George A. McCall, Fourth Infantry, being convinced the enemy was in position in his immediate front, sent three of Lieutenant Alfred Pleasanton's Second Dragoons to report the situation to General Taylor. Taylor ordered the army, then at a halt, to be put in motion. Captain May's squadron of Second Dragoons that had been reconnoitering all morning through the chaparral moved to the head of the column. Wilcox described the action: "The fire was rapid, close, and incessant — musketry and canister — the latter from 100 to 150 yards; the former at times in the dense jungle within a few feet."[16]

While the Mexican infantry were pushed back after the loss of many of the officers, the Mexican artillery continued to hold its position, several pieces in the road at the ravine. General Taylor ordered Captain May to charge the batteries. The dense chaparral on both sides of the road compelled Captain May to charge down it in a column of fours. His squadron (two companies) swooped down over three guns near the ravine, then rode into the depression and up the opposite bank to charge over four guns, cutting and stabbing the cannoneers with their sabers. Rallying six of his men, May charged for a second time upon the few Mexicans, who returned to their pieces. One of the men in May's squadron captured Mexican general Romulo de la Vega. May's squadron consisted of his own company and Captain L.P. Graham's, both of the Second Dragoons. In the charge First Lieutenant Zebulon M.P. Inge, seven men and eighteen horses were killed; a sergeant, nine privates and ten horses were wounded; and one man was taken prisoner.[17]

Vera Cruz

Late in the afternoon of Friday, March 5, 1847, General Winfield Scott's huge armada approached Vera Cruz, Mexico. Scott's plan for the capture of Mexico City was to enter the country through Vera Cruz, rather than by General Zachary Taylor's approach from Monterrey. Speed was essential in order to get away from low-lying Vera Cruz before the yellow fever or *vomito* season arrived. Guided by the blockading squadron of Commodore David E. Conner, Scott landed two miles below the city to be out of range of the Mexican guns at Fort San Juan de Ulua on an island guarding the city. To bolster his manpower Scott proposed to transfer nine thousand men from the combined twenty thousand under generals Taylor and John Wool.[18]

The men in Scott's armada who made an amphibious landing near the reef and island of Sacrificious were organized into three divisions, two of regulars and one of volunteers. Generals William J. Worth and David E. Twiggs were in command of the regular divisions; General Robert Patterson commanded the volunteers. When Commodore Matthew C. Perry replaced Connor, he lent Scott long-range naval guns to breach the walls of Vera Cruz. The six guns blasted a breach fifty feet wide in the stone walls. The city fell to Scott on March 26 and 27, 1847.[19]

On the 24th, before the city was blasted into submission, a small enemy cavalry force was discovered off to the extreme left of the American forces. A company of mounted rifles was sent to engage them. The rifles split into two columns and hit the Mexicans in the flanks. The Mexicans fled but were pursued until sunset. The mounted riflemen counted three enemy dead on the road while four riflemen were seriously wounded. Following the engagement Brevet Second Lieutenant Dabney H. Maury received favorable mention in Colonel Persifor F. Smith's report.

Associated with the landing at Vera Cruz was a battle at the nearby village of Medelin, south of Vera Cruz. On March 25, 1847, the Americans knew an enemy mounted force was in their rear. Under the command of Colonel William S. Harney, Major Edwin Sumner of the Second Dragoons marched towards the Medelin River with Captain Seth B. Thornton's squadron and fifty dismounted men under Captain Croghan Ker.[20]

When Colonel Harney arrived they observed a small party of Mexican lancers holding a stone bridge skirted by dense chaparral. An American reconnoitering party found the bridge heavily fortified and fell back after receiving a volley that killed a corporal and wounded two men. Sumner's men retired a short distance and requested two pieces of artillery. Reinforced by Captain William J. Hardee's company of Second Dragoons plus a company from the First Tennessee under Captain Benjamin F. Cheatham and four companies of the Second Tennessee under Colonel William T. Haskell, Colonel Harney attacked at once. First Lieutenant Henry B. Judd, Third Artillery, advanced his two pieces near the bridge and went into battery.

"Ker's men moved forward in line on the left of the road," Wilcox wrote, "the volunteers on the right, Hardee in rear near the guns, and Sumner with the mounted cavalry a short distance in rear." Lieutenant Judd's artillery fired only a few minutes before all advanced, charged the bridge and leaped over the barricade, Colonel Haskell in the lead. After giving way the enemy reformed. Sumner charged the Mexican lancers, broke their formation and chased them six miles to the town of Medelin. There they encountered a second party of lancers and drove them off as well. Lieutenant Lewis Neill of the Second Dragoons took two lance wounds in his body and arm. Colonel Harney wrote in his report that Major Sumner came up in gallant style and charged the enemy. The footmen fled into the woods but the lancers were completely routed. Major Sumner and Lieutenant Henry H. Sibley had several personal encounters with the enemy, "who," Harney reported, "were, in every instance, either killed or wounded." Despite the feud between them, Colonel Harney was not adverse to writing a complimentary report of Sumner's action.[21]

On April 2, 1847, after Vera Cruz fell, Colonel Harney led two squadrons of Second Dragoons under Major Sumner, a section of artillery and several infantry companies to Antigua. Antigua was on the main road to Mexico City. Crossing a river 250 yards wide and three and a half feet deep, the dragoons charged the forty-some Mexicans holding the town and took possession. Moving on they broke up Mexican cavalry pickets and took the village of Plan del Rio, about fifty miles from Vera Cruz. From April 13 until the 17th Harney's men scouted and escorted wagon trains.[22]

Plan del Rio became the site of an American camp in preparation for the attack on Cerro Gordo (Fat Mountain), a battle of some significance for Major Edwin V. Sumner. Cerro Gordo itself was a hill overlooking the National Road to Mexico City. Mexican lieutenant Colonel Manuel Robles examined Cerro Gordo; in his opinion it was a position from which to harass the invaders but, because it could be easily turned, was not the place to dispute a passage or to attempt a decisive battle. Nevertheless General Santa Anna ordered Cerro Gordo to be fortified.[23]

Important to the geography of Cerro Gordo was the Atalaya, a crest with an intervening depression. The Americans drove the Mexicans from the first to the second ridge, down its slope and up the steep side to within about 200 yards of the summit.

"In this spirited collision," Cadmus Wilcox wrote, "the American loss was 97 killed and wounded. Of the latter were Major Sumner, commanding the Rifle regiment, being disabled for a few days; Second Lieut. D.H. Maury, Rifle regiment, severely wounded."[24] Sumner's wound was caused by a musket ball hitting him on the forehead. The story was told that the ball bounced off his skull, which indeed it did, but the implication among the troops was that Sumner was invincible and gave rise to his nom de guerre, "Bull," or a later version, "Bull of the Woods." Another version of this story credits a metallic emblem, a star, worn on Sumner's cap, as helping to deflect the musket ball that still inflicted a wound. Although Sumner soon recovered, rumors circulated that night that he had been killed.

No doubt Sumner's skull was no thicker than normal and the ball that hit him had lost most of its velocity. But as time passed there were those who thought Sumner's thick skull that could repel a musket ball was accompanied by a limited capacity for brains. Robert Utley wrote, "A skull thick enough to deflect a musket ball gave 'Bull' Sumner his sobriquet and also enclosed a mind full of frontier and military lore but often obtuse in applying it."[25]

One correspondent reporting from Plan del Rio described the events leading up to Sumner's wounding this way:

> I have just returned from the scene of conflict, and a bloody one it has been on this side, the farthest Mexican fort. No one was seen in possession of it last

evening, but this morning it was found to be occupied by the enemies [sic] light troops, and to force it at once was deemed indispensable.

For this purpose the rifles under Major Sumner, besides a detachment of artillery and infantry were ordered to charge up the rugged ascent. This they did gallantly, driving the Mexicans after a desperate resistance. They were obstinate in the defence [sic], and great numbers of the enemy were killed, while on our side the loss was also severe.

Major Sumner's wounding was reported in several newspapers. One account stated, "Major Sumner was shot in the head by a musket." Another, "Major Sumner was shot in the head by a musket ball, but it is thought will recover." Even *Scientific American* carried a piece on Sumner's being hit by a musket bullet. The bullet was flattened to the thickness of a dime, the periodical reported, "and retained on its surface the print of the Major's hair."

Also reported was the capture of General Santa Anna's coach, "appropriated to the use of Major Sumner." Writing to his sister on April 30, 1847, John Sedgwick stated, "Santa Anna's carriage, with between twenty and thirty thousand dollars, was captured, which furnished an easy conveyance for our wounded officers."[26]

Second Lieutenant Dabney H. Maury described the incident this way in his *Recollection*. After receiving his wound and being carried from the field, he met Sumner, who was in temporary command of Colonel Persifor Smith's Mounted Rifles. Sumner, whom Maury described as "a rough old dragoon," met the wounded Maury and after learning what was happening hurried forward. Almost immediately Sumner was hit on the forehead by a musket ball. Afterwards Sumner came up and spoke very kindly to Maury, calling him "my brave boy." Those words, Maury wrote, "compensated for all the wound and pain and for some previous roughness of manner to me."[27]

William Woods Averell described Maury, a nephew but more like a son to the oceanographer Matthew Fontaine Maury, as "about five foot nothing" in height. He was a great reader of the best literature and a bright, interesting and profitable conversationalist. He became a Confederate general during the Civil War.[28] Ten years later another wounded lieutenant would almost forgive Sumner when he spoke kindly to him and expressed concern for his wounds.

On April 18, 1847, Sumner received a lieutenant-colonel brevet "for gallant and meritorious conduct at Cerro Gordo." The next day the dragoons occupied Jalapa, a town situated in a declivity of the mountain. Wilcox described it as having narrow streets full of streams, flowers, fruit trees and shrubbery in profusion. The threat of yellow fever in the low lands around Vera Cruz forced Scott to depart quickly for the high ground. He remained a month at Jalapa while supply wagons went back and forth to Vera Cruz for supplies. On May 23 he set out for Puebla.[29]

Little to no fighting took place during the months of May, June and July

1847, as General Scott resupplied his army and looked after the sick and wounded. The War Department was slow. Neither the money Scott needed nor the uniforms the men needed arrived. When Scott began his move upon the Mexican capital he had 10,300 troops; the Mexicans nearly 30,000. Wilcox quoted Scott, saying that when he advanced upon the City of Mexico Scott had temporarily severed connection with Vera Cruz and "the scabbard was thrown away, and we advanced with the naked blade."[30]

Soldier-turned-historian Cadmus M. Wilcox opened the fifteenth chapter of his *History of the Mexican War* with these words: "All doubts and suspense terminated on August 6th by orders announcing the advance from Puebla upon the City of Mexico. " Before dawn on August 7, 1847, General David Twiggs' division — the "Cerro Gordo division"—was in motion preceded by Harney's cavalry. Twiggs was followed by General John A. Quitman on the 8th then by General William J. Worth and finally by General Gideon J. Pillow on the 10th. Twiggs' division took the lead, as it was General Winfield Scott's rule that one of the only two regular divisions should always be in front. Worth's division landed first at Vera Cruz, then Twiggs led off from there to Jalapa; Worth led from Jalapa to Puebla, then Twiggs was in the lead again.[31]

The enemy appeared on the 10th when the Americans arrived at the hacienda Buena Vista near Lake Chalco. Harney ordered Sumner to charge them with one squadron while the remainder of the cavalry followed in support. The enemy retreated hurriedly and Sumner failed to overtake them although he pursued them a mile and a half.[32]

On the 18th Worth's division, again preceded by Harney's cavalry, moved from San Augustin on the main highway leading north to the Mexican capital, about twelve miles away. A reconnaissance in the direction of Padierna, four miles west of San Augustin, was under the command of Captain Robert E. Lee assisted by Lieutenant Pierre G.T. Beauregard. They were supported by two companies of the Eleventh Infantry and Captain Philip Kearny's company of First Dragoons. Another reconnaissance of San Antonio, Mexico, was supported by Captain Seth B. Thornton, Second Dragoons. As this recon team rounded a bend in the road they faced a battery of Mexican guns about 800 yards ahead of them. The Mexicans fired and Thornton met his death. This reconnaissance preceded the Battle of Contreras, or Padierna as the Mexicans called it. It was primarily an infantry and artillery fight. The victory yielded to the Americans an open road to the capital, 700 enemy dead, 813 prisoners, twenty-two pieces of artillery (half of large caliber), thousands of small arms, quantities of shot, shell and powder, 700 pack mules and many horses.[33]

Thornton's death was brutal. Captain Seth B. Thornton of Sumner's dragoons had been in the war since it began. In fact the year before his death, he had led a patrol into the ambush along the Rio Grande that precipitated the war. Now, ordered by General William Worth to advance, Thornton went forward with the dragoons to scout the enemy lines at San Antonio. An 18-pound shot hit him square in the body killing him instantly and tearing off his arm and smashing his breast and side. Thornton was buried immediately by the side of the road.[34]

Scott's army moved on to the next battle at Churubusco. In that engagement Sumner was in command of Major William W. Loring's Mounted Rifles and Captain Henry H. Sibley's company of Second Dragoons. They supported General James Shields' two regiments that were engaged in the rear of the Mexican lines and in danger of being out-flanked.[35]

Captain Robert E. Lee, seeing the Mexican cavalry were on the American left and outnumbered the American force, reported that to General Winfield Scott. Scott directed Major Sumner to support that wing with the rifle regiment.[36]

Later, before Shields' command gained the road, the enemy was in flight, but retired in good order. At this point Colonel Harney came up with two squadrons of cavalry and using the saber freely, charged the enemy's rear. Wilcox wrote:

> In the excitement of the chase, the leading squadron, composed of Phil. Kearny's company of the First [Dragoons], and Capt. Andrew T. McReynolds' company, Third Dragoons, failing to hear the recall when sounded, continued on to the immediate vicinity of the San Antonio Garita [a garita was a gated entrance to a town or city] where Captain Kearny, in advance, lost an arm from a discharge of grape and canister.... Lieut. Richard S. Ewell had two horses killed under him.[37]

In September of 1847, Mexican general Antonio Lopez de Santa Anna set up a defensive position a short distance west of and under the guns of Chapultepec. A length of buildings over 600 feet long running north and south was known as Molinos del Rey, the King's Mills. They manufactured gun powder and cast cannons at a foundry located at the mills. At the northern end was a flour mill. These buildings were constructed as if to be a fortress. West of the flour mill about 500 yards was a bastioned fort containing on the inside the Casa Mata, a large powder storehouse. Deep irrigation ditches and a ravine or *barranca* protected these strongholds as well as guns on the well-fortified Castle of Chapultepec. General Scott was determined to attack and destroy these works.[38]

Supporting General Worth's division were 270 men under Major Edwin V. Sumner made up of three squadrons of dragoons and one company of mounted rifles. Also joining Worth were the Eleventh and Fourteenth Infantry along with the Voltigeur (light infantry) regiment. Three field artillery pieces from the Fourth Artillery under captain Simon H. Drum and two 24-pounder siege guns under ordnance Captain Benjamin Huger (pronounced u'-GHEE) also supported Worth. The troops were in position the night of September 7, 1847, and the assault began early the next morning. Sumner's cavalry took a position on the extreme left to operate as circumstances directed.[39]

Mexican general Juan Alvarez, commanding the cavalry, advanced at a gallop towards Worth's left when the Americans moved forward to assault the Casa Mata. Along with sections of Captain James Duncan's battery, Third Artillery, under lieutenants Henry J. Hunt and William Hays, the Voltigeur regiment moved to the ravine. Major Sumner advanced and crossed the ravine. He formed his command within pistol shot of the Casa Mata and along with an occasional shot from Duncan's battery kept General Alvarez in check. Sumner had six men killed, and five officers and thirty-three men wounded. Here Sumner remained until the end of the fighting, changing his position to conform to Alvarez' maneuvering.[40]

In summing up the battle Wilcox wrote it was a brilliant but costly victory for the American army. Of Sumner he had this to say: "There has been seldom witnessed a more brilliant display of courage than was shown by Major Sumner and his small command of 270 when, in the presence of two armies, they dashed by the Casa Mata within musket range, crossed the ravine, and displayed in front of General Alvarez with his 4,000 lancers." Quoting *Mexican History*, Wilcox added, "He [Alvarez] did not destroy as he should have done, this feeble force (Sumner) which offered battle."[41]

Timothy D. Johnson in his book *A Gallant Little Army* described a hand-to-hand combat between a Mexican lancer and an American dragoon sergeant. At Molinos del Rey the Second Dragoons under Sumner provided valuable service by keeping the lancers at bay. On one occasion a lone Mexican lancer rode out from his lines, suggesting an invitation for individual combat. The dragoon sergeant took up the challenge. As they charged each other at a gallop, the dragoon veered to the left at the last instant and swinging his saber decapitated the Mexican. The sergeant returned to his lines, bringing the lancer's horse as a trophy.[42] Actually a dragoon was at no disadvantage against a lancer. The dragoon could parry the lance with his saber and take advantage of the length of the lance to use the leverage against the lancer.

General Scott's next objective after Molinos del Rey was the Castle of Chapultepec, literally the hill of the grasshoppers, as he moved on to take Mexico City. As was Molinos del Rey, Chapultepec was covered with deep and wide ditches and required much reconnaissance by the engineers. "Chapultepec, fortified by nature and art, is an isolated mound, rising 150 feet above the valley," Wilcox wrote, "nearly precipitous on the northern, eastern and part of the southern side, it declines gradually to the west to a cypress grove separating it from Molinos-del-Rey."[43] Captain Robert E. Lee with lieutenants Pierre G.T. Beauregard and Gustavus W. Smith of the engineers were prominent in conducting the scouts. Scott called his generals together to hear the engineers' report and to express their opinions based upon the results of the several reconnaissance missions. Then they would express themselves as to their thoughts as to the best approach. The meeting ended when Scott decided first to attack Chapultepec and then the western gate or *garita*. According to Wilcox, "General Scott, having selected the point against which he would direct his efforts, ordered a concentration of forces there, but Santa Anna, ignorant of Scott's intentions, was forced to divide his army to guard the many garitas of the city."[44]

On the night of September 11, 1847, Major Sumner, following orders, held his command of six companies of Second Dragoons in readiness for immediate service. In addition to his own six companies he also commanded Company F, First Dragoons, the company of wounded Captain Phil Kearny. Following General Worth's orders Sumner kept track of a large enemy force on Worth's left and rear. Worth ordered Sumner to attack the fleeing Mexicans after Scott's army captured Chapultepec. General Scott then ordered Sumner to return to Tacubaya, a short distance to the southwest, to protect headquarters while the rest of the army fought at the gates of Mexico City.

Upon entering Mexico City, Scott put Sumner in command of the Brigade of Horse in Occupation. The Second Dragoons escorted a large train to Vera Cruz to bring up needed supplies. On January 12, 1848, Sumner left Mexico to return to the United States on sick leave. Sumner had been suffering for about five weeks with an ulcer on the inside of one of his thighs. He landed in New Orleans on February 16, 1848.[45]

By the end of March, Sumner was back in Carlisle, Pennsylvania, as superintendent of the Dragoon Recruiting Service, remaining at Carlisle until August. On October 31, 1848, General Stephen Watts Kearny died at Jefferson Barracks. Sumner attended his funeral on November 2. Sumner returned to Fort Leavenworth on January 1, 1849, with the rank of lieutenant colonel commanding the First Dragoons. The following day he assumed command of the post and served in that capacity until the mid-1850s.[46]

Sumner's main task now was to protect the emigrants moving west. News of gold discovered in California encouraged adventurers to seek it and added to the numbers moving west. The *New York Tribune* of June 6, 1849, carried an item from the *Cleveland Herald*, reporting on the number of people moving west. It provided some statistics. The average distance the teams made was fifteen miles per day. The whole region around the fort was one tented field for miles in all directions. By the lowest estimate there were 50,000 animals on the plains. Citing Colonel Sumner the paper reported, "Col Sumner, the commanding officer at the post, who has much experience on the Plains, and knows their peril, says he fears there will be more deaths on the road to California this Summer, than there was in Mexico during the War." According to the *Herald* these data came from a letter written by one A.G. Lawrence,

Esq., of Cleveland to a friend. Lawrence was at Fort Leavenworth and wrote his letter on May 15, 1849.

Sumner left Fort Leavenworth on June 13, 1850, for Fort Laramie, arriving there July 6. He departed on July 25 for the upper Arkansas River to establish Fort Atkinson just outside what is now Dodge City, Kansas. On September 24, 1850, the fort having been completed during the first week of September, Sumner turned it over to Second Lieutenant Henry Heth and his eighty-man Company D, Sixth Infantry. Along with Captain Mansfield Lovell, Fourth Artillery, Sumner returned to Fort Leavenworth on October 7, 1850. Secretary of War Charles M. Conrad ordered Sumner on April 1, 1851, to assume command of the Ninth Military District, also known as the Department of New Mexico.[47]

PART TWO: THE COMMANDER

5

The Southwest

Historian Robert M. Utley wrote that the regulars came home from the Mexican War in high spirits. Both officers and men significantly outperformed the volunteers in every test of military ability. "The Regular Army," he wrote, "embarked on its post war duties with zest. But a variety of influences soon smothered this spirit and turned the talented and ambitious to other pursuits." Among the older officers who had laid the groundwork for the new professionalism in the 1830s and 1840s and still had years to serve were men such as Edwin V. Sumner, Philip St. George Cooke, William S. Harney and Robert E. Lee.[1]

The new territory added to the United States following the Mexican War strained the overextended capabilities of the army to defend the settlers coming to occupy the new lands. Colonel William A. Ganoe understood things this way: "At this time [1848–50] the army went seriously to work in garrisoning the new territory in order to make it habitable. Little by little nearly all the troops were occupying tiny posts over the prairies."[2]

Two schools of thought developed as to how to protect the emigrants from Native American depredations: the fixed-post concept and the roving-patrol idea. The idea behind the fixed-post concept, to which Edwin Sumner subscribed at least for a time, was to scatter small posts across the Indian Territory. Indians would not venture on distant raids, according to proponents, because their families and their possessions would be within striking distance of at least one of these fixed posts. These posts would also serve as way stations for travelers. The argument against this idea was that the posts would be hard to supply because they were numerous and often not on any kind of convenient or economic supply route such as a river or railroad line.

The roving-patrol concept envisioned a few permanent, large bases that could be served either by steamboats on rivers or by railroads. Each spring when the grass grew in quantity, strong mounted columns would set out and patrol. But critics of this plan argued that a regiment on patrol in June was no deterrent to the hostiles in November. Secretary of War Jefferson Davis was a proponent of this strategy.[3]

Trapping and trading with the Indians in the west since the 1820s, Tom Fitzpatrick, an old mountain man turned Indian agent, argued that neither approach would work, for the reasons listed above. Fitzpatrick, his hair turned white from an 1832 adventure with the Grosventres Indians in what is now Idaho, believed that the government should either pay an annuity to the Indians of greater value than plundering would provide or create a military force of sufficient size and strength to be able to stop their plundering. The government took this advice and compromised with half measures. The annuity was not enough to discourage raiding and the army became fragmented into small posts hardly able to defend their own parade grounds.[4] On May 6, 1851, the *New York Tribune* carried the story that appeared in the *St. Louis Republican* concerning the army in New Mexico. Colonel Sumner was in St. Louis on his way to Fort Leavenworth and then on to Santa Fe. In addition to troops to bolster the companies in New Mexico, Sumner took along farm animals, seeds, grain, farm implements and irrigating appliances.

The *Tribune* was in error in stating that Sumner was in the First U.S. Infantry. He never was. He was still in the First Dragoons until 1855. The paper went on to say that if the army could establish farms in the areas of good soil it would attract settlers to the area.

On May 12, 1851, John Greiner, an old-line Whig who would become acting secretary for the territory of New Mexico in 1852, wrote about Colonel Sumner in a letter from Independence, Missouri, to an unidentified recipient. Greiner called Sumner "the most business-like, energetic man in the army." His letter confirmed the newspaper account. He confessed that the government's plan was a "visionary one."[5]

Greiner reported on the drought: "There has been no rain in this country for eight months." Cholera too was a problem and he wrote that probably thirty men in Sumner's command had died from the disease.[6]

News of the cholera epidemic was reported in the *Syracuse Standard* on June 17, 1851, from a St. Louis source of three days prior. Eight to ten men were reported dead each day because of the disease, and two surgeons were reported dead.

In July of 1851, Lieutenant Colonel Edwin V. Sumner, First Dragoons, assumed command of the Ninth Military District (New Mexico) in his brevet rank of colonel. Under orders (issued the previous April) from Secretary of War Charles M. Conrad, Sumner was to institute a new order. He was to get the troops out of towns and place them in a network of posts designed to protect settlements in New Mexico, block Indian raids into Mexico proper and utilize the countryside for forage, food and fuel. The soldiers were to build their own forts (thus getting rid of civilian carpenters), harvest the forage for their mounts and cut their own firewood. Sumner was to organize campaigns against the tribes of the Navajos, Utes and Apaches. All this was to be done with an eye to strict economy.[7]

John Greiner reached Santa Fe on July 17, after a fifty-three-day trek. He reported there had been no rain in New Mexico for a year. For hundreds of miles not a single spear of grass could be seen. The wheat crop had been entirely destroyed and the corn crop as well. Corn was selling for $5.00 a bushel; flour sold for $15.00 per hundredweight. In his October 1, 1851, letter he described the conditions. The country was infested with "savage Indians, treacherous Mexicans and outlawed Americans." The country appeared to be at cross purposes. The civil and military authorities worked against each other. Specifically, Sumner refused to acknowledge the governor's right to send Indian agents with him into Indian country. "There is hardly an American here that stirs abroad without being armed to the teeth," Greiner reported.[8]

In a letter Greiner wrote on February 29, 1852, he stated, "The Governor [James S. Calhoun] wishes to arm the Mexicans to fight the Indians, but Colonel Sumner refuses to give him the arms to do it with." Still in Santa Fe on March 31, 1852, Greiner wrote that the next day was April Fool's Day and it might prove to be the correct day for him to take on the title of "Indian Agent and acting Superintendent of Indian affairs." He referred to the territory as "this wilderness of sin." Colonel Sumner had fewer than a thousand men, of no earthly account, to control an estimated 92,000 Indians, many of them at war. One mounted dragoon, he reported, weighed 225 pounds and was mounted on a horse he described as "poor as carrion." He concluded with an observation about "heavy dragoons on poor horses, who know nothing of the country, sent after Indians who are at home anywhere."[9]

On July 31, 1852, Greiner wrote that Colonel Sumner was claiming to be acting governor. Sumner said he would remove his troops as soon as the secretary took his post, for no other reason than to embarrass the civil authorities. Sumner, according to the way Greiner saw events, wanted to make it appear that the civil authorities could not govern New Mexico.[10]

Sumner started a comprehensive plan to relocate the troops to more strategic locations. He immediately moved the department headquarters and supply depot from Santa Fe to Fort Union, northeast of what is now Las Vegas, New Mexico, and just west of Interstate 25. He began building a string of forts. He established Fort Massachusetts, recognizing his birth state, on the department's northern frontier and in what would become southern Colorado. Just west of today's border between New Mexico and Arizona in the north-central parts of these two adjacent states, Sumner established Fort Defiance to control the Navajos. He built Fort Conrad below Socorro and Fort Fillmore just to the north of the U.S.–Mexico border.

In 1852, Sumner built Cantonment Burgwin outside what would later be Taos, New Mexico. This post was named for First Dragoon Captain John H.K. Burgwin, who was killed in 1847, when he tried to quell a rebellion. The cantonment provided quick military response to Ute and Apache threats to settlements and supply trains. Sumner personally chose the site for the post. Cantonment Burgwin, like many other posts on the frontier, was hastily constructed. The upright logs that formed the walls of most of the buildings were set in the ground about two feet deep without any protection against decay from moisture or from insects.[11]

Sumner personally resorted to a new product to serve him as a ration while he traveled over the dry and barren Southwest: canned or preserved meat and meat biscuit. *Scientific American* reported he used it and nothing else for days: "Only four ounces were sufficient for his daily sustenance, keeping him healthy and strong." Meat biscuit was a commercially unsuccessful product made by Gail Borden (1801–1874) who developed condensed milk and founded the dairy company that bears his name. A quantity of Borden's meat biscuit went along with Doctor Elisha Kent Kane on the Second Grinnell Expedition to the arctic in 1853.[12]

Sumner's work was not without its frustrations. At one point in 1851, he hastily recommended cavalry be replaced by infantry because horses so frequently broke down. He knew better, and this remark was probably a result of such frustration. A year later he recommended that New Mexico be abandoned altogether: "I consider it certain that some radical change must and will be made in the government of this territory sooner or later; that the people of the United States will not consent to bear this heavy burden, endlessly, without receiving the slightest return, and without even the possibility of bettering the condition of this people." Sumner expressed his opinion of things in New Mexico in a letter he wrote in May 1852. The letter was reported later in an eastern newspaper.[13]

Sumner had some experience dealing with conditions in New Mexico, arriving there as he did with Stephen W. Kearny early in the Mexican War. As Joseph C. Dawson III wrote, "Regular officers such as Major John Washington, Major John Munroe and Lieutenant Colonel Edwin Sumner drew assignments in New Mexico. In both territories [California and New Mexico] Officers operated ad hoc military governments, ... they created governments using civilians—either appointed or elected—who answered to military officers."[14]

Sumner was openly contemptuous of civilian officials at this time. He may have driven Indian agent James C. Calhoun to an early grave. Sumner moved his headquarters to Albuquerque to avoid having to be present to welcome Calhoun's replacement. As an affront, Sumner took along the national flag that flew over the plaza. Sumner not only did not get along with Governor William C. Lane; he also maintained a long feud with the citizens of the territory. In retaliation the local newspapers were critical of his campaigns against the Navajos. Still, Sumner was father to many lasting achievements. Secretary of War Conrad set incompatible goals: a firm defense, a vigorous offense and a strict economy. Although he tried to meet these goals, Sumner failed. "But," Utley wrote, "in the process he sketched the broad outlines of a defense system that endured without basic change for forty years.... [That] neither these nor still later changes fundamentally altered the framework testified to the general soundness of the defense scheme laid out by Colonel Sumner in 1851–52."[15]

On August 17, 1851, Sumner left on his Navajos expedition from Santo Domingo Pueblo, southwest of Santa Fe, with four companies of cavalry, one of artillery and two of infantry. Sumner marched to Canyon de Chelly in what is now Arizona with the cavalry and two mountain howitzers, leaving the rest at Canyon Bonito with Major Electus Backus. Sumner and his men encountered some Indians on the ridges of the canyon, but they were beyond the range of his weapons. Sumner reported, "This expedition was not as desisive [*sic*] as I could wish, but I believe it was as much so, as I ought to have expected. It was hardly possible to close an Indian war of many years standing by one expedition." Newspaper stories critical of Sumner's campaigns appeared in the local papers and were carried back east in the *New York Tribune* and the *St. Louis Republican.*[16]

An excerpt from the *Tribune* dated January 13, 1852, taken from the *St. Louis Republican,* with the banner "Santa Fe Monday October 20, 1851" is an example. It reported Sumner's campaign against the Navajos was a failure.

Part of Sumner's efforts to pacify the territory was to teach the Indians farming, but in this he had little success. His inspection trips did not encourage him. Sumner saw little hope for the area's being anything but a drag on the United States. In May 1852, he wrote, "The truth is, the only resource of this country is the government money. All classes depend upon it, from the professional man and trader down to the beggar." Sumner's report to Secretary of War Charles M. Conrad was printed in the *New York Tribune* on January 10, 1853. Sumner left New Mexico in July 1853, turning command over to Lieutenant Colonel Dixon Miles, the man who would surrender Harpers Ferry during the 1862 Maryland Campaign.[17]

6

Kansas and Popular Sovereignty

The Mexican War ended with the signing in February 1848 of the Treaty of Guadalupe Hidalgo. It added a half million square miles to the United States, and questions concerning those square miles created a political fissure that helped to split the country. Would slavery be permitted in these new lands? As early as August 8, 1846, with the war in Mexico just underway, the Pennsylvania representative to Congress, David Wilmot, offered an amendment to a House appropriations bill. A fundamental condition to the acquisition of any territory from Mexico, the amendment declared, should be that slavery should never exist in any portion of it. That amendment and the idea to preclude slavery from any part of the newly acquired land became known as the Wilmot Proviso.[1]

Enter Lewis Cass. Elected to the Senate from Michigan in 1845, Cass was the presidential candidate of the Democratic Party three years later. Based upon his understanding of the Constitution, Cass believed popular sovereignty should allow the people in the territories to decide for themselves whether or not slavery would exist within the territorial limits. As territorial governor of Michigan, Cass encouraged popular participation in territorial affairs, promoted local self-government and obeyed the wishes of the people without regard to his own right of appointment.[2]

By 1850, various advocates advanced four distinct proposals in answer to the problems of newly acquired territory. The first was the Wilmot Proviso—passed by the House but never by the Senate—that slavery should be excluded entirely. Those people considered to be "Free Soil" advocates supported this proposal. Southern rights advocate John C. Calhoun argued for the second proposal, that slaves were property and should be allowed as any other property would be. The South, in general, approved this approach. The third proposal was the idea that the Missouri Compromise line of 36 degrees,

30 minutes, be extended to the Pacific and would be an equitable division. Men likely to support Henry Clay as well as followers of Lewis Cass supported the third and fourth proposals. The fourth, popular sovereignty, would allow the people of each territory to decide for themselves.[3]

The Kansas-Nebraska Act of 1854, of which Senator Stephen Douglas was the political midwife, brought popular sovereignty to life. It nullified the old Missouri Compromise of 1820 by permitting slavery to exist wherever the people voted to establish it. Douglas argued that the Compromise of 1850 made the 1820 Missouri Compromise and the line it established inapplicable to the question. It

Colonel Edwin Vose Sumner in his middle years.

would, however, Douglas argued, remain in effect until Nebraskans settled the question. Congress would have no part in the discussion.[4] The doctrine of popular sovereignty mandated that the will of the people would be known based upon their votes on issues. But just exactly who were to be the voters? The bloody conflict of the 1850s that tore Kansas apart had its roots in the unfertile soil of this uncertainty. Free Soil settlers from the East understood residency as a qualification for voting. Most of the older states required a year's residency to vote in federal elections and six months for local elections. But widespread internal migration undermined the idea that voting should be tied exclusively to residency. The lack of firm standards for voting led to irregularities, disputed outcomes and downright fraud. Another concern was alien suffrage. Many Western states allowed un-naturalized immigrants to vote.

Kansas held no single standard of popular sovereignty. Missourians believed Kansas must be a slave state if Missouri's economy was to be maintained. Hence many from Missouri came to Kansas to vote. Flaunting their presence, the Missourians openly offended the Free Soil voters. Encouraged by the New England Emigrant Aid Society to settle in Kansas, Northerners outnumbered Southerners in the Kansas territory. However, the territorial administration was under Southern control, having usurped its authority by rigged elections. To counter this legislation the Northern settlers tried to establish their own government. Of the two governments author Carol Bundy wrote, "One was legal but corrupt, the other illegal but representative."[5]

Governor Andrew H. Reeder, a former Pennsylvania lawyer, was now a popular sovereignty Democrat and a Pierce administration appointee. No statesman, Reeder shared Pierce's Southern point of view. He saw his appointment, according to William C. Davis, as an opportunity for personal gain through land speculation. His first official act on November 24, 1854, was to order an election of a delegate to Congress. He defined "residence" as the voter's actual dwelling or his practice of inhabiting the territory to the exclusion of any other home and with a bona fide intention of remaining permanently. Yet John W. Whitfield, former Indian agent and a "Southern rights" candidate largely popular with Missourians, won the election handily. A Leavenworth man told how. Despite Governor Reeder's definition of residency the whole area was overrun on Election Day by hordes from Missouri. They took possession of the polls, browbeat and intimidated judges, forced their votes into the ballot box and drove off all whom they suspected of voting for the other candidate. Voting was done not by secret ballot but by colored ballots. So by the color of the ballot the potential voter carried, his choice of candidate was clearly evident.[6]

Although Sumner had been at Fort Leavenworth in 1850, his time there, for the most part, was before the hostilities between Free Soil and proslavery men. When the Kansas-Nebraska Act was passed in 1854, Sumner was in Europe.

Overseas Assignment

As far back as February 1837, Colonel Stephen W. Kearny, through General-in-Chief Alexander Macomb, asked Sumner about visiting Europe to observe foreign cavalry units. Sumner was interested in the many cavalry improvements made by European armies. However, he did not get to go at that time. But in 1854, he got his chance, visiting Spain and France, mainly. Landing in Liverpool on April 17, 1854, Sumner traveled through London and Paris on his way to Madrid, where he arrived on April 24 with dispatches for the U.S. minister to Spain, Pierre Soule. Sumner was favorably impressed with what he saw of Spanish cavalry units, noting that drunkenness was unknown there and only one man was in confinement.[7]

Sumner was not impressed with the French. He had an interview with the emperor and one with the empress that did not go too well. He visited the elite Saumer Cavalry School as well as observing several cavalry corps in Paris. Although he believed the United States had nothing to learn about cavalry from the French, he did apply for a complete set of French cavalry equipment. He then left Paris for Berlin and returned to the United States on September 19, 1854.[8]

Sumner's session with the Empress Eugénie may have been exaggerated. Mr. Donn Piatt (1819–1891) wrote a questionable account of Sumner's meeting with the Spanish wife of Napoleon III. According to Piatt, an American lawyer, journalist and secretary of the Paris Legation during the Pierce administration, Sumner was sent to Spain to present dispatches to the U.S. minister there in Madrid, Pierre Soule. The papers Sumner carried stated the United States position on the *Black Warrior* affair and the U.S. offer to purchase the island of Cuba.

In February 1854, Cuban officials had seized an American merchant vessel, the *Black Warrior,* on its way from Mobile to New York. Supposedly the ship violated Cuban customs regulations. In spite of protests by the American consul, the cargo was confiscated and the captain heavily fined. The incident caused a great stir in the United States, particularly in the South where elements of the slave power wished to annex Cuba. The event was, however, overshadowed by the Kansas-Nebraska Act.

According to Piatt's story about Summer's meeting with the Empress Eugénie, Sumner told her he had been in her country, and she asked why. Sumner explained that he carried dispatches, dispatches concerning what he called "the Black Warrior outrage." The empress took offense to the term "outrage." Piatt represented her as saying, "You want war, gentlemen — you want war, so as to seize upon Cuba; and you think we cannot prevent it, with this Crimean war on our hands; but we have plenty of arms, plenty of soldiers, and if worst comes to worst, we'll turn the negroes upon you." Sumner shot back an angry reply. The empress left the room to Sumner and several embarrassed American diplomats. Judge Mason scolded Sumner as they left the palace. "Talk to me about scaring us with niggers," Sumner was supposed to have said; "I'd half a mind to box her imperial ears."[9]

On May 27, 1898, the *New York Herald* printed a rebuttal to Piatt's account. Sumner's daughter Mrs. W.W. Teall told how her brother had made Donn Piatt retract the story. She pointed out that while her father was not very diplomatic, he was not a rough frontiersman but was noted for courtly manners.[10]

The First Cavalry

On March 3, 1855, Edwin V. Sumner received a promotion to colonel of the newly-formed First U.S. Cavalry in recognition of his long service in the mounted arm. Sumner organized his command that spring at Jefferson Barracks, Missouri, then in June established his headquarters at Fort Leavenworth,

Kansas. He campaigned against the Sioux that summer and returned to Fort Leavenworth on November 2, 1855.

Officially a colonel, Sumner was to become a pawn on the chess board the Pierce administration made of Kansas. Professor Durwood Ball described the politics. The year 1856 was an election year, and Franklin Pierce was seeking re-nomination by the Democratic Party. His success rested on making popular sovereignty work. The federal army was seen as a law enforcement tool available to Pierce, and Colonel Edwin V. Sumner was the senior commanding officer of troops in the Kansas Territory.

Governing Kansas at this time was the hapless incompetent Wilson Shannon, a mediocre Ohio politician. He arrived in Kansas clinging to the belief that the territorial legislature was legal, its opposition not.[11] Shannon's boss, Secretary of State William Marcy, instructed him to request federal regulars to assist the enforcement powers of United States Marshals—but only as a last resort. Marcy understood the mistrust of standing armies among the population. Meanwhile, Secretary of War Jefferson Davis instructed Colonel Sumner at Fort Leavenworth and Lieutenant Colonel Philip St. George Cooke at Fort Riley to fill Shannon's requisitions of federal troops to act as a *posse comitatus* when necessary. Davis instructed Sumner that he was to furnish a military force to aid the governor when the governor decided the United States Marshals were unable to suppress insurrection.[12]

The *Syracuse Daily Journal* expressed its displeasure with President Pierce when it wrote that President Pierce "shakes his puny fist at the outraged settlers." The paper believed that Free Soil settlers would be treated as outlaws by the administration and driven into submission by United States troops.[13]

Sumner disagreed with the Pierce administration's military policy in Kansas. Anticipating new invasions especially from Missouri, Sumner wanted to be able to intervene against all armed bodies regardless of from whence they came. Davis instructed Sumner through Adjutant General Samuel Cooper that he, Sumner, could only answer the governor's requisition for a military force to overcome armed resistance to the laws and against the peace and quiet of the territory. Sumner's concern was that the territorial authorities, all Democrats, would sic his regulars on Free State settlers but allow Missourians to roam and plunder freely.[14]

Davis ordered Sumner not to disarm bands entering Kansas, reminding him that he was neither to consider where men may have come from nor whether they were armed or not. Sumner was only empowered to act when called upon by the proper authorities when armed resistance was made against the laws of the territory.[15] (See Item 1 in the appendix for Davis' instructions to Sumner.)

Sumner cautioned Governor Shannon against permitting U.S. Marshal Israel B. Donelson to summon a civilian posse to serve federal warrants in

Lawrence, Kansas, a Free State community. Doing so, Sumner realized, would create a confrontation between the two opposing groups, Free Soil and proslavery. Shannon refused and Sumner reported to Secretary Davis that the use of civilian forces made bloodshed unavoidable. Davis praised Sumner's restraint. On May 21, 1856, Donelson's posse of five to eight hundred men sacked Free Soil Lawrence. This coincided with the savage caning of Colonel's Sumner's cousin Charles Sumner, the abolitionist senator from Massachusetts, on the Senate floor by Preston Brooks.[16]

On June 14, 1856, the *Syracuse Journal* carried a story from the *New York Daily Times*. Ossawatomie, a Free State town, was sacked by a Georgia mob on June 5. The printing office was destroyed, houses were burned, sixteen horses were stolen, and the jewels were taken from ladies' ears and fingers.

This background led to the major events of Sumner's action in Kansas. The Free State legislature planned to convene in Topeka on July 4, 1856. Governor Shannon, not wanting to have to deal with this hot issue, left the territory in late June on what he called personal business. Before leaving and turning things over to acting governor Daniel Woodson, who was willing to serve the proslavery cause, Shannon instructed Sumner to disperse the Free State body should it try to convene.

Initially Sumner sent Major John Sedgwick, First Cavalry, to Topeka to prevent the legislature from assembling, but Acting Governor Woodson insisted that Sumner be present as well. Sumner went with five companies of cavalry supported by artillery. In spite of the military array, the Free State assemblage tried to call the members to order. At this point Colonel Sumner intervened. He told the assembly that he was about to perform the most painful duty of his life. However, under the president's proclamation, they could not meet as a legislature and he had to disperse them. On July 4, Sumner declared:

> God knows I have no party feeling and will hold none so long as I hold my present position in Kansas. I have just returned from the borders where I have been sending home companies of Missourians and now I am here to disperse you. I now command you to disperse. I repeat that this is the most painful duty of my whole life. But you must disperse.[17]

When asked if the legislature was to be dispersed at the point of a bayonet, Sumner replied that he would use the whole force at his command to carry out his orders. Some agitated legislators compared Sumner to Oliver Cromwell, who had broken up the English parliament. When Sumner returned to Fort Leavenworth on July 6 the new commander of the Western Department, General Persifor F. Smith, placed him on extended leave. Many saw the leave as a reprimand. Lieutenant Colonel Joseph E. Johnston, now commanding officer at Fort Leavenworth, stated that Sumner left the fort "in high dudgeon" and that he felt, according to Johnston, "ill-used by an ungrateful administration."[18]

The consequences of President Franklin Pierce's decision to commit his administration to support the Kansas-Nebraska Act doomed him to be a one-term president. He became a fly caught in the spiderweb of the partisan struggle for Kansas. Rather than holding a special election to decide which of the two legislatures would govern Kansas, Pierce chose to side with the proslavery side. Enemies of the Pierce administration capitalized on the Topeka episode. For a time Sumner and Davis were at odds. Writing to Adjutant General Samuel Cooper, Sumner explained his actions in Kansas had "borne hard" against both sides. "The Missourians," Sumner wrote, "were perfectly satisfied so long as the troops were employed exclusively against the Free State party; but when they found that I would be strictly impartial, that lawless mobs could no longer come over from Missouri, and that their interference with affairs in Kansas was brought to an end, then they immediately raised a hue-and-cry that they were oppressed by the United States Troops."[19]

The Pierce administration received much criticism for its handling of affairs in Kansas. The *Syracuse Daily Journal* carried the following accusations against Pierce and his administration in its Monday evening issue of June 16, 1856. The paper accused the slave power in Kansas of pillaging towns, murdering settlers and plundering the houses of Free-State men. It named General Whitfield and Colonel Buford as leaders of the "marauding ruffians."

The paper went on to editorialize that since President Pierce had been disappointed in his re-nomination he had changed tactics and no longer was interested in supporting the proslavery faction. "Indeed," the paper continued, "we already perceive indications of this change of tactics in the report that Col. Sumner and Gov. Shannon had ordered the dispersion of a force of the Ruffians under Gen. Whitfield.... But now, since his masters have turned the cold shoulder upon him, he will in all probability return the compliment, by refusing to help them in conquering Kansas."

Ever the legalist, Jefferson Davis complained that there was nothing in the various instructions to Sumner that said he should take preemptive actions against armed groups. Attempting to distance himself from Sumner's dispersal of the Free State men in Topeka, Davis asked what language in the president's proclamation gave Sumner the authority to use force to disperse an illegal legislative body. Sumner had the power, Davis confirmed, to intervene when lawless acts were fully realized but not when serious consequences were merely anticipated.[20]

The *Philadelphia Inquirer* printed an item on page 2 of its August 6, 1856, edition stating that the president sent a message to the Senate in reply to a resolution made by that body that no order had been issued by the War Department to any officer in Kansas to disperse any unarmed meeting of the people of the territory. It went on to report that the secretary of war was not satisfied that circumstances were such as to justify Colonel Sumner in using force to disperse the Topeka assembly. Davis called upon Sumner to communicate more fully regarding his actions at Topeka.

A Contemptible Quibble

Reporting a story from the *New York Herald* on August 12, 1856, the *Syracuse Journal* reported on the Senate resolution that called upon the president for more information concerning the instructions governing Colonel Sumner's actions in Kansas. It quoted Secretary of War Davis that no orders has been issued to any military officer in command in Kansas to disperse any unarmed meeting of the people of that territory or to prevent by military power any assemblage of the people.

The paper then went on to state that the first letter of instructions from Secretary Davis to Col. Sumner had directed him to obey the governor of Kansas, and to employ his troops when the governor might think it necessary "for the suppression of insurrectionary combinations or armed resistance to the execution of the law." Since the Pierce administration recognized the present government of Kansas, then, the paper argued, was not Colonel Sumner correct in disbanding the Topeka Legislature? "The denial, therefore, of the Secretary of War," the paper concluded, "of any authority from him to Col. Sumner to disperse any unarmed meeting of the people of the territory is a contemptible quibble."

This quarrel between Secretary Davis and Colonel Sumner caused no permanent split between them. They had been friends since their dragoon days at Jefferson Barracks. During February 1858, Sumner made frequent visits to Davis when he was bedridden with eye inflammation.[21]

Violence flared unabated while Secretary Davis fretted, trying to split the legal hair that President Pierce's dispatch to Governor Shannon to disband Marshal Donelson's posse following the sack of Lawrence, Kansas, would transform the army's mission there from posse service to military constabulary duty. Davis could ponder this technical distinction; Kansas settlers of either political persuasion needed protection, protection largely withheld as the administration dealt with legal nuances. As a posse, the soldiers served court officers; as an armed constabulary, federal troops patrolled without the legal cloak of federal marshals or county sheriffs.[22] Commenting on how things appeared to the man in the Kansas street was an up-and-coming young lieutenant named James E.B. Stuart. To his niece from Fort Leavenworth on June 6, 1856, Stuart wrote, "You have no idea how delighted we would be to have you with us. Do you think you could trust yourself among border-ruffians? I am afraid we will have hot work yet here in Kansas, murders are committed on both sides every day, a soldier was shot from his horse while riding along the other day. Every one goes armed."[23]

Immediately following the sack of Lawrence on May 21, old John Brown, disillusioned with nonviolent abolitionism and ineffective Free State resistance to the territorial government, took action. Late on the night of May 24, 1856, Brown and his men killed three members of the Doyle family near Pottawatomie Creek. Moving on, they killed Allen Wilkinson, then Dutch Henry Sherman. None owned slaves, but they were supporters of the proslavery party. The Doyles were illiterate and believed blacks to be inferior. These simple men, Henry Sherman the possible exception, were not just murdered but butchered.[24] On June 11, 1856, Major John Sedgwick was back at Fort Leavenworth and wrote to his family in Connecticut. While he said no one could condone the action of Israel Donelson in burning the town of Lawrence, Kansas, and committing other outrages, no life was lost. But the reaction to this sacking resulted in severe crimes. Sedgwick told of five men being taken from their beds, having their throats cut and their bodies mutilated, more horribly than anything done by savage Indians. "I sincerely think that most of the atrocities have been committed by the free-soil party," Sedgwick concluded, "but I cannot think that they countenance such acts—that is, the respectable class."[25]

But the respectable class changed its mind, if it ever held the attitude Major Sedgwick ascribed to it. Judge James Hanway, a Free State settler, understood the public attitude concerning the killings in this light. He thought public opinion was divided. But later he believed that Free State men considered John Brown and his men to have performed a justifiable act that saved their homes from threatened raids of proslavery men.[26]

Thomas Wentworth Higginson, the magnificent activist and fighting preacher, wrote in his informal biography *Cheerful Yesterdays* that regarding John Brown's extreme acts in Kansas, the so-called "Pottawatomie massacre" of May 24, 1856, Kansas Free State men were of one mind. Higginson stated that he had heard of no one who did not approve of Brown's actions. Kansas's Free State leader, Governor Charles Robinson, endorsed the act and told Higginson so.[27]

Oswald Garrison Villard, publisher and historian, tried to explain and partially justify Brown's actions. "There have been advanced many excuses for the killings," Villard wrote, "and a number of them deserve careful scrutiny." Citing the lynch law that brought order out of chaos in 1849 San Francisco, Villard stated that there may be times in a newly settled country when it becomes necessary for the conservative elements to take the law into their own hands, particularly if there is an absence of judicial machinery. But even wild justice must follow a certain procedure, a kind of drum-head trial to give the accused men an opportunity to be heard. And such extra-legal proceedings should be conducted for only the briefest of periods.[28]

On June 5, 1856, Sumner and his troopers converged on Brown's camp on Ottawa Creek telling Brown that he, Sumner, was operating under orders from President Pierce and Governor Shannon to disperse all armed bands. Sumner released Brown's prisoners. Having no warrant, the marshal who came along with Sumner could not put Brown under arrest. Sumner was therefore at that time acting as a posse. At the same time Sumner met with some 250 Missourians who had come to release Brown's prisoners, and Sumner broke up this band as well. Sumner referred to his actions here as a sign of his impartiality.[29]

One of Brown's captives released by Sumner was Henry Clay Pate, captain in the territorial militia and a deputy U.S. marshal. Pate told of his party being taken to a camp on Middle Ottawa Creek and guarded, but they had not been treated unkindly, he said. They were held captive for three days and three nights before Colonel Sumner and a company of dragoons released them.

Colonel Sumner reported from Fort Leavenworth his rescue of Pate's command and his dispersing about 250 men under J.W. Whitfield and militia general Coffee, who were out to rescue Pate and his men. With Colonel Sumner at this time were Major John Sedgwick and Lieutenant James E.B. Stuart plus about fifty cavalrymen. Sumner informed them that he was there by order of the president and proclamation of the governor to disperse all armed bodies assembled without authority. Shortly after Sumner's address the militia moved off, saying they would not resist the authority of the general government. "Whether this is a final dispersion of these lawless armed bodies is very doubtful," Sumner wrote. Sumner believed the governor's proclamation should have been issued six months earlier. "As the matters now stand," he continued, "there is great danger of a serious commotion."[30]

The Cleveland, Ohio, *Plain Dealer* on June 16, 1856, reported on Sumner's releasing the captives. He read the proclamation of Governor Shannon to both groups. Sumner challenged Henry Pate's claim that he was there on orders from Governor Shannon. Stating that Pate was not grateful for being released from Brown's captivity, held as he was by what the paper called "murderous abolitionists," the newspaper went on to report that Pate had slandered Colonel Sumner and sent him a challenge. The item, titled "Interesting from Kansas" concluded by reporting that a private in one of Colonel Sumner's companies had taken the matter and gone out with Henry Clay Pate to answer the insult to his commander.[31]

Major Sedgwick, a Northern man by birth, wrote his account of the dispersal of Brown's band:

Things are getting worse every day, and it is hard to foresee the result. One of these things must happen: either it will terminate in civil war or the vicious will band themselves together to plunder and murder all whom they meet. The day after writing my last letter I started with a squadron of cavalry to go about forty miles to break up an encampment of free-soilers who had been robbing and taking prisoners any pro-slavery man they could meet.[32]

Two clergymen, Charles J. Ellicott and Samuel J. Andrews, writing in the July 1863 issue of the *North American Review,* may have been too otherworldly to have bothered to get their facts straight. They claimed that Colonel Sumner, "commander of the United States forces in the Territory," invaded Kansas to establish "by fraud and intimidation, the slave system of Missouri."[33]

7

The Cavalry

On March 4, 1855, Lieutenant Colonel Edwin Vose Sumner, First Dragoons, became colonel of the newly formed First Cavalry Regiment. Under the forward-looking, reform-minded secretary of war Jefferson Davis, who understood the need for more mounted patrols, the War Department added the new First and Second Cavalry regiments. Supporting Sumner were Joseph E. Johnston, lieutenant colonel, and John Sedgwick and William H. Emory, majors.

Joe Johnston was happy in neither his position of second-in-command nor his rank of lieutenant colonel. He protested to Secretary of War Jefferson Davis. He believed he should have been promoted over Sumner by virtue of his having been a brevet colonel during the Mexican War. Johnston also claimed that he had held the rank of lieutenant colonel prior to Sumner's holding that rank. Nothing came of his petitions, however.

Colonel Albert Sidney Johnston commanded the Second Cavalry Regiment with Lieutenant Colonel Robert E. Lee as second in command. The two majors at the time this regiment was first organized were William J. Hardee and William H. Emory. Emory served for a brief time before transferring to the First Cavalry. The opening made by Emory's transfer was offered to Braxton Bragg, who declined. The position was filled by George H. Thomas. Other men in the Second Cavalry to earn some fame in the future civil war were captains Earl van Dorn, E. Kirby Smith and George Stoneman. Among the Second Cavalry lieutenants to gain future fame were Charles W. Field, John Bell Hood, Nathan "Shanks" Evans, Richard W. Johnson and Kenner Garrard.[1]

In a letter to his wife dated July 1, 1855, from Jefferson Barracks, Robert E. Lee wrote: "I have got a fine puss, which was left me by Colonel Sumner. He was educated by his daughter, Mrs. Jenkins, but is too fond of getting up on my lap and on my bed; he follows me all about the house and stands at the door in an attitude of defiance to all passing dogs."[2]

Mrs. Jenkins was Sumner's first child, Nancy, born at Sackets Harbor, New York, on February 12, 1823. She married Leonidas Jenkins at Fort Atkinson, Iowa, on September 2, 1845. Leonidas Jenkins, a West Point graduate of 1841, was a lieutenant in the First Dragoons when he died of yellow fever on October 18, 1847, at Vera Cruz, Mexico.[3]

To begin the organization of his regiment at Jefferson Barracks, Sumner chose to address the issue of horses. He required 855 mounts at a cost of $135.00 each for a total of $115,425. He requested a good number of mares as they were fleeter, hardier and less susceptible to disease than stallions. He suggested to Quartermaster General Thomas S. Jesup to buy horses at Cincinnati, Ohio, in order to get horses from Kentucky and western Virginia. Sumner tested horse flesh by having the animal run a mile. From 1832 with the founding of the mounted rangers, the method of purchasing horses was based upon requisitions placed by the particular branch of the service, i.e., cavalry, artillery, transportation, etc. This procedure lasted with little change until about 1908 with the establishment of the U.S. Remount Service of the Quartermaster Corps.[4]

On June 19, 1855, Colonel Sumner established the headquarters of the First Cavalry at Fort Leavenworth. In so doing he replaced his friend Lieutenant Colonel Philip St. George Cooke, Second Dragoons, who left on June 9 for Fort Pierre on the Missouri River in Nebraska Territory. John Sedgwick, an artillery man during the Mexican War, had been interim commander at the fort and was now a major in the First Cavalry. Sumner went east on July 5 and among other business, while visiting relatives in New York State he hired fifty carpenters to construct stables and barracks at Fort Leavenworth.

Secretary of War Jefferson Davis was giving serious thought to new arms for the mounted regiments, just as he was considered adopting the rifle musket for the infantry. Developments in France had made the muzzle-loading rifle, traditionally slow to load, a practical infantry arm. It used an undersized, soft-lead bullet that easily slid down the barrel; the bullet expanded because of the force of the gas released by the combustion of the powder charge and gripped the spiraled rifling as it passed down the barrel. The bullet was known as the Minié bullet, named for its inventor. In 1855, Davis ordered the new cavalry regiments to be armed with the Colt Navy model .36-caliber revolver. Much lighter in weight than the Colt Dragoon revolver, the Colt Navy had adequate range and power. Based upon his inspection of weapons in the Department of New Mexico, Major William A. Thornton suggested that the Sharps carbine replace the U.S. Model 1847 musketoon. Thornton was also in favor of a new model saber, as well as better saddles, stirrups and bits.[5]

The First Cavalry Regiment was ordered to join with Brevet Brigadier

General William S. Harney in an expedition to punish the Indians for the so-called Grattan Massacre. This would be the First Cavalry's first campaign. The Grattan Massacre was an unfortunate encounter between soldiers and Indians caused mainly by inexperienced, very junior officers in command at Fort Laramie. In June of 1853, a Miniconjou warrior took a shot at a soldier operating a skiff used as a ferry across the Platte River. The post commander, First Lieutenant Richard B. Garnett, sent Second Lieutenant Hugh Fleming with twenty-three men to arrest the Indian. Invading an Indian community on such an errand was always full of risk and a challenge even for experts. Young Fleming, only a year out of West Point, was no expert. As a result of his handling the situation six Indians were shot. How many may have been killed or seriously wounded is not recorded, but Fleming and his command withdrew minus their prisoner. This bungled operation put the Indians in an ugly mood.[6]

A year later Lieutenant Fleming was in command at Fort Laramie. Second in command was Brevet Second Lieutenant John L. Grattan, West Point class of 1853. In addition to being inexperienced Grattan was a brash hothead. On August 18, 1853, a Mormon emigrant reported at the fort that an Indian had butchered a cow that had strayed. Grattan, waiting for a regimental vacancy, saw this as an opportunity for advancement and pressed the indecisive Lieutenant Fleming to authorize an expedition.

The Indian who slaughtered the cow was a young Miniconjou living in the Brule camp. Chief Conquering Bear of the Brules counseled Lieutenant Fleming to wait for the Indian agent so proper restitution could be made. Complicating the problem was the fact that the Mormon wanted to be moving on with the rest of his train. Fleming gave in to Grattan and the next day Grattan, with twenty-seven privates, two noncoms and two 12-pounder guns marched into the Brules' camp. The guns were trained on the tepees during the forty-five minute parlay, which failed to produce the Indian they were after. Losing his patience, Grattan ordered his men to fire. Chief Conquering Bear fell mortally wounded, then Grattan ordered his guns to fire. They were set at too high an elevation and merely shredded the tops of the tepees. Sioux Indians swarmed over the soldiers and scattered them. Joined by the Oglalas, the Brules raced after the fleeing soldiers, shooting them down as they fled. One wounded survivor reached the fort but died several days later. The enraged Indians pillaged a warehouse and engaged in petty horse stealing. In November a small party of Brules attacked a stage, killing three men and wounding a fourth.[7]

To direct the operations against the Sioux, Colonel William S. Harney, on leave in Paris, France, was called home, given a brigadier general's brevet and put in charge. When he was finished with the organization at Fort Kearny in July 1855, his command numbered about six hundred men, a combination of infantry, artillery and mounted units that included part of Harney's own regiment, the Second Dragoons. Lieutenant Colonel Philip St. George Cooke led the mounted troops.[8]

On September 3 Cooke, with two companies of dragoons and two companies of mounted infantrymen, was on Blue Water Creek above the Indian village. Little Thunder was the chief having taken the place of the dead Conquering Bear. The battleground is in what is now Nebraska, north of Lewellen and due east of Oshkosh, two Nebraska towns on U.S. Route 26. The village was caught between Cooke's men to the north and Harney's troops below the village.

At daybreak Little Thunder and his headmen came out under a white flag for a talk. Harney told them if they were peaceful, they would surrender the warriors who had been causing the trouble. While the chief and his party went back to talk with their people, the infantry advanced. The troops fired when they came within range. The sound of gunfire signaled Cooke's troops. Caught between two columns, the Indians tried to escape up a ravine. Rushing to the edge of the ravine, the infantry fired into the mass of Indians below. The cavalry followed, cutting down the fleeing fugitives. Participating in this battle were three men who would be prominent soldiers eight years later at Gettysburg: Captain Henry Heth and lieutenants Gouverneur K. Warren and John Buford.[9]

Colonel Sumner and the First Cavalry received orders from Washington on August 21, 1855, to join General Harney on the plains. Sumner and his regiment were to pursue the Indians in retaliation for the Grattan Massacre. Sumner was to move out on or before September 20 by direct route to forts Kearny and Laramie. On September 14 Sumner wrote to Harney that he would have four hundred men — about eight companies — at Fort Kearny on October 2. If there were no orders at Fort Kearny for Sumner, he would follow on to Fort Laramie. Harney issued Special Order No. 61 from his headquarters at Fort Pierre, Nebraska Territory, which ordered Sumner to go into winter quarters somewhere that offered the best forage within a radius of from ten to a hundred miles of Fort Laramie. Sumner never got the order. On October 8, with his command between Fort Kearny and Fort Laramie, Sumner began his return to Fort Leavenworth. He could go no farther without sacrificing the greater part of his horses, horses that had cost the government $135.00 a head. After an eight-hundred-mile trek the First Cavalry was back at Fort Leavenworth on November 2, 1855. For this action, Harney brought charges against Sumner. Harney continued to press charges against Sumner until January 1859, but Sumner was never court-martialed.

Harney's expedition had some positive results. Chief Spotted Tail of the Brule gave himself up and was sent to Fort Leavenworth, where he became a friend of Sumner's. When Spotted Tail returned to his people he cautioned his young braves against making war after having seen the number of whites and their arms and equipment.[10]

8

The Cheyenne Expedition

In September 1850, the First Dragoons built a new fort near what is now Dodge City, Kansas. First named Fort Mackey, then renamed Fort Sumner for its builder, it was again renamed Fort Atkinson on June 25, 1851. Serving as a base from which patrols went forth to protect the Santa Fe Trail, Fort Atkinson was the site of councils held between the government and Indian tribes. There the government persuaded some tribes to meet at Fort Laramie, where in 1851, the Fort Laramie Treaty was signed with the Cheyennes and Arapahoes. The southern equivalent of the treaty was signed at Fort Atkinson with the Comanches, Kiowas and Plains Apaches on June 26, 1853.[1]

At first both Indians and whites believed the Fort Laramie Treaty would solve problems of travel along the migration trails. William Bent was encouraged to build a new "fort" on the Arkansas River, about thirty-seven miles east of the original Bent's Fort, now known as Bent's Old Fort. The new trading post was fully stocked for trade by the summer of 1853. But that same summer brought anxiety along the trail.[2]

The idea for a large-scale military campaign against the Cheyennes and other tribes began in 1855. Indian Agent John W. Whitfield, the same proslavery man who would be active in Kansas a year later, believed the Cheyennes and other tribes on the plains needed a "sound chastisement." A year later in 1856, with Whitfield now in Kansas, Colonel William S. Harney believed the Indians needed the same kind of lesson he had given the Sioux. By November 11, 1856, an expedition against the Cheyennes was in the planning stage. The plans were completed by March 1857. On April 4 the army issued General Order No. 5, which directed an expedition against the Cheyennes under the command of Colonel Edwin V. Sumner, First Cavalry.[3]

As was true for so many battles between Indians and whites, the event that triggered this new expedition was the perception of Indian atrocities and

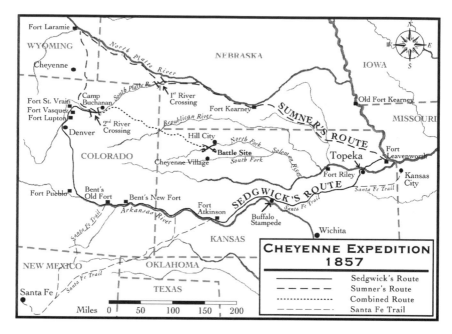

Map showing the area covered by the 1857 expedition against the Cheyenne. It shows the northern route taken by Colonel Sumner and the southern route taken by Major Sedgwick. The sites of two significant events along the way are shown as well.

the need to "teach them a lesson." In mid–1856, a train of emigrants went into camp at the crossing of the Republican River. Things had been quiet and the cattle and oxen were permitted to graze without much of a guard. There had been no signs of Indians. But just as everyone was at his ease, Indians swooped down upon the whites from a line of bluffs that ran parallel to the stream. The battle was short. Only a few managed to escape and make their way to Fort Kearny to tell of the massacre. Although at the time troops were trying to keep the peace in Kansas, when word of the massacre reached Secretary of War Jefferson Davis late in the year, he ordered Colonel Sumner at Fort Leavenworth to take the field as early as possible in 1857.[4]

The specifics of the order were that two squadrons of the First Cavalry (a cavalry squadron was two companies or more, or a third of the regiment) should be equipped and supplied for distant service to move along the line of the Arkansas River as soon as the weather permitted. Another squadron would move at the same time along the Platte River. It would pick up a squadron of Second Dragoons at Fort Kearny, and then add three or four companies of Sixth Infantry at Fort Laramie.

Colonel Sumner was permitted to go with either column, each of which could take one or more prairie howitzers. A supply of forage, enough for at least ten days, was to be sent out in advance of the columns, which would march when the grass was growing well enough to provide sufficient grazing for the stock.

Second in command of the First Cavalry, Lieutenant Colonel Joseph E. Johnston would have no leisure time while the rest of the regiment was away. The orders directed him to take the remaining squadron to move south to survey the southern boundary of the Kansas Territory, a good assignment for a former topographical engineer.[5]

When the two new cavalry regiments were established they were to have half of the captains and lieutenants, company-grade officers, appointed from civilian life. The other half plus the officers of the rank major and above were to be appointed from existing units within the army.

Having to fill the officer positions in the two new cavalry regiments with men drawn from civilian life — the way Colonel Sumner himself had entered military service — may seem as though it ought to have been unnecessary by 1855, with West Point being better established than it had been in 1819. But in any graduating class, only a percentage went into the mounted service, not enough for the needs of two new regiments. During the years from 1855 to 1860, inclusive, one hundred seventeen officers were appointed to the army from civilian life. During the same period two hundred eleven young men graduated from the military academy. Morris Schaff, class of 1862, described the first graduation ceremony that he witnessed as a cadet, that of the class of 1859. Each cadet was called from his seat in the chapel to receive his elaborately engraved diploma, drawn from a drum, the head of which had been removed. Class standing determined the order in which the cadets were called forward to receive their diplomas. Class standing determined the branch of the army they would be going to. From first in the class down to the last, the cadets were assigned to the engineers, the topographical engineers, then ordnance, artillery, infantry, dragoons, cavalry and lastly mounted rifles. With eight branches into which the class was distributed, there were not enough to fill the new cavalry regiments without resorting to civilians.

The branches of the army as listed were in priority sequence, mounted rifles on the bottom. Morris Schaff told the fate of one not-so-gifted scholar, Harold Borland of Arkansas, who did manage to graduate at the bottom of his 1860 class. After six years at the academy he was recommended for the mounted rifles, "the only thing under the heavens for which he could be recommended," Schaff wrote. If he was not too gifted academically, he was clever. Borland, known as "Ginger" to his fellow cadets because of the color of his hair, was asked by Ordnance Captain James G. Benton to state into how many pieces a 12-pound shell would burst. After some thought Ginger replied, "Not less than two."[6]

The First Cavalry was a new and largely inexperienced regiment. Lieutenant Colonel Johnston had been a topographical engineer, as had William H. Emory, although Johnston served for a time with the Voltigeurs and foot riflemen during the Mexican War. Major John Sedgwick had been an artillerist in Mexico. The cavalry was new to these men, but they worked to acquire all that was needed for the expedition. Horses and mules as well as beef cattle for fresh meat along the way were needed in quantity. Next was forage for the animals, food for the men, then clothing, shelter tents, weapons, ammunition and wagons to haul it all. Meanwhile, the troops underwent training.

The logistics required for the men to be equipped and supplied for distant service, as the orders stated, were staggering. Ammunition was needed for a variety of firearms. The troops all carried Colt Model 1851 .36-caliber Navy revolvers, but, depending upon the company, the carbines varied. Three companies carried the U.S. Model 1854 .58-caliber rifled carbine. One company carried Sharps Model 1852 percussion carbines. Another company was armed with Springfield Model 1855 pistol-carbines. In some companies the men carried Merrill, Latrobe and Thomas .54-caliber breechloading percussion carbines.[7]

The Merrill, Latrobe and Thomas carbine was but one model, not three as the reader may think. Equipped with the Maynard primer (the government would consider nothing else at this time), the government bought one hundred seventy of these carbines at $35.00 each. Mechanically the arm was an adaptation of the earlier Jenks carbine, the one Sumner preferred when he tested it for the Ordnance Department at Carlisle Barracks. The first model was known as the Merrill, Latrobe and Thomas carbine and was made by Remington under contract for a Baltimore, Maryland, firm. The breech was opened for loading by a lever on top of the small of the stock. James H. Merrill became associated with Thomas, Latrobe and Thomas in 1855, and the firm brought out the carbine described. The mechanism was cumbersome, and not a success. In 1858, Merrill patented a simpler and more practical breechloading mechanism.[8]

The colors of the horses varied from one company to another for the practical reason that in the midst of combat a trooper could more easily identify his company should he become separated from it. The men in Captain William N.R. Beall's Company A rode sorrel horses; Captain Delos B. Sackett's Company B rode grays; while captain Thomas J. Wood's Company C rode sorrels as did Company F and Company I under captains William D. DeSaussure and George T. Anderson, respectively. Bays were ridden by the men in Companies D, H and K, whose commanders were James McIntosh, Edward W.B. Newby and George H. Steuart. Captain Samuel D. Sturgis, Company E, had his men mounted on roans, while the men in Captain William S. Walker's Company G rode blacks. Again for easy identification the two buglers per company rode white horses and blew their various calls on copper bugles.

These horses were provided to the enlisted men by the government, but officers had to furnish their own. They could be of whatever color the officer wished. Each officer usually had two horses.

William Y. Chalfant may have made a mistake in the spelling of George H. Steuart's last name. There is no listing in Heitman's *Register* for a George H. Stewart but there is for George H. Steuart. George H. Steuart was in the West Point class of 1848 and in the Second Dragoons. He became a captain in the First Cavalry on December 20, 1855. Mr. Chalfant may have made this mistake based upon the account of Private Robert Peck. Peck named the company commanders and spells Steuart's name Stewart.[9]

Of the company commanders, Sackett, Wood, Steuart and Sturgis had been dragoons. Beall and McIntosh had been infantry officers before becoming cavalrymen. DeSaussure, Anderson, Newby and Walker had served in state volunteer units during the Mexican War. While most of the companies of the First Cavalry Regiment were with Sumner and Sedgwick trying to keep the peace in Kansas, Steuart and his Company K rode to Fort Kearny in 1856 and made an attack upon a Cheyenne war party.[10]

With the spring thaw of 1857, solid ice on the Missouri River broke and the river became navigable once again. New recruits began to arrive at Fort Leavenworth to fill the vacancies in the companies. As late as April 29, 1857, less than a month before the expedition was to depart, another three hundred recruits arrived. Training was hectic to get the new men ready for the upcoming campaign. But with these new men the companies were at full strength — eighty-four privates per company — plus four sergeants, four corporals, two buglers, and one farrier plus the captain and one first and one second lieutenant.

For his service a private earned $12.00 per month. A corporal earned $14.00, and if and when he rose to sergeant's rank he would earn $17.00. A first sergeant earned the princely sum of $22.00 per month.[11]

Among the three hundred troopers to arrive at Fort Leavenworth after the ice broke on the Missouri River was Private Robert Morris Peck, a printing office apprentice not yet eighteen years of age. He enlisted in Company E, First Cavalry, in Covington, Kentucky, sometime in November 1856, and with a lot of other recruits went to Jefferson Barracks. They trained and drilled throughout the winter and at the end of February went by steamboat up the ice-chocked, muddy Missouri River to Kansas.[12]

Farther on in his narrative Peck described Colonel Sumner and Lieutenant Colonel Joseph Johnston and named some of the officers in Sumner's company and regiment. Sumner, whom Peck described as being well into his advanced years, had snow white hair and a beard to match. To young private Peck, "he was still quite vigorous, every inch a soldier, straight as an arrow, and could ride like a Cheyenne." To Peck he was the ideal commander and,

Peck believed, the men idolized him. It seemed to Peck that Sumner, known as "the old Bull o' the woods," was always happiest when there was a fight in sight.

Mr. Peck wrote this piece in 1901. He may have remembered Colonel Sumner from his pictures taken during the Civil War, when Sumner's hair and beard were indeed "white as snow." But in a picture of Sumner taken about 1855, his hair and mustache were dark and he wore no beard.[13]

Of Lieutenant Colonel Joseph E. Johnston, Peck and his fellow soldiers did not think so highly. "Old Joe" Johnston was too cautious, lacking Sumner's aggressive dash. Peck named other officers as well. The majors were John Sedgwick and William H. Emory; the captains Wm. N.R. Beall, Delos B. Sackett, Thomas Wood, James McIntosh, Samuel D. Sturgis, William Dessansure [sic], William Walker, Edward W.B. Newby, George Burgwin Anderson, and George H. Stewart [sic]. George B. McClellan had been a captain in the regiment but had resigned before Peck enlisted. Among the lieutenants were James E.B. Stuart, George D. Bayard, David Stanley, Eugene A. Carr, Frank Wheaton, Eugene Crittenden, Eli Long, David Bell, Jos. H. Taylor, Jas. B. McIntyre, Elmer Otis and John A. Thompson.[14]

It is not clear who replaced Captain George B. McClellan nor which company he was to command. Francis B. Heitman lists March 3, 1855, as the date of appointment for all the First Cavalry captains. McClellan's biographer Ethan S. Rafuse gives the date of March 22, 1855, as the date he accepted his captaincy in the First Cavalry. "But before he could assume his new duties," Rafuse wrote, "he was tapped for the premier peacetime assignment of his prewar army career: service on a special three-man commission to study European military systems and observe operations in the Crimea." Stephen W. Sears gives McClellan's date of appointment to captain as March 3, 1855.[15]

On April 15, 1857, even before all the new troops arrived, Colonel Sumner issued orders designating which companies of the First Cavalry would form the several columns. The southern column, under Major John Sedgwick, would comprise companies D, E, G and H. Companies A and B were to be the northern column under Colonel Sumner; they were to be joined by companies E and H of the Second Dragoons when Sumner's column reached Fort Kearny. Then when it arrived at Fort Laramie, companies C, D and G, Sixth Infantry, would be added to Sumner's command. Lastly, companies C, F, I and K of the First Cavalry under Lieutenant Colonel Joe Johnston would move south to survey the southern boundary line of Kansas Territory. In addition they were to keep on the lookout for hostile Kiowas.[16]

The campaign had its chroniclers. One of Sedgwick's soldiers, Private Robert Morris Peck, in curly, black-haired Captain Samuel D. Sturgis' Company E, kept a record of the column's march he published years later, from which excerpts have already been taken. Colonel Sumner's head wagon master and former dragoon, Percival G. Lowe, published his experiences in his book, *Five Years a Dragoon ('49 to '54) and Other Adventures on the Great Plains.* Disgruntled first lieutenant James Ewell Brown Stuart's letters to his wife add to the literature of the expedition. A young second lieutenant in company H, Eli Long, kept a diary from May 18 until September 14, 1857. Appointed from civilian life, Long made the army his career and rose to become a Union major general of volunteers during the Civil War. Because of his last name, Long, he was confused with Sumner's son-in-law Armistead L. Long.[17]

The forces assembled for the Cheyenne Expedition were divided into the southern wing under Major John Sedgwick and the northern wing under Colonel Edwin V. Sumner. They would move essentially southwest and northwest, respectively, and in general circle what is the present state of Kansas — except for its southeastern portion and its southern boundary — and encircle eastern Colorado as well. The two columns were to meet on or about July 4 at a site midway between what are now Denver, Colorado, and Cheyenne, Wyoming.

Sedgwick traveled more south than west from Fort Leavenworth to below Topeka, Kansas, where he would follow the Santa Fe Trail to Fort Atkinson near the site of present-day Dodge City, Kansas. From there his column would follow the Arkansas River to Bent's New Fort and on to Pueblo, Colorado, where he would swing due north to meet Sumner.

Colonel Sumner's column, ordered to forts Kearny and Laramie in what would become today's Nebraska and Wyoming, moved pretty much on a straight line northwest from Fort Leavenworth. They picked up the Oregon Trail near the present border of Kansas and Nebraska and followed it to Fort Kearny, where they met the dragoons that were to join them. From Fort Kearny they moved on a northwest line to Fort Laramie following the Oregon Trail and the south bank of the "too thick to drink, too thin to plow" North Platte River. From Fort Laramie, now accompanied by infantry companies, Sumner's column marched due south to meet Major Sedgwick.[18]

9

The Campaign Begins

The Cheyenne Expedition began with Major John Sedgwick's column leaving at 9:00 A.M. on May 18, 1857. The men of senior captain Samuel D. Sturgis' Company E, riding their roan horses four abreast, led the way with the pleasant-faced Sturgis at their head. The last troops to pass Colonel Sumner and his staff went by at 10:00 A.M. Far in front of the column after it had passed in review rode four Delaware Indian scouts led by a chief named Fall Leaf. These scouts were to prove to be the best. Major Sedgwick and his adjutant, Second Lieutenant Lunsford Lindsay Lomax of Company D, and a bugler rode some distance behind the Indian scouts.

With Captain Sturgis in the lead rode First Lieutenant Frank Wheaton and Second Lieutenant Eugene W. Crittenden. Next came Captain Edward W.B. Newby accompanied by First Lieutenant James B. McIntyre and Second Lieutenant Eli Long leading their Company H. Company G followed with only Second Lieutenant George D. Bayard to lead it. The captain, William S. Walker, was on leave to be married, and First Lieutenant J.E.B. Stuart of G Company was to go with Colonel Sumner, still at Fort Leavenworth. The last company, D, was headed by Captain James McIntosh and First Lieutenant David S. Stanley. Two prairie howitzers brought up the rear. News of the troops' leaving Fort Leavenworth was reported in the *New York Tribune* on June 12, 1857. Four days later in its June 16 edition the paper reported on the expedition in more detail, naming the companies and the company commanders that comprised the two columns. Even Joe Johnston's Kansas boundary survey was covered.[1]

Sedgwick's column halted at Salt Creek after three miles of travel to allow the wagon train, the remuda of spare horses and mules, and the beef herd to catch up. That evening they went into camp by the tiny proslavery hamlet of Eastin. Soon a mounted officer with several men on foot came into camp. These soldiers had been in jail in Leavenworth City because of excessive celebration in anticipation of their departure for the plains. Colonel Sumner paid their fines so they could join their units.

On Tuesday morning, May 19, the routine of the trail began. The men were up at first light and began their daily routine after roll call. At 7:00 A.M. they broke camp, having groomed, watered and fed their horses, had their breakfast and packed their tents and gear in the company wagons. This routine would hardly vary except they would be on the march by 6:30 A.M. the next day and from then on. On this day's march they passed more proslavery settlements going into camp on Grasshopper Creek opposite Lecompton, the proslavery territorial capital.[2]

Private Peck described the settlements in this part of Kan-

John Sedgwick as a Union major general. Sedgwick, a long-time subordinate to General Sumner, was killed by a sniper in May 1864. Massachusetts Commandery Military Order of the Loyal Legion and the U.S. Army Military History Institute.

sas: "As we (Sedgwick's command) marched westward, we found the settlements of Kansas few and scattering, generally being confined to the timber along the watercourses, most of the prairie being yet unoccupied." The men crossed the Kaw River on horseback but the wagons crossed one at a time on a ferry. The ferry was a flatboat pulled back and forth by means of a rope stretched between trees on each bank of the river. After crossing they hit the old Santa Fe Trail just west of Topeka.

Private Peck encountered a tribe of Kaw Indians and formed a low opinion of them:

> Just south of Council Grove the government had established a reservation, agency and mission for the Kaw tribe of Indians, where teachers, preachers, farmers and mechanics were trying to teach them the arts of peace — more particularly, how to earn their bread by the sweat of their brows—but with indifferent success; for Mr. Lo [a derogatory name for Indians from the supposedly Eastern concern for them and expressed as "Lo, the poor Indian"] invariably develops an inherent horror of labor, and would sooner raise hell and hair any time than corn.[3]

On May 20, the first day Sedgwick's men began to break camp at 6:30 A.M., they crossed the Kaw River on the ferry; Colonel Sumner and his two companies were leaving Fort Leavenworth on their northwest trek. Viewing the procession's ceremonial departure was the new post commander, Lieutenant Colonel George Andrews, Sixth Infantry. With Colonel Sumner at the front of the troops were First Lieutenant James Ewell Brown Stuart, Company G, acting regimental quartermaster and commissary officer, and Second Lieutenant Albert V. Colburn of Company B, regimental adjutant. Within this small clutch of men were the orderly bugler and a four-mule ambulance to be used as a mobile headquarters. Next came Company A, its captain, William N.R. Beall, First Lieutenant John N. Perkins and Second Lieutenant Richard H. Riddick, all in the lead. Behind the men of Company A, mounted on sorrel horses, came Company B on grays, led by First Lieutenant Phillip Stockton. Captain Delos B. Sackett of Company B was in Washington, D.C., on special orders.

Transportation that went along with Sumner included the ambulance,

Samuel D. Sturgis as a brigadier in the Union army. Massachusetts Commandery Military Order of the Loyal Legion and the U.S. Army Military History Institute.

fifty wagons drawn by six-mule teams, two prairie howitzers pulled by four-mule teams, the remuda of extra horses and mules, and the beef herd. In charge of the transportation was ex-dragoon Percival G. Lowe, who was put in charge of the wagon train on May 1, 1857, at Lieutenant Jeb Stuart's request.[4]

The regimental band accompanied Sumner and after playing the traditional "The Girl I Left Behind Me," cased their instruments. Later they would be stored in a wagon. Following the route taken by Major Sedgwick for the first several miles, Sumner too halted at Salt Creek to allow the wagon train and animals to catch up.

As Sumner's column marched on a northwesterly line they passed through the last two towns to represent civilization until they reached Fort Kearny.

The towns, Palmetto and Marysville, were divided by the Big Blue River. Marysville, the larger of the two, could boast of twenty log houses, a weekly newspaper and atrocious whiskey.[5]

On May 31 Sumner crossed the Big Sandy and camped on the Little Blue River about eighty miles southeast of Fort Kearny. The next day Lieutenant Jeb Stuart resigned as regimental quartermaster and commissary officer, his place being taken over by Second Lieutenant Riddick. Lieutenant Jeb Stuart had a grievance.

10

Trouble Along the Way

The Angry Lieutenant

Working from his sickbed in the last days preceding the departure of Colonel Sumner's northern column, First Lieutenant James E.B. Stuart saw fit to contradict his colonel. Writing to the adjutant general, U.S. Army, in Washington on June 1, 1857, from a camp on the Little Blue River, Oregon Route, Stuart spelled out in great detail his dispute with Colonel Sumner. The dispute arose when Sumner asked Stuart to sign receipts for ordnance already loaded into wagons that had left the fort. Stuart signed them but objected to being held accountable for items he did not count before the wagons were loaded and sent out. Sumner then relieved Stuart of his position as regimental quartermaster.

Lieutenant Stuart, West Point class of 1854, had received his promotion from brevet to second lieutenant in March 1855, when he went from the Mounted Riflemen in Texas to the First Cavalry. He served as regimental quartermaster from July 1855 until the end of May 1857. He was good at his job. In May of 1856, he rode into Fort Leavenworth one night requesting forage and rations for Colonel Sumner's command camped south of Westport, Missouri (present-day Kansas City), about thirty-four miles from Fort Leavenworth. The route, according to acting post wagon master Percival G. Lowe, was over a crooked, narrow, rutted, little-used road. "Stuart had been a quiet witness of a very hard struggle, and but for his piloting we should not have gotten there [Sumner's camp] that night for he was the only one of the party who had been over the road," Lowe wrote.[1]

Stuart went on to explain to the adjutant general how Colonel Sumner's clerk had given him the invoice and receipts for the ordnance of the command that was already in the wagons and had started out. Upon being summoned to Sumner, Stuart asked the colonel if he had referred to the regulations in regard to ordnance and said that he, Sumner, was required to take charge of it. Stuart went on to great length to explain the circumstances of his being removed from his position of regimental quartermaster. In closing Stuart wrote that the offence he was charged with committing was "objecting to take charge temporarily of the ordnance &c."[2] The letter was signed "J.E.B. Stuart 1st Lt. 1st Cav." Colonel Sumner penned his remarks to the adjutant general on the back of Stuart's letter. The tone of Stuart's letter shows he felt he had been wronged by Colonel Sumner, yet he performed well on the campaign. There is no evidence that Sumner held any grudge against the headstrong lieutenant.

Upon arriving at Fort Kearny, Sumner met the two companies, E and H, of Second Dragoons that were to join the expedition plus one hundred recruits for companies B, C, D and G, Sixth Infantry, who had been ordered to go along with Sumner to Fort Laramie to join their companies. During June 4 and 5 the new regimental quartermaster, Second Lieutenant Riddick, who replaced Jeb Stuart in the assignment, worked with wagon master Percival G. Lowe to see to the loading and packing of supplies, forage, grain and other items to replenish what had been consumed along the way.[3]

The Buffalo Stampede

On May 30, 1855, while First Lieutenant James E.B. Stuart was ending his role as regimental quartermaster and possibly composing in his head his June 1 letter to Adjutant General Samuel Cooper, miles to the south Major Sedgwick's column was coming upon prairie-dog towns and into Buffalo country. The day before they entered the Great Plains was marked by the change in the grass. The taller grass ended and shorter buffalo grass took over the landscape. First Lieutenant James B. McIntyre and a Delaware Indian scout each killed a buffalo. That evening the men ate buffalo meat, the first for most of them. Most soldiers found the grass-fed bison lean, tough and stringy.

Lieutenant Eli Long recorded in his diary for May 29 that two buffalo were killed: "Saw two or three herd of Buffalo an Indian killed one and [Lt. James] McIntyre also killed one." Long did not go hunting, because his horse was pretty well used up and he had left his revolver in his trunk. Other travelers reported favorably as to the quality of buffalo flesh. One young bride, making the trip in 1849, found the flesh of the buffalo enjoyable and was pleased to have it. "When rations were low it came in very handy," she wrote.[4]

Major General John Gibbon wrote that when he was on the plains in 1860 as a young officer he had enjoyed a baked buffalo head. The skin was left on when baking the head and it was placed in a fire pit full of coals in the ground. This was covered with several inches of dirt and a fire built over it. The head baked overnight. Gibbon's soldiers were inexperienced in the art of frontier baking, and it had to be baked for a second time. They managed to get grit on the meat when they unwrapped the protective skin. Still in all, Gibbon wrote that the meat was soft and tender and the tongue like marrow.[5]

Breaking camp that Saturday, May 30, 1857, Sedgwick's command set out for the Little Arkansas River, about a twenty-mile march. While they found neither water nor timber along the way they did find large herds of buffalo, giving the officers a little sport. Some enlisted men tried in vain to hunt on foot. At the end of the day the officers had killed twenty of the shaggy denizens of the plains.

The sport of buffalo hunting was dangerous, as much for the hunters as the hunted, or at least as dangerous for the horses used in the chase. George Armstrong Custer shot his horse in the head with his revolver during one long chase and fell hard to the ground. Hunting with Orlando B. Willcox in August 1850, a soldier name Godwin killed his horse when he shot him through the neck. Nathan "Shanks" Evans shot his mare through the ear on the same hunt and no buffaloes were killed.[6]

Willcox was an artillery man and sometimes used a six-pounder as his weapon of choice: "Killed another in the afternoon with a six pounder gun at about four hundred yards, with canister shot; he was one of a group of three I shot at." The effect of the gun must have been impressive for about two months later Willcox recorded this entry: "The Dr. got out a six-pounder and several buffalo were shot down within short range of our camp. The meat of the calves & heifers delicious; the udder particularly." On the other extreme, Lieutenant James W. Abert preferred a double-barreled shotgun when hunting on horseback. The heavy, solid one-ounce balls made a mortal wound.[7]

Sometimes when a hunter could approach the herd downwind and thus get within range undiscovered, he could shoot from ten to fifteen before the herd spotted him. Buffalos seemed unconcerned when members of the herd fell over. Only if the wind changed direction or a wounded animal gave the alarm would the herd run on, moving in a gallop "when the long hair on the fore-arm flutters about like a pair of sailor's trowsers."[8]

Eli Long told of the technique of buffalo hunting on horseback. When the hunter got near enough to fire into the buffalo's left flank (apparently the hunter rode on the left flank whenever possible) he had to instantly wheel his horse to the left to avoid being gored. "It is a noble sight," Long wrote, "to see the old bulls come down gradually to their knees oscillating from side to side like a balloon as if reluctant to give up their free and savage life."[9]

Trooper Robert Peck, young and certainly impressionable, wrote about the wildlife he saw along the march. "The first settlement of prairie-dogs that

I noticed was at the Little Arkansas," Peck recollected, "but from that time on throughout the trip we were seldom out of sight of these interesting little animals."[10]

Frequently along the route, Major Sedgwick's column came across signs that former travelers had come that way. When they made camp on May 30 they found a large pile of stones with a faded headboard. It marked the grave of a captain and eight privates from a dragoon company killed by Indians some years earlier. The names, the date and the company to which these men belonged were secrets the weathered board did not reveal.[11]

Major Sedgwick and his men were not the only ones traveling. A Majors and Russell wagon train heading for New Mexico was camped in the middle of a prairie-dog town just above the military camp. It seems an odd place to camp, as the burrows might have caused a sprain or other injury had they been stepped into by man or beast. A wagon train of immigrants with twenty-five hundred head of cattle was camped across the stream from the army. Although they claimed to be headed to California, many of the officers believed they were Mormons on their way to Utah. The suspicion of the army officers was understandable in light of recent Mormon troubles and a pending expedition to be sent against them.[12]

On Sunday, May 31, they moved out with the Big Bend of the Arkansas River as their objective for the day. They met two trains heading east. One was a Mexican train that had lost twenty-five mules to a stampede by a great buffalo herd. Sedgwick's train was a long, strung-out column of cavalry, supply wagons, remuda and a beef herd. As the column snaked its way down into the Arkansas River valley, the plain ahead seemed to be one dark mass of buffaloes.

The men witnessing the sight below and ahead of them saw something unique to their age, vast herds of American bison. To try to visualize their numbers and the extent covered by these immense herds taxes our imagination today even as we read vivid descriptions of them. The buffalo ranged in its heyday from the plains of Texas to above the border with Canada and from the Missouri River and upper Mississippi to the slopes of the Rocky Mountains. Sometimes there were as many as 10,000 animals in a single herd. Their numbers have been estimated at over sixty million at their peak. In the summer of 1868, General William T. Sherman and his command rode for three days through one continuous herd. At the height of the bison's commercial slaughter, between 1872 and 1874, more than 5,100,000 hides were shipped, and this number does not include the hides used locally by native tribes. It is estimated that each Plains Indian used three buffalo hides each year.[13]

Francis Parkman recorded these entries in his journal in 1846: June 6, "Saw the hills dotted with thousands of buffalo." September 1, "We had not gone a mile, when the prairie in front was literally black with buffalo." September

3, "A long line of buffalo stretched over the prairie.... The roaring and fighting of the bulls were incessant."[14]

On September 29, 1850, Orlando B. Willcox made the following entry in his diary: "Sunday. Buffalo in thousands and thousands around us all day. Large districts perfectly black with them. The river from Pawnee Rock very extensive and all the country around alive with herds. [Mansfield] Lovell had a fine chase, killing a couple of cows and a calf."[15]

Catherine Haun, the young bride of an Iowa lawyer, made the trek across the plains in 1849. She and her husband had decided to follow the path of the gold rush as part of a large, well-equipped wagon train in hopes of a better life in a better climate. She wrote of her encounter with the buffaloes:

> This was the land of the buffalo. One day a herd came in our direction like a great black cloud, a threatening moving mountain, advancing towards us very swiftly and with wild snorts, noses almost to the ground and tails flying in midair. I haven't any idea how many there were but they seemed to be innumerable and made a deafening terrible noise as is their habit, when stampeding, they did not turn out of their course for anything. Some of our wagons were within their line of advance and in consequence one was completely demolished and two were overturned. Several people were hurt, one child's shoulder being dislocated, but fortunately no one was killed.[16]

Fully aware of the destructive power of a vast herd of stampeding buffalo, still Mrs. Haun appreciated the importance of these shaggy beasts to the western traveler of her day. She told how the people of the wagon trains walked and gathered buffalo chips in bags and used them for fuel. She believed the travelers over the plains could not have survived without "this useful animal." The travelers made frequent use of the buffalo's hump, tongue, marrowbone, tallow, hide and chips.[17]

Former private Robert Peck admitted he hesitated to tell later generations of the size of the herds he had seen lest they would believe he was greatly exaggerating. He told of first seeing buffalo at Cottonwood Creek about fifty miles west of Council Grove. At first the herds were small in numbers and scattered. Soon, however, their numbers increased amazingly. The distance through the herds east and west, Peck reported, varied from one hundred fifty to two hundred miles.[18]

Peck described in some detail a stampede that nearly overran and trampled Sedgwick's command. As Sedgwick's strung-out column approached the Big Bend of the Arkansas River and crossing a level stretch of about eight miles, a mammoth herd of stampeding buffalo was bearing down upon them about two miles away. Fortunately for the column Major Sedgwick had the common sense to turn control over to Captain Samuel Sturgis.

Sedgwick, although an experienced officer, had little experience on the plains. Before he transferred into the First Cavalry he had served in the artillery for nearly twenty years. "The sight of that brown mass of animals—so vast in extent that we could see no end in flank or depth —," Private Peck wrote, "thundering towards us in an irresistible torrent, made him turn pale, as he appealed to Sturgis: 'Sturgis, what'll we do?'" (See Item 2 in the appendix for Peck's description of the oncoming buffalo.)

Captain Samuel Sturgis, West Point class of 1846, served in the Mexican War as a second lieutenant in the First Dragoons. In 1855, he held the rank of captain and fought the Mescalero Apaches along with Lieutenant Colonel Dixon S. Miles and Captain Richard S. Ewell. Sturgis had been in buffalo stampedes before and knew what needed to be done. He sent the bugler back to have the wagons formed into a corral and the beef cattle and the other animals herded inside. The bugler was to inform the company commanders that Sturgis was temporarily in command. Then Sturgis had the men gallop back to the train and form a "V" about one hundred yards ahead of the wagon corral, the point of which faced the onrushing herd. One man in four held the horses, as the cavalrymen were to fight their shaggy foe on foot. The corral of wagons was contained within the wide open end of the "V." Private Peck estimated the herd was about two miles away when Captain Sturgis took command. They were coming from the north.

At the command to commence fire the troopers poured a sheet of lead into the charging herd from their "Sharp's [sic] rifles," Peck stated. So hot and heavy was the firing into the mass of charging animals that the herd began to split apart. They actually climbed over one another. Parting as they did, the herd ran on either side of the hastily constructed corral but went right on running as fast as ever.[19]

William Chalfant named the firearms distributed among the companies but not in enough detail to know which company had what type of arm. Since only one company had Sharps and Private Peck mentioned that arm, we can be pretty sure the Sharps were in Captain Samuel Sturgis' Company E. Whatever poor company had the Model 1855 pistol-carbine it is to be hoped that company was with Joe Johnston and his surveying party.

The men butchered the better cuts of meat from the younger buffalo and stowed it away in their wagons. The rest they left for the wolves. The threat of the stampede over, they moved on and made camp that night on the Big Bend, camping on the river bank. From Big Bend their road westward lay along the north bank of the Arkansas River.

While Private Peck was vividly impressed by his near-death experience with the buffalo stampede that he described it in detail in his "Recollections," Lieutenant Eli Long, a budding buffalo hunter, had only this to record in his diary: "Buffalo immense herd were stampeded and crossed the road right in front of the column." What makes this entry curious is not only its nonchalance, but that the day before, his entry included his starting after a herd but not getting "a shot at them, failing to get my Hoosier horse George within shooting range." Then Long's entry for Saturday June 6 contained this line: "Lt. [George D.] Bayard the most indefatigable sportsman in the command killed a white wolf and took its scalp." Perhaps it is because Lieutenant Long was back with the wagons and not on the firing line that he seemed so indifferent to the stampede that so impressed the young Private Peck.[20]

German emigrant Eugene Bandel was a soldier in the First Cavalry. He was part of Lieutenant Colonel Joseph Johnston's Kansas border survey. He wrote, "I would see great herds of buffaloes in every direction, as numerous as the stars in the heavens." Later he wrote, "We marched about twenty-one miles over very level prairie covered with buffaloes, who have left scarcely enough grass to keep our animals alive. A good many of our mules gave out today." Bandel explained how much of the buffalo carcass was wasted as only the tongue, liver and a few choice cuts were taken. "Of a buffalo weighing from eight hundred to a thousand pounds, hardly fifty pounds of meat will be taken by the men of the command. I killed one on the road today but did not take any of the meat, having plenty of it in our wagons already."

Probably the men in Lieutenant James Abert's expedition to the southwest in 1845 made the best use of the buffalo carcass. Abert wrote that bulls were rarely shot for meat other than in the spring. In other seasons the meat from the bulls was rank and unpleasant. Abert told how the hide along the backbone was slit and the meat cut off from both sides of the vertebrae. (For a more detailed description of the butchering process see Lieutenant James Abert's description in the appendix, Item 7.[21])

The River Crossing

At the request of the regimental quartermaster, First Lieutenant Jeb Stuart, Percival G. Lowe took charge of the transportation for the Cheyenne Expedition. Lowe assigned "Nick" Beery as chief wagonmaster for Major John Sedgwick's southern column, explaining that it was to go up the Arkansas River by way of the Santa Fe route to about where Pueblo, Colorado, now stands, then up to about the site of Denver and down the South Platte River to Fort St. Vrain, about thirty-five miles north of the site of Denver or near present-day Greeley, Colorado. There he would meet Colonel Sumner's column on or about July 4, 1857.

Lowe recorded in his diary for June 6, 1857, "Command left [Fort] Kearny, and without incident of importance camped four miles below Beauvais' Crossing of South Platte June 13." "Without incident" evidently covered the days in between June 6 and 13. The fourteenth was a day of rest, and Lowe ordered the canvas covers taken off the wagons to let the sun dry out the dampness that was sure to have accumulated. The next day, June 15, Lowe and his assistants left camp at five o'clock that morning and rode to the river crossing. The river, high from the melting snow in the mountains, was about half a mile wide, and the current ran about three to four miles per hour.[22]

Percival G. Lowe was born in New Hampshire on September 29, 1828. He was a brother to Thaddeus Sobieski Constantine Lowe, a balloonist for the Union army during the Civil War. Before joining the dragoons in 1849 he had worked first as a newsboy at the age of fifteen then as a dry goods store clerk in Lowell, Massachusetts. He had been to sea twice; first along the coastal waters and then on a whaling ship. Between sea adventures he had learned the daguerreotype business.

When Lowe's five-year enlistment in the dragoons came to an end in 1854, he believed he had learned all he could in the army and saw a better future for himself as a civilian employee of the Quartermaster Department. One thing he had learned as a dragoon was about to help him here on the South Platte River crossing.

Back in 1850, Lowe, as a dragoon en route to Fort Laramie, had to cross this same quicksand-bottomed South Platte River. He learned how from famous Mountain Man Tom Fitzpatrick, the same mountain man-turned-Indian agent who was critical of the fixed post and roaming patrol concepts explained earlier. The quicksand had to be beaten down to become firm before the wagons could cross. Without a firm roadbed or river bottom, the wagons could be mired and sink or could be upset if one side of the wagon sank into the sand more quickly than the opposite side. The way to pack the sand and make it firm was to cross with many animals, maybe having to go back and forth several times if the herd was not large. The animals needed to be encouraged to move quickly or else they would get hopelessly sucked into the quicksand. Their many feet and hooves in time would make the river bottom firm enough for the wagons to cross. But no time could be lost or the bottom would become soft once again.[23]

Now Lowe began his preparations to get Colonel Sumner's column — men, trains and animals — across the swollen South Platte River. At the crossing site the river was half a mile wide and on average about two feet deep. Pointing out the landing site on the far north bank, Lowe selected a quick-witted teamster named Eskridge to remain on the south bank and keep his eye fixed on the far site. Eskridge was to watch Lowe as he walked across the river to the landing site on the north bank. Eskridge was no mere observer. His job was to signal Lowe if he began to drift from a straight line, because the strength of the current, estimated to be about three to four miles an hour, would carry Lowe downstream. As he walked across Lowe found the river bottom to be very uneven. In some places the water was but a foot deep, in others three to four.

There was a small island just upstream from the crossing where many tall, slim willows grew. Lowe and some of his men who followed him cut a number of these into poles about ten to twelve feet long. They allowed the leaves on the top to serve as a kind of banner. Lowe, now across the South Platte, stood at the landing site and, keeping an eye on Eskridge, directed the men with the willow shafts to push them into the quicksand bottom in a straight line from Lowe to Eskridge. The willow shafts were put in where the river was the shallowest so the current, weakest in the shallow water, would not wash them away so easily. It was a tedious struggle according to Lowe, but they got them placed in a straight line from bank to bank.

The cavalry rode up about the time Lowe got finished setting the willow poles. Lowe explained the method of crossing to Colonel Sumner and quartermaster second lieutenant R.H. Riddick. The crossing must be made close to the line of willows. Lowe wrote that Sumner needed no long explanation, as he had been there in 1850. So Percival G. Lowe, chief wagonmaster, started out first to show the way and the head of the column followed, keeping up fairly well. Before long, however, some of the files began to drift with the current and the column began to bow, the center about three hundred yards below or downstream from the line of willow markers. Many horses floundered, Lowe recorded, and several men nearly drowned. None did, but with the column drifting, Lowe's river bed did not get the compression he wanted.

"That tumbling, boiling cauldron of sand and water was dangerous for the strongest and most experienced men with teams," Lowe wrote. "Be it remembered," he added, "that the man, horse or wagon standing still will soon sink in the sand; one must keep moving constantly or sink." Lowe asked Sumner if he had any instructions. Sumner replied, "Be very careful." Just as Sedgwick deferred to an experienced junior officer when confronted with the buffalo stampede, Sumner allowed his capable subordinate to supervise this dangerous but important crossing.

Lowe did not explain why he crossed the beef herd last. Having them cross earlier would have helped to compress the quicksand. One can only surmise that Lowe had his reasons. Lowe and his men were stripped down to their underwear and even though they were on saddle-mules, in no time they were soaked with the cold river water.

When the wagons crossed Lowe had a dozen teamsters on saddle-mules riding along the crossing to help any wagon and team in trouble. As a wagon was ready to cross, a mounted teamster tied a rope on the halter of the lead mule and led it into the river. Two more mounted men rode at the lower or left side (called the "off side" by the teamsters) to whip up the mules and keep them from drifting downstream. They tried to keep a fifty-yard distance between wagons and no more than six wagons in the river at any one time. If the men rode on the left or "off side" and were crossing essentially from the south bank to the north bank, the riders were on the upstream side of the wagons.

"Most of the teams had more or less trouble," Lowe wrote, "causing outriders to get off into the water to help out, so that all clothing was soon wet through. The day was dark and cloudy, the water cold from [the melting] snow-clad mountains and the north wind cold, and all suffered much." As soon as a team was across, the teamster unhitched his saddle-mule and came back to help.[24]

All things considered, the crossing went well. However, an ambulance with all the medical supplies was lost. When about half of the wagons were safely across the river, the ambulance headed into the stream. It was the lightest load and all thought it would cross with the least trouble. But in mid-stream the mule team became tangled, the leaders swung around and the saddle mule sank into the quicksand and got caught under the wagon tongue. Then the left wheels sank into the sand and it rolled over in the deepest part of the river. The driver of the team was a boy of eighteen who would have drowned had Lowe not come to his aid. One wagonmaster froze, sitting on his horse like "a wooden man," Lowe thought. Others in the icy stream cut the harness and the mules scrambled out of the river on their own. All the medical supplies for the command were washed downstream never to be rescued.

With nothing but buffalo chips for fuel, the men who had been in the icy stream for a number of hours had to warm up with hot coffee and whiskey toddies. They were able to change into dry clothes. However, they had plenty to eat and were cheerful at day's end. Colonel Sumner expressed his satisfaction to Lowe as to his management of the crossing, and when Lowe complained about losing the ambulance, Sumner told him to be well satisfied.

In his river adventure rescuing the boy, Lowe lost his hat. Jeb Stuart got one of his own from his trunk and had his servant deliver it to Lowe. The loss of a hat on the hot western prairie was a true misfortune.[25]

Sumner reached Fort Laramie on June 22. The Second Dragoon companies E and H were ordered to go to Utah to serve with General Harney. Here at Fort Laramie, Sumner's command received supplies for the remainder of the campaign, adding another one hundred fifty head of cattle to their herd. Companies C, D, and G, Sixth Infantry, joined Sumner's command.

Two days earlier on June 20, Sedgwick's column had passed by Bent's Old Fort. The remains were nothing more than "a few old mud walls." The next day Lieutenant McIntyre shinnied up the center pole of a deserted medicine lodge to retrieve a fox skin, something one of the Indian scouts could not do. McIntyre planned to send it home to his wife.[26]

On the morning of June 27, 1857, Colonel Sumner left Fort Laramie, putting his troops on the road and marching almost due south to join Major Sedgwick near the old site of Fort St. Vrain, a former trading post. Lowe was acting as a scout. The scouts with Sumner could do little more than follow a trail. When Lowe reached the South Platte River prior to meeting Sedgwick on July 4, he found it swollen from recent rain and melting snow from the mountains. Lowe made it across with his horse and was able to return, but with difficulty each way. Seeing Lowe's trouble crossing the river, the scout who was with him told Lowe and teamster Simeon Routh that maybe next time he, Lowe, would take the advice of a scout. Lowe told him in no uncertain terms how useless he was as a scout. At that point Lowe saw the dust of Colonel Sumner's column approaching.

Lowe selected a campground farther downstream and then rode out to meet Sumner, who was anxious to know about the crossing. Lowe gave him the disappointing news. After going into the camp Lowe selected, the command fired a thirty-two-gun salute with their prairie howitzers in honor of the Fourth of July. In addition to the celebration they were answering a similar salute fired by Sedgwick's men farther up the river on the opposite side.[27]

The Cheyennes

Just as the so-called Grattan Massacre and General Harney's punitive expedition that followed resulted from a dispute over a cow, Colonel Sumner's Cheyenne Expedition of 1857, resulted, in part, from a dispute over a horse. In neither case did cool heads prevail early on, and as Grattan's actions infuriated the Indians, Captain George H. Steuart's actions infuriated them once again. At his capture on May 12, 1864, by Union forces, Steuart, a Confederate general by this time, was vituperative and considered by one Federal officer as a "little creature who insulted everybody who came near him." Another of his captors said Steuart was a man of "little mind, without character."[28]

The horse in question was one of four that in the spring of 1856 were in the possession of a Cheyenne camp. The horses were, however, claimed by white men. The Indians claimed the horses were strays they had found on the prairie. The Indians were to surrender the horses and their white owners would pay for their rescue and care. The Cheyennes agreed, but only regarding three horses, stating that the fourth was found in a different location on the prairie and had been in their possession before the other three. Then too the Cheyenne, Two Tails, who had the horse refused to give it up. To keep the peace, some of the tribe wanted to force Two Tails to give up the horse, but he refused.

Two Tails' insistence to keep what he believed to be his led to an arrest order for certain Cheyennes. Arrest was a concept foreign to the Indians, who believed going into captivity meant certain death, so they naturally resisted the arrest order. To enforce the order the soldiers fired and an Indian was killed.

Shortly thereafter an old trapper was killed by some Cheyennes. Not long after, a party of Cheyennes saw a wagon coming along. Wanting tobacco, they sent two of the group out to beg some from the driver. He became frightened at the approach of the two and shot at them. In response they shot arrows at the driver, wounding him in the arm. The rest of the group rode out and, using their quirts, drove the two tobacco-seeking Indians back into camp.

To this attack the whites sent out Captain George H. Steuart, later known as Maryland Steuart (George Bird Grinnell spelled his name Stewart) with forty-one men of his First Cavalry Company. It being a cold, rainy day, Steuart found the Indians huddled up in their buffalo robes. Seeing the troopers charging straight at them they dropped their weapons and robes and ran away on foot, even leaving their horses behind. In Captain Steuart's encounter with the Cheyennes, ten were killed and left on the field and another eight or ten were badly wounded.[29]

Steuart's attack prompted a Cheyenne attack on a small Mormon train where several were killed including a child, and a woman was abducted. His action also led to the Indians' belief that the government wished war and encouraged the young men of the tribe to go to war and attack trains. These were the actions and activities that brought about Sumner's campaign against the Cheyennes in 1857.[30]

Following these troubles nearly all the Cheyennes, Northern and Southern, gathered on the Solomon River in northwestern Kansas where they spent the winter. In camp were two medicine men, Ice and Dark. The two were to use their spiritual powers against the whites. The power of these two was such, the Cheyennes came to believe, that they had nothing to fear from the white soldiers. So powerful was the medicine of these two men that the bullets fired from the soldiers' guns would simply roll harmlessly out of the muzzles and fall to earth. "These two medicine men," wrote George E. Hyde, "persuaded the young warriors that they had a medicine which would make the guns of the soldiers useless and that the bullets of the whites would not harm the Indians."[31]

Afterwards the tribes parted; the Northern Cheyennes going north, the Southern Cheyennes going south. The Northern Cheyennes encountered some soldiers. Who they may have been Grinnell didn't say, but the encounter convinced the Cheyennes to turn south again and unite with the Southern Cheyennes. When warm weather came the combined tribes set out to meet the soldiers and destroy them.[32]

Ice, or White Bull as he was known later, must have been a recognized and respected medicine man. Several years later he made a war bonnet for Roman Nose, a Northern Cheyenne who belonged to the Crooked Lance Society. Since early childhood Roman Nose had proposed to become a warrior. He sought out his friend Ice to make him a protective charm. Ice made a war bonnet, using nothing manufactured by the white man. The crown of the bonnet was made from buffalo hide on which Ice mounted a single buffalo horn. Two long tails of eagle feathers trailed behind the headpiece, red feather on the right and white on the left. Skins of a bat and small birds tied to the crown adorned the bonnet. Even the paint used was made from clay, ground stones and pulverized animal bones.[33]

Like Achilles and his vulnerable heel, the war bonnet too was vulnerable. Ice warned Roman Nose never to shake hands with anyone after he first put on the bonnet. When in a fight, Roman Nose must imitate the call of one of the birds whose skin was fashioned onto the bonnet. Neither could the bonnet keep him from being killed if he ate food taken from the dish with a metal implement. While wearing his war bonnet Roman Nose was mortally wounded at the battle of Beecher's Island and buried on a traditional scaffold in the Republican River Valley about September 21, 1868. Until then it seemed to have the powers Ice and Roman Nose believed it possessed.[34] Convinced of Ice's power and his strong medicine, the Cheyenne warriors were confident of victory.

11

Sumner and Sedgwick Meet

On July 4, 1857, the nation's eighty-first anniversary, the two columns came to the fast-flowing and treacherous South Platte River but on opposite sides and barely within proximity of one another. It was the sound of their individual firings of their national holiday celebration salute that told each commander of the other's arrival. Sedgwick and his men had come down from the timbered foothills of the Rockies and were back on the plains again. Marching down the South Platte they passed the ruins of old abandoned adobe trading forts, namely forts Lupton, Lancaster and St. Vrain, the latter the nominal site for the reunion of the two commands. Upon hearing the firing of the holiday celebration, Major Sedgwick sent one of the Delaware scouts to Colonel Sumner's camp, downstream about fifteen miles away. Eli Long's entry for the national holiday is in agreement with Private Peck's account. Long, however, added that it rained and hailed during the afternoon.[1]

Robert Peck wrote that one of the Delaware scouts left Sedgwick's camp to report to Colonel Sumner. P.G. Lowe wrote that it was the Delaware Fall Leaf himself who delivered the report. This difference is not important except to illustrate how events are remembered. Peck wrote of his experience in 1901, forty-four years after the event. On the other hand the Delaware scouts traveled with Sedgwick's column, not with Lowe and he may not have been as familiar with the scouts as Peck would have been.

Whoever the Indian messenger was, he had no easy time crossing the South Platte River to bring Colonel Sumner news from Major Sedgwick. Lowe wrote, "Someone cried, 'A horseman on the south side of the river!' and all rushed for a sight of him. After long exertion, everyone having given him up for lost a dozen times, the horseman emerged from the river, and proved to be 'Fall Leaf,' one of the Delaware Indian guides from Major Sedgwick."[2]

Fall Leaf had to repeat his adventure as he returned to Sedgwick with Sumner's order for Sedgwick's column to move downstream opposite Sumner the next day. Fall Leaf's struggle to cross the rapid-flowing South Platte River was the prelude for another attempted crossing of this dangerous river.

On July 5 Sedgwick's command marched downstream and reached a point opposite Sumner's camp about noon. Earlier that morning before Sedgwick arrived, Sumner made an attempt at crossing the South Platte.[3] This time it was the men of Sumner's command who worked to make the crossing, with Sumner, his adjutant Lieutenant Albert V. Colburn and Lieutenant Riddick being the only officers participating in the work. Lowe and his men were not to take part unless asked, and Lowe confessed that he was glad.

The first thing to be done was to stretch a rope from the north bank to an island in the middle of the river. Three metallic, water-tight wagon beds were fashioned into a raft. After a long, hard struggle of wading, swimming and pulling, by noon the soldiers had the rope stretched to the island. In many places the water was over a man's head. One of the metal wagon beds came loose from the makeshift raft and raced downstream in the rushing current.

Three cavalrymen who were working with the rope in midstream lost their hold. One man managed to grab hold of some overhanging willows with one hand and with the other take the hand of one of his fellow workers until they could be rescued by others. However, the third trooper, a man named Daugherty, was swept under by the current and drowned. Of trooper Daugherty's drowning Lowe wrote, "Fifty men saw this fine soldier, Daugherty by name, go down to his death, with no power to assist him, in that stream of yellow sand and water, and his loss caused deep regret."[4] At five o'clock, with Major Sedgwick's command camped opposite Sumner's, the colonel gave orders to abandon the river crossing at this point.

On July 6 the two commands moved eighteen miles downstream, the turbulent South Platte still keeping them apart. The next day Colonel Sumner established Camp Buchanan, in honor of the president. Sedgwick's command now was able to cross over to the north bank. Lowe along with his wagon masters and teamsters helped the trains across without serious accident. The lost metallic wagon-box was found on a sand bar here where the river widened, became shallower and less threatening.

On July 13, 1857, Lieutenant Riddick found the remains of trooper Daugherty on an island below their camp site. He had the soldier's remains buried on the island they named Daugherty Island. Nothing more was recorded about this service, and Daugherty's lonely grave was one of many graves in the West, unattended, hardly marked and scarcely remembered.

Accidents

The death of trooper Daugherty was an example of the numerous accidents experienced by all — military and civilian — who traveled west. Firearms accidents were common even among men used to handling them. Robert Peck wrote of coming upon a party of miners, one of whom had shot himself through his hand when he pulled his rifle, muzzle first, out of a wagon. He was careless, and for the rifle to have fired it may also have been cocked. His hand was amputated by the military surgeon in Sedgwick's command.[5]

Lieutenant Eli Long had an accident with the pistol he described as "a Colt's Army size revolver," a description too general for precise identification. However, it may have been the four-pound, four-ounce Colt revolver in .44-caliber. That would have been more suitable for buffalo hunting than the lighter .36-caliber navy model. At over four pounds no wonder Lieutenant Long kept it in his trunk part of the time. But it went off accidentally, he stated, "the ball whistling along by the side of the horses head."[6]

On September 12, 1850, Orlando B. Willcox recorded in his diary: "One of the camp women was shot dead the other day by the accidental discharge of a gun in a wagon on the road."[7]

A sentry coming off his post carelessly lifted his carbine by the muzzle. It went off, wounding his arm so severely it had to be amputated the next morning.[8]

John F. Finerty of the *Chicago Times* traveled as a reporter with General George Crook in 1876, and had become pretty well experienced with frontier life when he nearly shot himself. "Just then we halted," Finerty recorded, "and at the remount the muzzle of my carbine struck the hammer of my revolver, which by some oversight was left down upon the cartridge. An explosion followed. I felt as if Somebody hit me a vigorous blow with a stick on the right rear of my pantaloons."[9] At the Battle of Solomon Fork against the Cheyennes in 1857, First Lieutenant David S. Stanley, First Cavalry Regiment, accidentally fired his revolver as he dismounted in order to take deliberate and steady aim at an Indian. No one was hurt.[10]

At times tethered cavalry horses and mules would stampede, pulling up their picket pins. These foot-long pins, similar to landscape timber spikes the modern reader may be familiar with, were like a mace of old as they flailed the air at the end of a long leather tether attached to the halter of a frightened, runaway horse.[11]

These were the kinds of accidents male travelers recorded. Women told of domestic accidents to families and especially to children. Children frequently fell out of the wagons. It was not uncommon for a child to get caught beneath a wagon wheel.[12]

The Force United

At Camp Buchanan the two columns were united on July 7, 1857. Colonel Sumner believed the Cheyennes he was after were far to the southeast. As a consequence the soldiers' next task was to make up a mule train carrying supplies on their backs and makeshift pack saddles for the overland pursuit. Sumner's instructions to Lowe for the organization of the mule train were that it be able to accompany six companies of cavalry and three of infantry and be the mobile, fast-moving column needed to support the men seeking to find and engage the Cheyennes.

The civilians under wagonmaster P.G. Lowe built several shops under the pole-supported awnings of the wagon covers. The blacksmith shop was busy shoeing and saddlers were making pack saddles from whatever material they could find. Lowe had no one except a few Mexicans who knew anything about packing. A kind of school with Mexican instructors and army officers acting as translators taught the rudiments of packing mules to several of the enlisted men. The mules were to carry one hundred fifty pounds each. The saddle-mules had to be trained to carry a load rather than being ridden.

The men themselves were to travel as light as possible. All extra baggage was left with the wagons. For clothing the men took only what they wore. Their saddle blankets would be their bedding. Except for one two-mule ambulance for the sick, no wheeled vehicles followed along. The only shelter was one tent fly to serve as headquarters and adjutant's office and another fly to serve as a hospital.[13]

By July 13, 1857, one hundred eighty mules were ready to carry the supplies for Colonel Sumner and his men. Captain William S. Ketchum took charge of the infantry companies and Major John Sedgwick the cavalry. Second Lieutenant Albert V. Colburn became acting adjutant general of the expedition; Second Lieutenant Lunsford Lomax became acting adjutant for the infantry and cavalry. First Lieutenant Frank Wheaton became acting quartermaster and commissary officer because Lieutenant Richard H. Riddick was to go to Fort Laramie with P.G. Lowe. Second Lieutenant George D. Bayard took charge of the artillery, now a complement of four guns. Lieutenant James E.B. Stuart returned to Company G as acting commanding officer, replacing George Bayard. Captain William Walker of Company G was on leave and never part of this expedition.

This same day, July 13, Percival G. Lowe supervised the transfer of Colonel Sumner's combined command back over the South Platte River to its southern bank without incident. Lowe and his teamsters would not be coming with the soldiers. Instead he was ordered to make the one-hundred-fifty-mile trip back to Fort Laramie; refit his train, making as many six-mule teams as possible; load his wagons with corn and other supplies; and meet Sumner and his men at the South Platte River crossing named Beauvais' Crossing on or about August 1. This was the same crossing they had made on the way to Fort Laramie, about one hundred seventy-five miles southeast of the fort.

Lowe and Lieutenant Riddick had some work to do before leaving for Fort Laramie. To pull his one hundred nine wagons with five hundred four mules, Lowe made up twenty-five six-mule teams, eighteen five-mule teams and sixty-six four-mule teams. Some worn-out cavalry horses and about fifty injured or horseless cavalrymen went along under the command of Lieutenant Riddick. Soon after departing, Lieutenant Riddick found the remains of trooper Daugherty and buried them on "Daugherty's Island."[14]

The men said their goodbyes; Sumner complimented Lowe on his performance and while shaking hands told Lowe his salary had been increased by twenty-five dollars per month. Of this departure Robert Peck wrote: "I doubt whether Colonel Sumner and the more experienced men anticipated such an easy job, for it was said of the 'old bull o' the woods' that whenever he started on such a trip he never expected to get back in twice the time of his rations."[15]

Back east on July 13 in Alexandria, Virginia, that city's *Gazette* printed an account from Indian agent Thomas S. Twiss. Twiss corrected a story that had originated from a telegraph message from St. Louis that Sumner and his whole party had been killed by Indians. The report was either greatly exaggerated or wholly without foundation. The next day the same paper printed a second rebuttal of the story.[16]

The Pursuit

The trail Sumner's men followed was an Indian trail. Tracks from the dragging of travois by migrating Indians were deeply scored into the ground, as were the ruts made by the wagon wheels of Indian traders. Sumner followed the South Platte until July 17, when he left the river to march southeast across the plains. He followed a road that First Lieutenant Francis T. Bryan of the Topographical Engineers had made a year before when he surveyed a road from Fort Riley to Bridger's Pass.[17] Sumner was headed for the Republican River and was crossing a hard stretch of land. Old, dry buffalo chips littered the ground, but no buffalo were seen. Three men became ill from drinking bad water and had to be transported in the ambulance, sharing space with medical supplies, two tent flys and a load of ammunition. The sun was merciless. Four men were overcome and needed attention. Even tough, reliable Captain Sturgis suffered from the effects of the sun.[18] The heat on the plains often rose to over 100 degrees and coupled with a constant wind made traveling during the afternoon unbearable. Sumner halted his column during these hours, resuming the march around 5:00 P.M. During these breaks the men made "shebangs" to provide some shade by placing saddle blankets over four sabers stuck into the ground. Water was scarce. A light rain fell one night and the men caught what they could in their waterproof raincoats, called talmas.

Conditions improved by July 22. They struck water and killed several antelopes, the first large game they had seen in a number of days. Sumner made his camp in a grove of cottonwood trees where there was plenty of grass for his livestock. This camp was on the Hackberry Creek near its mouth, where the water sank into the sand before reaching the Republican River. The water was running under the sand about a foot deep. Sumner's soldiers were now deep in Cheyenne country.

Sumner essentially followed the Republican River. Now that they were in Cheyenne country Sumner gave orders for the officers and men to keep their arms and ammunition in good order. About ten days after they separated from Percival G. Lowe, Lieutenant Riddick and the wagon train, Sumner's horses and mules began to fail. Their weakened condition would play a part in the battle looming ahead. William Y. Chalfant gave a good account of the condition of the cavalry mount. In order for a cavalry horse to maintain weight and general good health while on the march it had to have about twelve pounds of grain a day plus an equal amount of hay. The horses carried heavy packs when they were away from a wagon train in addition to the cavalryman and his equipment. Away from the wagon train, as were Sumner's horses now, the grain ration was cut and after it was gone, horses as well as all the livestock had only what nature provided. As we have seen, expeditions began in the spring after the grass began to grow again. Poor diet, poor water, heat and overexertion all contributed to the breaking down of the cavalry mount. As she lost weight — remembering Sumner's preference for mares — her saddle fit poorly and caused saddle sores. Colonel Sumner may have remembered his ration of straw cut fine and rye meal that he fed his horses back at Carlisle and yearned for that horse food now.[19]

To conserve the mounts, Colonel Sumner ordered the troops to dismount and walk every alternate hour. The order applied to officers as well, even though they supplied their own horses. On July 23 they camped on Big Timber Creek, an area familiar to Sumner from his work there in 1850. There now they came upon the site of a former Cheyenne village, evidenced by the circle of tipi rings and fire pits. Sumner issued orders to increase security. The men slept in their clothes, including boots, their firearms by their sides. The guards were extra vigilant. Robert Peck told how the command marched *en echelon*: "Colonel Sumner had taken the precaution to march the command in three columns, 'en echelon' (a sort of stair-step fashion), from which they could be brought quickly into line, to meet an attack from the front, rear, or either flank."[20]

By July 24 the ambulance broke down, probably because it carried all the spare ammunition, a load beyond its capacity. The ammunition boxes were repacked on the mules—Lowe's mule-packing school proving to have been time well spent — and the ambulance was converted to a two-wheel cart. Later that day scouts reported another abandoned Cheyenne village. Then the next day they found another one, much larger. This one had a medicine lodge built around a cottonwood tree in the center of the village. On July 26 the twenty-day supply of rations carried by the pack-mules was close to being used up. Colonel Sumner gave some thought to sending a messenger to First Lieutenant Riddick with the wagon train of new supplies gathered at Fort Laramie. Sumner calculated Riddick would reach the South Platte crossing within the next several days. Sumner thought of ordering Riddick to move south until he came across the trail Sumner's expedition scratched into the surface of the plains and prairie and to follow it until they caught up with Sumner and his hungry force. Although Sumner estimated it would be at least another twelve days before Riddick would arrive with the badly needed supplies, Sumner, on second thought, decided to wait a few days more to see if he could locate the Cheyennes before ordering the supply train to move down to meet him. Private Peck's statement that the "old bull of the woods" would have his command subsist on their pack-mules or horses if he struck a warm trail was coming true. That night a guard fired his carbine when his challenge went unanswered, and a man sprang upon his horse and vanished into the night. The officer of the guard, First Lieutenant David S. Stanley, believed the young German recruit on guard who had fired to have been nervous and jumpy. The next day, however, they found unshod hoof-prints and concluded they were being watched. Indeed they were.[21]

Marching on, they reached the north fork of the Solomon River on July 27. Across the stream from their camp was the site of yet one more Cheyenne camp, this one only recently abandoned. Persuaded by the evidence found in the camp, Colonel Sumner decided against sending for Lieutenant Riddick. More fresh signs of Indians were found the next day, and excited anticipation filled the camp while two freshly killed buffaloes helped to fill empty stomachs. But there was no grass for the horses at this camp site; they would have to fill their stomachs with water.

Two Indian dogs came into the American camp that evening, giving further proof the Cheyennes were near. All cooking was done during day time and no fires were permitted after dark. The men slept with their carbines. The horses and mules were kept close by. Sumner's habit was to camp in a square, picketing the animals on the outside and having the sentinels report every half hour that all was well. He claimed never to have had a horse stolen on the plains. This night the sentinels probably reported conditions at their posts to the officer of the guard in low voices.[22]

On July 29, 1857, the day of the battle, the men rose to verbal commands. Each man was to carry a bit of food in his haversack in case he got separated from the command during the battle. Leaving camp at 6:30 A.M., they struck out in an east-by-southeast direction following a fresh trail made by a half-dozen unshod Indian ponies. The formation was three columns, three cavalry companies being the flanking columns with the cavalry guard, artillery and the three infantry companies forming the center. A Delaware scout reported to Colonel Sumner at 10:30 A.M. that the scouts had sighted about five or six Cheyennes, who retreated as the scouts advanced. Later one of the Pawnee scouts reported more Cheyennes moving along the north bank of the south fork of the Solomon River. In the Solomon River valley the Cheyennes gathered and waited for the soldiers of the First Cavalry. It was time to prepare for battle.[23]

Lieutenant Long recorded, "The Pawnee guides reported that they saw Indians ahead 5 or 6 the Col gave the command trot march, we then trotted down to a wide but shallow creek supposed to be Solomon fork."[24]

The Battle

Private Robert Peck described the build-up to and the battle of Solomon Fork in his "Recollections." About 10:00 A.M. on July 29 the Delaware scout Fall Leaf sent one of his scouts back to the column to report to Colonel Sumner the sighting of a small party of Indians that retreated as the scouts advanced.

This party turned out to be a reconnoitering party of Cheyennes who came out to watch the cavalrymen and their "walks-a-heap" infantry companions. As the soldiers approached, the party of Cheyennes fell back onto the main body. Colonel Sumner was concerned the Indians would retreat and get away. He therefore pushed on ahead with the six companies of cavalry, even though that meant leaving the infantry and artillery behind. There was also the fear that the Indians were planning to draw the soldiers out by making use of a decoying party, then, with the soldiers well strung out, fall on the scattered force with their whole force.

When Sumner got word that the Indians had been sighted, he halted the command and sent orders to all company commanders to see that their men were prepared for action. Dismounting, the men tightened saddle-girths, examined arms and equipment and made what last minute preparations were needed. Little preparation was necessary, Private Peck recalled, because the men had frequently been admonished on the trip to keep their "kits" in good order. The men remounted and Colonel Sumner addressed his combat-ready troopers.

He had a very loud, strong voice, Private Peck remembered, and his voice along with his well-known fighting proclivities earned for him the name "Bull o' the Woods," by which sobriquet his men were fond of speaking of their old white-headed, white-bearded fighting colonel.

At the sound of the bugle, the first bugle call sounded in several days, the cavalrymen moved out. Soon the bugle called the command to trot and before long the infantry fell behind. The artillery batteries under Lieutenant George D. Bayard kept up until crossing a miry stream. The mules pulling the artillery pieces bogged down.[25]

Private Peck was of the opinion that it might seem reckless of the colonel to scatter his command and attack an enemy of unknown size with only the cavalry portion of his command. Peck believed, however, that Colonel Sumner thought the Indians might get away without a fight, so he wanted to bring one on. He would either whip the Indians or hold them in place until the rest of his command came up. Private Peck estimated that deducting the "sick, lame and lazy" (as he described some of his comrades in arms) plus those attending to the pack-mules and the artillery battery, each company of cavalry had on average fifty men. About three hundred mounted cavalrymen were all Sumner had that were ready to go into action.

One of the foreign-born soldiers confronting the Indians that day was twenty-six-year-old, German-born Sebastian Gunther. He told his story many years later to Mr. S.L. Seabrook. Gunther remembered that when the cavalry came in sight of the Indians, Colonel Sumner continued to advance his men at a slow cavalry walk but went from column into line. Every carbine was in its boot, every old horse pistol was in its holster and every saber was sheathed, Gunther recalled. When the distance between the whites and the red men was about two hundred yards Sumner ordered his bugler to sound "Trot!"

Trying to express the tension that gripped each trooper, Gunther described what he believed each cavalry man must have felt: "Still the trot goes on and no sign from the commander. The men wonder: will he use the carbine, the pistol or the sabre."[26]

Coming down a hollow from the upland prairie, the troopers spread out onto the Solomon River valley. At the lower end of the wide valley were a few scattered cottonwood trees. Through binoculars some of the company officers saw Indians lounging under the trees, then saw them mount their horses and ride out to meet the advancing troopers. The Cheyenne warriors, encouraged by the medicine and administrations of Ice, had been waiting for several hours and had let their horses graze while they relaxed.

Lieutenant Long recorded this scene in his diary: "We saw the warriors coming up to meet us on their ponies stretched out in line. They had their shields and all their warlike utensils flying. They came up boldly to within about one hundred yards of us about I think 350 of them."[27]

Private Peck went on to write that by the time the Indians had approached near enough to make an estimate of their numbers, it seemed to him that they outnumbered Sumner's cavalry. He secretly wished the infantry and artillery were with them. Old Bull, he thought, had bitten off more than he could chew; but Peck added that if Sumner thought so, he never let on but proceeded as if things suited him. "The men used to say," Peck wrote, "they believed he would fight a buzz-saw." Fall Leaf quickly rode forward when Sumner's men were nearly within rifle range, and he halted about half way between the two lines. Suddenly he halted his horse, raised his rifle and fired at the Cheyennes. Then Fall Leaf returned, drawing the fire from several of the Cheyennes. Peck recalled, "We heard Colonel Sumner say in a loud voice to Lieut. David Stanley, who was beside him: 'Bear witness, Lieutenant Stanley, that an Indian fired the first shot!'"[28]

Even in those days officers must have had certain rules of engagement. Soldiers like Private Peck had little patience for them. "It is probable that he had been hampered by one of those milk-and-water orders from Washington," Peck thought, "and he seemed relieved to be able to establish the fact that an Indian fired the first shot, pretending not to have noticed that said shot was fired by one of his own Indian scouts and not by a Cheyenne." Peck was glad they would not have to be burdened by "demands of the weak-kneed sentimentalists of the East."[29]

While still out of range of Sumner's carbines, the Indians crossed the river and attempted to circle around his right and to get at the pack train in the rear. Meanwhile the Cheyennes were working to outflank the soldiers on their left as well. Sumner ordered Captain Beall and his sorrel horse Company A on the left to move to head them off. Then to the surprise of many, Lieutenant Jeb Stuart among them, Sumner roared, "Sling—carbines! Draw—saber!" Colonel Sumner seemed determined to offset the disparity in numbers, Private Peck believed, by a bold dash that would create a panic among the enemy. At first Peck believed Sumner had made a serious mistake when he ordered a saber charge. He was not alone in that initial opinion. But the sight of three hundred bright sabers flashing in the sunlight caused the loping red men to pause. "The sight of so much cold steel seemed to cool their ardor," Peck wrote. Those Indians who moved against Sumner's flanks also hesitated. Upon seeing the Indians' hesitation, Peck had to admit to himself that Old Bull knew what he was doing after all.[30]

Colonel Sumner did not know the reason the Indians would not stand a saber charge. He probably never knew. What effect on the outcome his order to have fired a volley prior to his saber charge would have had can only be speculated. Certainly a volley might have killed and wounded some of the warriors and their ponies. It might have weakened the Cheyennes' resolve to see the bullets hit among them rather than falling harmlessly from the carbine muzzles as Ice the medicine man had predicted. Robert Peck wrote that the charge was made when they were almost in rifle range. Had Sumner ordered his men to deliver a carbine volley when they were almost in range, the bullets would have fallen to earth in front of the Cheyennes and would have lent support to Ice and his forecast.[31] Remember the variety of arms carried by the companies of the First Cavalry. It is also worthwhile to note that Sumner was concerned for his flank when he ordered Company A to protect it. Sumner came under criticism at Antietam for ignoring his flanks when he ordered John Sedgwick's division into the West Woods on the Antietam battlefield. Sumner knew as well as any experienced officer the importance of flank protection.

When the Cheyennes saw, however, that the cavalrymen were charging with their sabers, a weapon Ice had not considered, they were of little faith. Their chief, admired by the white soldiers for his bravery and his horsemanship, tried to steady his warriors by riding out in front of them along their line. When Colonel Sumner bellowed the order to charge, a command preceded by "Gallop — march!" the men of the First Cavalry charged, bringing their sabers to "tierce point." Tierce point was a command, given as "In tierce — point." In the tierce position, the edge of the saber was to the right and the man's fingernails were in the down position, towards the ground. At the command "point" the right arm was thrust forward and the edge of the saber was up.[32]

George E. Hyde told of the charge from the Indian's perspective. When Sumner's six companies of cavalry fronted into line the Cheyennes began to advance, the warriors singing war songs. They truly believed in the medicine of Ice and were certain the white soldiers' guns would fail them. After Sumner's orders to draw sabers and to charge, according to Hyde, "For the first and last time in the annals of Indian warfare a large force of cavalry swept forward to attack a body of mounted Indians with the steel." Before the soldiers were within striking distance of the Cheyennes the Indians turned, scattering in every direction.[33]

"All their chief's fiery pleading," Peck wrote, "could not hold them, for every redskin seemed suddenly to remember that he had urgent business in the other direction." They delivered a volley of arrows as a parting shot before scattering in various directions, although mostly going south. "Col Sumner before giving the command charge," Lieutenant Eli Long recorded in his journal, "gave the command draw sabre and we charged with drawn sabre but soon returned them and made use of Colts [sic] revolvers instead."[34]

Sumner's cavalrymen became scattered also in pursuit of the fleeing Indians. But the cavalry horses were jaded after the long campaign, while the Indian ponies were fresh and full of vigor. The pursuit had covered about seven miles, according to Private Peck, when the bugles sounded "recall."[35]

Second Lieutenant Eli Long was officer in charge of the guard that day, in charge of the bodyguard for Colonel Sumner. At the command "Charge!" Long's horse must have understood and it went racing ahead. Lieutenant Long and Fall Leaf were the first to reach the stream bank and fired at several Indians, some of whose horses were mired in the quicksand of the stream bottom. Long was reported to have fired eight shots at a group of three, wounding one. How he managed to fire eight shots from a six-shot revolver and perhaps a single-shot carbine would be interesting to know. Perhaps he also carried a brace of the horse pistols that Private Sebastian Gunther referred to. Company A, after thwarting the Indians' attempt to flank the soldiers, joined with company E; together they got close to a group of Indians but did not manage to kill any. Company E, remember, had the Sharps carbine, the darling weapon of so many Civil War historians. It does not appear that the carbines figured much at all in this fight. Neither does it seem that the soldiers were very proficient in the use of their revolvers.[36]

The Surprised Lieutenant

First Lieutenant James E.B. Stuart was surprised to hear Colonel Sumner's command to charge. Stuart kept a diary and wrote lengthy letters to his wife, Flora. Dated July 30, 1857, the day after the battle, from camp on the Solomon Fork, Stuart described the battle and his part in it to "My Dear Darling wife": "Yesterday after about 17 days steady march from Camp Buchanan we overtook about 500 Cheyennes drawn up in order of battle & marching boldly & steadily towards us. We fronted into line as soon as possible (the six companies of Cavalry) the Infantry being too far behind to take any part in the action, also Bayard's Battery which the Col stopped 3 or 4 miles back as unable to keep up."[37]

Stuart explained to his wife that it was his intention to fire a carbine volley and then charge with the drawn revolver, using the saber as a last resort. Stuart believed most of the company commanders thought likewise.

"But much to my surprise the Col ordered *draw Sabre charge* when the Indians were within gun shot," Stuart wrote. Stuart wrote that the horses of the troopers were worn out and mostly unable to keep up with the Indians.[38]

One estimate put the Indians killed at thirty, while George Bird Grinnell wrote that the number killed was but four. He gave their names as Coyote Ear, Yellow Shirt, Carries the Otter and Black Bear. Coyote Ear was Indian trader George Bent's father-in-law.[39] Those killed — the number reported by Grinnell seems low — were on foot because their horses became stuck in the soft river bottom. Most of the Indians killed died fighting viciously on the sloping hill across the river. A number on foot got away on the backs of their comrades' horses who paused to rescued them. Contrary to the general rule that the Indian would fight to the death rather than surrender, Private Peck reported that one Cheyenne who had lost his horse surrendered to the soldiers when he saw he had no chance to escape.[40]

More characteristic of the fighting Cheyennes was the warrior Private Rollin M. Taylor fought in a desperate hand-to-hand fight shortly after he crossed the boggy Solomon River. While trying to run down a Cheyenne on foot, Taylor's horse stumbled into a prairie-dog hole, throwing Taylor onto the ground. Taylor lost his revolver but retained his saber. The Indian shot three arrows at Taylor, producing a flesh wound to his right shoulder and one to his scalp as the arrow went through his hat and parted his hair. Using his bow to parry the saber and trying to cut the trooper with his knife, the Cheyenne warrior fought well until Taylor inflicted a severe blow to the Indian's right arm. With his bow cut to pieces, the Indian still tried to knife Taylor until the loss of blood made him stagger and fall. Taylor drove his saber into the fallen Cheyenne. As he lay dying the Indian made signs to ask if Taylor planned to scalp him. Taylor signed that he would not, and the Indian smiled as his life ended there near the river bank. When a Pawnee scout came by and wanted to scalp the dead Cheyenne, Taylor threatened to kill him with his saber if he tried.[41]

At least one soldier witnessed Private Taylor's duel with the dismounted Cheyenne. The first sergeant of Company B was a French-Canadian from Quebec named Eugene Roy. Roy had served in the U.S. Army during the Mexican War and after returning to Canada, came back to the United States and reenlisted in 1856. The following is his account of Private Taylor's battle with the Cheyenne:

> The Indians decided to fight with the energy of despair for they knew we would give them no quarter. They fought until the last with an inconceivable desperation. When I got near to one of them he fired four or five arrows with an unbelievable rapidity. I struck him with my saber but my horse became unmanageable and when I returned he was on foot fighting with a young man named Taylor. He used only his saber and the Indian his bow to parry the saber blows. They were too close together for us to shoot. There were two more Indians at a distance from us who tried to flee and I waited the outcome of the duel before chasing them.
>
> After a few uneasy moments Taylor, with his saber in his left hand and his right on the hilt, thrust it into the Indian up to the middle of the blade like an infantry soldier would use his bayonet.

Sergeant Roy's account also seems to indicate that the Pawnee scout may have indeed scalped the Indian Private Taylor had slain.[42]

While the number of Indian deaths is unclear, Colonel Sumner had two of his troopers killed and twelve men wounded. In the corner under a hastily constructed hospital tent fly were the bodies of Private George Cade, Company G, and Private Martin Lynch, Company A. Cade's body bore the mark over his heart where an arrow apparently had gone clear through him. Lynch bore the wounds from arrows and two bullet holes fired from his own revolver. Not content to sit idly by holding pack mules while his company charged after the fleeing Indians, Lynch had drawn his saber and joined the charge. His horse, described as a fiery, hard-mouthed thing, ran away with him, and he got in among a number of Indians. He was shot with arrows and after falling from his horse, was shot again with his own revolver. An Indian was in the process of scalping him when his companions reached the scene, killed several Indians, one of them with Lynch's pistol in his hand, and recovered Lynch's body. Based upon this incident alone, the number of dead Indians given by Grinnell seems too low.[43]

Three men were critically wounded: First Sergeant George C. McEawen of Company D was shot by a rifle through his arm and chest; Private Franz Piot of Company B received an arrow wound, the arrow passing entirely through his chest; and Private James M. Cooke had an arrow shot through his abdomen. Less seriously wounded were First Sergeant Henry B. Robinson, Company H, with a saber cut on his hand; Private Francis T. Freer, Company B, with an arrow wound in his hip; Private Alexander Wilkey, also of Company B, who received an arrow wound to his face; and Private Thomas Wilson of Company D, who had an arrow go clean through his arm. Finally, Private Rollin Taylor of Company E, who had the fight with the Indian, received arrow wounds to his shoulder and head. Colonel Sumner visited the wounded, talking encouragingly to the men. When the colonel spoke with Private Cooke, who had the stomach wound, Cooke told him, "I'll live to eat lots of hard tack and sowbelly for Uncle Sam yet."[44]

Lying among the wounded that Private Peck saw when he visited the hospital was First Lieutenant Jeb Stuart. Stuart told his wife about his wound and how he had received it. Chasing the fleeing Cheyennes, Stuart had come upon Lieutenant Lunsford Lomax, who Stuart believed was in serious trouble from an Indian on foot about to shoot Lomax. Stuart shot at the Indian, hitting him in the thigh, and the Indian returned the fire from an Allen revolver but missed. From Stuart's account in his letter to his wife, the cavalrymen were not very proficient in their shooting skills with the Colt revolver. Now Stuart was out of ammunition, so he called on other men nearby to come to the rescue. First Lieutenant David S. Stanley, who was Colonel Sumner's witness that an Indian fired the first shot to open the battle, rode up to shoot the Cheyenne warrior. Dismounting to be on foot to take deliberate aim, Stanley accidentally fired his last round upon dismounting. As Stuart wrote, "He [Stanley] began however to snap the empty barrels at the Indian." The Indian walked up to Stanley, pointing his revolver at him. At that point Stuart drew his saber and slashed the pistol-packing Cheyenne across his hand while at the same instant the Indian fired "his last barrel within a foot" of Stuart. The pistol ball hit Stuart square in the chest and lodged under his left nipple.

Stuart went on to tell his wife that the Indian was finally killed by Lieutenant McIntyre and an enlisted man from Company D. Colonel Sumner rode up and, Stuart wrote, "jumped off his horse like a cat and greeted me in the most affectionate terms. I felt really tempted to forgive him for all the past."[45]

Eli Long recorded Stuart's battle in his diary for July 29. After his encounter with the Indians, Colonel Sumner rode up and they all went forward to where Lieutenant Stuart was wounded:

> He [Stuart,] Lt. [James B.]McIntyre, [Lunsford] Lomax and [David] Stanley were after about 50 but could not catch but one, he had an old fashioned self-cocking 6 shooter, he stopped doubtlessly to save the rest and put out his hand to a Corpl. saying how do at the same time shooting at him but missed him. Lt. Stewart attacked him when he shot Stewart in the breast. McIntyre ran up in time to run him through with the sabre. Stewart was not wounded very badly the bullet not penetrating deep.

From Stuart's description of the Allen revolver the Indian fired to wound Stuart, it must have been an Allen pepperbox. Stuart received his wound when the Indian "fired his last barrel within a foot of me." The pepperbox was a pistol whose cylinder was elongated to have a barrel for each chamber. In the more common revolver, such as the Colt, only the cylinder, which contains the cartridge (or as in earlier models the bullet, powder and percussion cap on the nipple), revolves. The shorter cylinder rotates as the revolver is cocked, and all bullets are shot through a single barrel. With the pepperbox, both the chamber and its barrel rotate and each chamber fires its bullet through its own barrel.

The pepperbox revolver was manufactured in great quantity and was not an exclusive patent of Allen. William W. Marston, for example, made a pepperbox pistol in his New York City plant at Second Avenue and 22nd Street. W.W. Greener described the pepperbox as "a revolver without a barrel, the hammer being placed either above or below the chamber, and the pulling of the trigger rotated this chamber, and also cocked and fired the weapon. Thus it possessed the trigger-action mechanism of the modern double-action revolver."

It seems that Lieutenant David S. Stanley may also have had a pepperbox revolver. Stuart wrote in his letter, "He began however to snap the empty barrels at the Indian."

The Allen revolvers were made by Ethan Allen, named for but no relation to the man of Fort Ticonderoga fame. Allen got his first patent in 1837, for his successful pepperbox. Later he went into business with a brother-in-law, and his arms were known as Allen and Wheelock revolvers. Stuart's wound was probably inflicted by a .36-caliber ball.[46] (See Item 3 in the appendix for the text of Stuart's letters.)

The Aftermath

Just as Private Taylor may have protected the corpse of the Cheyenne he conquered from the attempted scalping by the Pawnee scout, Colonel Sumner protected the life of the Cheyenne who surrendered. The Pawnees wanted to put the captive Cheyenne to death by torture and have a scalp-dance over him. They offered Sumner six of the ponies they captured from the Cheyennes and agreed to forfeit the money they were to be paid when they reached Fort Kearny. Sumner was so disgusted with their performance and demands that he discharged them.

Less sympathetic was Private Peck. He had hoped the Cheyenne prisoner would be turned over to the Pawnees. He would have liked to have seen such a ceremony to have been able to write about it. After all, it was a sight few white men saw and lived to tell the details. Peck wanted an Indian to have that "post of honor."[47]

With no means of transporting the twelve wounded, Colonel Sumner left one infantry company under Captain Foote to take care of them. They were ordered to return to Fort Kearny when the wounded were able to travel. The troopers spent July 30 building a sod fort to protect the wounded from possible attack by returning Cheyennes. The compound measured fifty feet by fifty feet and was about five feet high. On July 31 after burying the dead and leaving a dozen head of beef cattle for the little sod cantonment, the First Cavalry saddled up about 10:00 A.M. and rode south following the main trail of the retreating Cheyennes.

About fifteen miles from the battlefield, Colonel Sumner's command came upon a Cheyenne village that had been hastily abandoned. The lodges were still standing and a great deal of property lay neglected. The soldiers took whatever they could make use of, particularly dried buffalo meat. Everything else was put to the torch.[48]

It took twenty-three misery-packed days for Colonel Sumner's column to reach the Arkansas River. The marches were long, hot and exhausting. The food was poor and scanty. As they traveled they came across freshly made graves of Cheyennes who had succumbed to their wounds. Trails indicated that the Indians were splitting up into smaller groups, so the prospect of encountering any real number of them for another battle diminished with each passing day.

When they reached the Arkansas River, Colonel Sumner sent Major Sedgwick with four companies of cavalry to follow the Cheyenne trail. When Sedgwick reached Bent's Fort he was to take possession of anything he could find in the way of rations sent out by the government for the Indians' annuities. At the same time Sumner sent an express rider to Fort Riley for a train-load of supplies. The supply train and Sedgwick's four companies were to meet and join with Sumner at Big Bend.

Sedgwick returned with hard tack, bacon, sugar, coffee and salt, but no clothing nor tents, and now the weather was beginning to get cold. While they heard at Bent's Fort that the Cheyennes were still on the run, broken up and badly demoralized, Sedgwick's men encountered hostile Kiowas and Comanches. According to Private Peck, Major Sedgwick showed a lack of nerve and again it was competent Captain Sam Sturgis who "saved the bacon."[49]

News of Sumner's fight with the Cheyennes reached Lieutenant Colonel Joe Johnston's surveying party on August 18, 1857. Johnston was waiting for supplies to reach him, sent out from Fort Leavenworth on July 24. They did meet a mail train that reported the news about Sumner's fight. As may be expected the news was not strictly accurate: "They related [that] Colonel Sumner had a fight with the Cheyennes somewhere near [Fort] Laramie. About fourteen Indians were killed; an officer was wounded, [and] a sergeant and two privates were killed on the American side."[50]

Meanwhile Jeb Stuart and the other wounded men were being cared for by Captain Foote's infantry company and Dr. Edward N. Covey at the little field hospital and sod fortification named Fort Floyd. Writing to his wife on August 1, 1857, Stuart described his condition and gave a description of the little fort. He was set up under the shade of a tent fly just a few paces outside of the sod fortification. Ordered by the doctor to be quite still for the first few days after receiving his wound, Stuart lay quiet and gazed up the river for a distance of about two miles.

During the night of August 4 between twenty to thirty Cheyennes attacked the small detachment but inflicted no casualties. Later that morning several of Sumner's Pawnee scouts (apparently Private Peck was inaccurate in stating that Colonel Sumner dismissed the scouts over the Cheyenne prisoner episode) arrived in camp, having been attacked by Cheyennes and lost their horses. The Cheyennes destroyed some letters they carried, but they relayed Colonel Sumner's order for Captain Foote to go directly to Fort Kearny.

Stuart's letters to his wife, written like a kind of diary, established that he arrived at Fort Kearny on August 17, 1857. They broke camp on August 8; the three men who could not ride were transported on Indian-style drags. Food was scarce, there were just the tough beef cattle to eat until Stuart and Dr. Covey shot two buffaloes on August 10. Stuart was now becoming impatient with Captain Foote. Awakening to a foggy morning on August 14, Stuart discovered that the Pawnee scouts had taken off during the night. Stuart blamed Captain Foote for their departure. On August 14 Stuart told of a heavy fog that enveloped them, and to add to their discomfort the Pawnee guides had left them in the middle of the night. Stuart blamed infantry Lieutenant Foote, whom he referred to as a "stupid numbskull," for driving the Pawnees away. According to Stuart, Foote had grown impatient because the Indians couldn't speak English. Then too he had them mounted one day and on foot the next. In Stuart's opinion Foote was no more deserving to command men than a six-month-old child. By Foote's folly, Stuart wrote, "we *all* suffer & the wounded particularly First Sergt McKeown are in great jeopardy." According to Stuart's letters it was he, Stuart, despite the advice of others, who navigated by the stars and traveled in a northeasterly direction that brought them to Fort Kearny and to safety.[51]

For all practical purposes Colonel Sumner's Cheyenne Expedition ended when Major John Sedgwick troops rejoined Sumner with the supplies from Bent's Fort. Another load of supplies and forage arrived from Fort Leavenworth as a result of Sumner's sending wagon-master Nick Berry to get them. Sumner also received orders for his command to proceed to Fort Kearny and there report to General Albert Sidney Johnston to join forces being sent to Utah to suppress the Mormons. Sumner himself was to return to Fort Leavenworth. In taking leave of his men, Colonel Sumner acknowledged the disappointment the men must have had on learning they were to go to Utah. Sumner went on to inform his tattered men that the War Department was ignorant of their depleted, worn-out condition. He tried to encourage them by saying he thought they would only have to go to Fort Kearny. By that time he would make their condition known to the War Department when he reached Fort Leavenworth, which he was hurrying to reach. Private Peck wrote that the men felt like cheering Sumner, but the rules prohibited such displays.[52]

It was not until September that the folks back east got word of Sumner's expedition. Both the *Syracuse Standard* on September 12 and the *New York Tribune* two days later printed accounts of the fight that had been published from St. Louis in the *Independence Messenger*. The *Standard*'s excerpt stated Colonel Sumner had overtaken the Cheyenne Indians and the ensuing battle had resulted in the indiscriminate slaughter of 400 to 500 men, women and children. The *Tribune* doubted the accuracy of the story, not believing that Colonel Sumner would make war on women and children.

The expedition that covered about a thousand miles between mid–May and mid–September 1857, and during which hardship and privation were commonplace, was reported in the Secretary of War's annual report for 1857, in a very concise and sterile way. On page 57 of volume 2 of the annual report the battle was accounted for in a few brief paragraphs:

XXIII July 29, 1857. Colonel E.V. Sumner, 1st cavalry, commanding expedition against the Cheyennes, with companies A, B, D, E, G, and H of his regiment, and companies C, D, and G 6th infantry, after a march with the former of more than a thousand miles, came upon a body of some three hundred Cheyenne warriors on Solomon's fork of the Kansas, in Kansas Territory, drawn up in battle array to oppose his march.

The report went on to say the Indians were all well mounted and well armed, "many of them with rifles and revolvers." The Indians were pursued about seven miles with a loss of nine killed. "Number wounded not known." The report contained the names and rank of the men killed and wounded and the companies to which they belonged. The secretary's account of the expedition ended with the following: "The troops, on the 31st of July, took the principal town of the Cheyennes, which had been abandoned, containing one hundred and seventy lodges and a large amount of property."

Despite the service of the Mormons during the Mexican War, Federal authorities now objected to the independent stand taken by the Church of Jesus Christ of Latter Day Saints in the Great Salt Lake area of Utah. The Mormons wanted to be governed by members of their own faith. The Federal government objected to their independent stand and their sanctioning of polygamy. By the summer of 1857, President James Buchanan feared a revolt in the Utah Territory and believed a show of force would establish order.

Troops for the expedition began to assemble at Fort Leavenworth in May 1857, about the time Major Sedgwick and Colonel Sumner departed on their campaign against the Cheyennes. After some false starts in selecting a commander, Colonel Albert Sidney Johnston assumed command. Although the soldiers suffered through the bitterly cold winter made all the more severe by the Mormons' scorched-earth policy, nothing much came of the operation militarily.[53] Colonel Sumner was as good as his word. On their way to Fort Kearny under Major Sedgwick the men met their supply train, which had been with Percival G. Lowe. Their orders to go to Utah were rescinded and they returned to Fort Leavenworth. Then the companies of the First Cavalry were scattered throughout Kansas to once again keep the peace and referee elections.[54]

The First Cavalry had a second opportunity to take part in the Mormon War. But until then, from November 1857 to the spring of 1858, Colonel Sumner faced two courts-martial. The First Cavalry got orders to transfer headquarters from Fort Leavenworth to Fort Riley on November 14, 1857. Coming along with Sumner were Lieutenant Colonel Joseph E. Johnston, Major William H. Emory and Lieutenant James E.B. Stuart. Sumner left his regiment on November 19, 1857, after being at Fort Riley but three days in order to go on extended leave.

On October 10, 1857, the *St. Louis Republican* reported that Colonel

Sumner was under arrest and a court-martial had been ordered. "He returned from the expedition against the Cheyennes a few days since," the paper concluded. Even before the first court-martial began at Fort Leavenworth in December 1857, rumors began to circulate that Sumner had mismanaged the Cheyenne expedition by allowing the Cheyennes to escape. These suspicions probably were more serious and damaging to Sumner than the actual charges preferred by Major George Deas of the Adjutant General's Department. The *Syracuse Standard* carried an item in its columns on October 21, 1857, from an earlier article in the *New York Times*. The story mentioned Sumner's order to disperse the Topeka Convention the year before and that he now was being court-martialed for his conduct in the Cheyenne Expedition. The paper went on to outline the battle correctly. It supported Sumner's action in attacking the Indians directly rather than waiting until the infantry and artillery arrived. The paper believed the Indians would not have waited for the Sumner's reinforcements to come up. The *Times* gave an interesting tactical explanation for why the saber and not the carbine was used in the battle:

> That the sabre was used and not the carbines and revolvers, is another charge. The explanation is, that had the troops been ordered to halt and fire, the officers, who were in front would have been obliged to retire to the rear, and if the Indians had charged after their fire, when the cavalry were deranged, carbines unloaded and officers in the rear, a great portion of the dragoons being new recruits, the consequences might have been disastrous.

The newspaper article ended by pointing out that the court-martial was the government's way of punishing Sumner for his peacekeeping actions in Kansas and carrying out orders odious to him and against the civil rights of the people.

However on October 22, 1857, the *New York Tribune* reported that the *Times* story was in error and that the court-martial was based upon charges brought against Sumner by Major Deas. Sumner was found guilty of a breach of protocol by not attending Major Deas when he inspected the hospital, guard house and barracks. Although from Pennsylvania and appointed to the military academy from that state, Deas served the Confederacy as a lieutenant colonel in the Adjutant General's Department.

Two charges were made against Sumner: neglect of duty and conduct unbecoming an officer. He was found not guilty of the conduct unbecoming charge but guilty of the other. He was to be suspended from rank and pay for four months. General Winfield Scott upheld the sentence of the court but remitted the penalty.[55]

Sometime during the early part of 1858, while on leave at home in New York, Sumner faced another court-martial on charges preferred by General William S. Harney. This court was held on March 11, 1858, and Sumner was once again at Carlisle, Pennsylvania. The first charge was of "conduct to the prejudice of good order and military discipline." The second charge was of "sending a challenge to another officer to fight a duel, in violation of the twenty-fifth of the Articles of War." The third charge was of "upbraiding another officer for refusing a challenge, in violation of the twenty-eighth of the Articles of War." Colonel Sumner pleaded not guilty to all charges, charges that were based upon a series of letters Sumner wrote to Harney. On March 16, 1858, Sumner was found not guilty of all three charges. The court declared, "Colonel Edwin V. Sumner 1st Cavalry, is released from arrest, and will join his regiment in Kansas."

This court-martial received much attention in the Syracuse as well as other New York newspapers. The *Syracuse Standard* carried this story in its March 13, 1858, edition. Citing the 25th Article of War — sending a challenge to an officer — of which Sumner was accused, the paper stated it was not strictly a challenge. When the so-called challenge was made, Sumner was undergoing a sentence of a former court-martial suspending him from command, rank and pay. So his conduct while undergoing the sentence took him out from under the 25th Article. These charges were nothing more than a governmental rebuke for his "repugnance to carrying out the behest of the slave power," the paper reported. "That was," the paper added, "an offense never to be forgiven by his pro-slavery enemies."

Earlier on February 25, 1858, the *Syracuse Daily Standard* reported on some irregularities that had caused the quarrel between Harney and Sumner. Harney was president of a court-martial in which Sumner was arraigned on what the paper called "some trifling charge." Since Harney had instigated the prosecution, Sumner naturally objected to Harney's conducting the proceedings.

On March 25 the *Syracuse Standard* made fun of the proceedings at Carlisle. The *New York Tribune* reported in its March 17, 1858, edition that Colonel Sumner was acquitted of both charges brought against him by General Harney and that the court deliberated less than fifteen minutes. The paper reported Sumner was to leave with his regiment from Fort Leavenworth on May 10 for Utah.

Sumner returned and assumed command of Fort Riley on April 15, 1858. On June 4 he left with the First Cavalry to take part in the Mormon War. After a march of 480 miles his column received word that the Mormon troubles were at an end militarily.[56]

On July 23, 1858, Sumner and the First Cavalry began a campaign against the Kiowas and were involved in Indian campaigns until December 1860. During this time Sumner reestablished Fort Atkinson, recommended the establishment of forts Larned and Wise and recommended that the government purchase the site of Bent's Old Fort.

12

The Utah Expedition
and Further Trouble
with Native Americans

Colonel Edwin Sumner's two-column expedition against the Cheyenne Indians, which left Fort Leavenworth in May 1857, was not the only such expedition undertaken by the U.S. Army that campaign season. The James Buchanan administration was determined to bring the Mormons in Utah to heel. Convinced the Mormons were in rebellion, the administration decided to appoint a non–Mormon governor and a fresh slate of territorial judges to administer the territory. The Mormons wanted only those of their faith to govern. To back up and support these new governmental appointees and to assure Mormon obedience, a force of United States troops would accompany these new officials. General William S. Harney, Colonel Sumner's old nemesis, was initially appointed to command the expedition. Harney balked at the assignment. General Winfield Scott cautioned President Buchanan against such a move, arguing that to organize a force such as would be needed to oppose the four thousand Mormons in Utah would require much preparation and could not get properly underway until late in the campaigning season.[1] Although Harney was replaced by Albert Sidney Johnston on August 29, 1857, he did not come onto the scene right away and Harney used his quasi-commander position to harass his old antagonist, Colonel Sumner. A kind of interim command fell to Colonel E.B. Alexander of the Tenth Infantry.

On August 2, 1857, four days after Colonel Sumner's fight with the Cheyennes and while Jeb Stuart and the other wounded troopers convalesced in the sod fortification, First Lieutenant Elisha G. Marshall at Fort Kearny, Nebraska Territory, wrote a letter to Adjutant General Samuel Cooper. Marshall reported that nineteen men and two herds of beef cattle numbering 824 destined for Salt Lake for the Utah Expedition had been attacked by about one hundred fifty Cheyennes only twenty-eight miles west of Fort Kearny. Of the nineteen men, one was killed and another one badly wounded. Two days later Lieutenant Marshall wrote to Samuel Cooper that he and his party had buried the slain man, a Mr. William Sandburn, but had been able to round up only forty-three head of cattle from the two herds.[2]

General Harney sent a copy of Lieutenant Marshall's letter to General Winfield Scott at army headquarters, which Scott had relocated to West Point. Harney included a letter of his own in which he informed General Scott that this was only the first of such depredations the unpunished Cheyennes would be causing. He pointed out that infantry were useless against Indians. Harney added, "I shall retain the two companies of the 2nd Dragoons at Fort Laramie, and have to request the General-in-chief will cause the two companies of the 1st Cavalry, ordered to this Post [Fort Leavenworth] under Colonel Sumner, to be stopped at Fort Kearney [sic] to furnish escorts from that place, as I have no disposable mounted force at my command for this service." Harney wrote this letter on August 8, 1857.

After General Scott read Harney's letter he wrote on the back of it (in red ink no less), that the loss of the cattle herd had been caused by a grave blunder. While passing through hostile Indian country the herd had been in front of the troops and without any guard for the herd's protection. Scott said he hoped that the expedition would not be jeopardized unduly by the loss of the herd. Scott sarcastically pointed out that the only measure taken by the general commanding was to issue a circular stating that in the future the commander would give protection to supply trains.

General Scott sent this off to the secretary of war. Then Scott wrote another letter to the secretary the next day, August 19, 1857, from his army headquarters located at West Point. In this letter Scott referred to his instructions issued June 29 to the commander of the expedition. Scott cited his instructions to point out to the secretary that Harney neglected Scott's orders. Specifically Scott ordered that "a small but sufficient force" must move separately from the main force to guard the beef cattle and other supplies that, because of moving slowly so the cattle would arrive in good condition, would encumber the march of the main body. "This detachment," Scott concluded, "though afterwards to become the rear guard, may, it is hoped be put in route before the main body, to gain as much time as possible before the latter passes it." (See Item 4 in the appendix for the complete text of General Scott's letter.)

General Harney blamed the Cheyenne troubles on Colonel Sumner's fight on the Solomon Fork; he said it had merely stirred up trouble and not killed enough Cheyennes to end their marauding and plundering. Harney claimed in his letter of August 22, 1857, to the assistant adjutant general that it was Sumner's failure to punish the Cheyennes sufficiently that allowed them to plunder so close to Fort Kearny. A party of some 150 Cheyennes attacked the cattle herd within thirty miles of Fort Kearny. Harney went on to fault Sumner for not sending at least two companies of his mounted force to Fort Kearny immediately after the battle to protect both public and private property.[3] (General Harney's complete letter is recorded in the appendix, Item 5.)

As stated at the end of chapter ten, Colonel Sumner returned to the command of Fort Leavenworth on April 15, 1858. He oversaw campaigns against various warring tribes into 1860. By 1858, Indian agents reported the hostility of the Kiowas and the Comanches, stating that they were audacious and insolent and expressed utter contempt for the officers of the government. Kiowas robbed Mexican trains and were committing depredations on the Texas frontier and along the Santa Fe Trail. Finally in 1860, two campaigns set out against them. One column of troops under Major John Sedgwick operated from Fort Riley and a base on the Arkansas River. The other column, under Captain Samuel D. Sturgis, advanced from Texas.[4]

In 1860, Sumner was in St. Louis in command of an army department. On April 3, 1860, Sumner issued orders for the start of an expedition against the Kiowa and Comanche tribes. Major John Sedgwick with six companies, four of the First Cavalry at Fort Riley and two of the Second Dragoons at Fort Kearny, would head an expedition against the Kiowas and Comanches. The initial destination was Pawnee Fork, Kansas Territory. The troops were to march well armed and carry an abundant supply of ammunition. "Instructions for the conduct of the Expedition, beyond the Arkansas [River], will be furnished hereafter," Sumner's order concluded. (For the complete order see the appendix, Item 6.)

Colonel Sumner asked for Delaware scouts, knowing firsthand of their value from his campaign of 1857. He offered command to Brevet Colonel Charles A. May or to Major John Sedgwick should May decline. Sumner's instructions to Sedgwick in either case were to hold no intercourse with the Indians until they were punished. He reminded Sedgwick that when in pursuit of Indians, a steady determined march would overtake them when they were traveling with their families. Sumner advised leaving the wagons at Pawnee Fork. When attacking a superior force, he said, turn their flank.[5]

From Fort Riley John Sedgwick wrote to his sister on May 12, 1860, describing the busy preparations he was making for his march. He has to think of everything necessary for five hundred men taking to the field for the entire summer. They would have wagons for the first two hundred miles to Pawnee Fork and from there pack mules would carry only what was necessary. For rations, Sedgwick told his sister, they were just enough to keep the men's bones together.

Sedgwick added that if successful they should return in September or

October. He was pretty sure he would get command, but orders had not yet arrived.[6]

On July 11, 1860, Colonel Sumner issued a report on the status of the campaign. Major Sedgwick, while examining the upper Arkansas River region, sent two detachments after a hostile party of Kiowas they encountered about twenty-five miles from Bent's Fort. Two warriors were killed and sixteen women and children were captured. Jeb Stuart, still a first lieutenant, headed one of the detachments with twenty men. Second Lieutenant George D. Bayard, who had remained with the quicksand-mired howitzers at the battle of Solomon Fork, was mentioned for his personal daring. He received a severe wound in his face. During the pursuit the men endured hunger, driving rain and hard riding.[7]

Early in June 1860, six companies of the First Cavalry, A, B, C, D, E and I, left from forts Washita, Arbuckle and Cobb under Captain Samuel D. Sturgis to take part in the campaign against the Kiowa and Comanche tribes. A total of eleven officers and 419 men marched from the Canadian River to the Arkansas River and then followed a trail northward. Captain Sturgis made a report on August 9, 1860. On August 7, 1860, Sturgis and his men came upon a large band of Indians numbering between six to eight hundred and comprised of members of the Kiowa, Comanche and, Sturgis believed, Cheyenne tribes. At first they appeared to be prepared to make a stand, but as Sturgis' column approached they turned and ran. After a running fight that covered about fifteen miles the Indians scattered in small parties in all directions so that pursuit was all but impossible.

Sturgis' report went on to state that twenty-nine Indians were killed and a large number wounded. Sturgis' losses numbered two friendly Indians killed, three men wounded, one man missing and three horses killed.[8]

Again on August 12, 1860, Captain Sturgis made a second report. After leaving their camp on Beaver Creek, a southern branch of the Republican River, on the morning of August 6 a party of Indians numbering from thirty to forty appeared about a mile away.

Sturgis ordered a pursuit, but as was common the cavalry horses, after a long march, were in no condition to overtake the Indians. After chasing them about eight miles, Sturgis' men were no closer to capturing the enemy than when they started, prompting Sturgis to write that this was but one more demonstration proving that after marching a thousand miles cavalry horses were no match against the fleet Indian ponies.

Later Sturgis' command encountered from six to eight hundred warriors determined to make a stand. Sturgis sent Captain James M. McIntosh's squadron to move and take the enemy in flank (as Sumner had stated to Sedgwick) while Captain Eugene A. Carr's squadron moved to the center either to make a charge or fight on foot as the situation might warrant. Once again

the Indians did not stand, and the jaded cavalry horses prevented their capture.

Sturgis made mention of some gallant fighting on the part of his men.
Private Michael Wheelan, Company B, was surrounded and attacked by nine
Indians. Though wounded in both legs he managed to kill two and wound
one, breaking the heads off three Indian lances with his saber. He was rescued
from further injury by three men from the train who saw what was going on.
Private Warren Hastings, Company I, was also left behind because his horse
was disabled. He was attacked by some ten or twelve Indians, one of whom
he killed and three of whom he wounded, but he was rescued by several of
his fellow troopers who had also fallen to the rear because their horses became
disabled. Two privates from separate companies each killed an Indian in
hand-to-hand combat.[9]

Meanwhile on August 8 Sedgwick received an order issued on June 30.
His column was to undertake the construction of Fort Henry A. Wise. A dis-
appointed Sedgwick journeyed up the Arkansas River to the fort site near
Bent's New Fort. Sedgwick's orders came from headquarters, Department of
the West, St. Louis. "With regard to abandoning the expedition against the
Indians," the order suggested, "it is difficult to judge what should be done."
Coming in too soon would be criticized for not continuing the pursuit longer.
On the other hand, the orders admitted, staying out too long would offer
Sedgwick too little time to shelter his command for winter. Sedgwick would
have to decide for himself but, the order suggested, "continue the pursuit
until mid August." The order ended with the note "Colonel May reports to
me that a large body of Kiowas are on the Solomon's Fork, near where we met
the Cheyennes in '57."[10]

Sedgwick lost no time in writing to his sister of his disappointment in
having to build Fort Wise. From a camp near Pawnee Fork where he had left
his wagons earlier he wrote the very day he got Sumner's order. He was not
happy having to build the fort so late in the season with only tents for shelter
and no implements to build it with. Sedgwick claimed he had not been so
disgusted since he learned back in 1857 he was to go on to Utah after having
been part of the Cheyenne Expedition.[11]

On September 12, 1860, Sedgwick provided his sister with some news
and interesting data. "It is not likely that I shall get married this winter. Our
stores are on the road from Leavenworth. There will be over three hundred
wagons, carrying six thousand pounds each, at an expense of eight cents per
pound for hauling, so that you can estimate something of the expense of keeping five hundred men for one year more than four hundred miles beyond civilization." The freight bill was over $144,000.

Major John Sedgwick wrote several letters to his sister from Fort Wise.
On November 17, 1860, he wrote, "The subject of politics loses all its savour

before getting out here. It is never mentioned except when the papers come in, and then a short topic. All concede Lincoln's election, and think any change will improve upon the present one." On November 30, he wrote, "Hurrah for Lincoln! I say." In his letter dated December 10, Sedgwick began with a paraphrase of Shakespeare. Perhaps it was a form of amusement. "Our winter of discontent has not as yet been made glorious by a mail, although the sun has favoured us almost daily for the last four months."[12] His letter went on to say, "We have heard of Mr. Lincoln's election and the probable difficulty he will experience, if not direct opposition, to his inauguration. It seems lamentable that this Union that we have boasted of and glorified so much should be broken up, but I hope our next news will be more satisfactory. How a disruption will affect me I cannot foresee; probably would result in my leaving the service at once."

On January 16, 1861, Sedgwick wrote from Fort Wise, "Colonel Sumner has gone on leave for several months, which leaves me the only field officer with the regiment.... All other evils compared with disunion are light, cemented as the Union is with so much blood and treasure."[13]

PART THREE: CIVIL WAR

13

Politics

Edwin V. Sumner was a Democrat. Yet he volunteered to serve as an escort to president-elect Abraham Lincoln in his twelve-day, nineteen-hundred-mile journey from Springfield, Illinois, to Washington, D.C. From St. Louis on December 17, 1860, Sumner wrote to Lincoln volunteering his services as well as those of his friend Major David Hunter.[1]

Sumner went on to inform the president-elect that he was reading everything he could find on current events and was becoming convinced that secession was treason. "Not in a state collectively," Sumner wrote to explain his political philosophy, "but in the individuals of a state who contravene the laws."[2]

When the train carrying the president-elect reached New York State the *New York Times* reported on its progress through the state. Henry Villard of the *New York Tribune* observed, took notes, wrote dispatches and telegraphed it all back to the city. Villard talked to president-elect Lincoln as often as he could. When he could not he talked to the people around Lincoln and got to know Colonel Sumner. Villard had known Edwin V. Sumner Jr. in Washington and had helped him get his appointment to the army.[3]

In Lincoln's party, along with Sumner, were three other army officers, Major David Hunter, Captain John Pope and Captain George W. Hazzard. As Lincoln and his party neared Washington, Frederick W. Seward, son of Senator William H. Seward, brought word that General Winfield Scott, alerted by Allan Pinkerton, believed there was a conspiracy plot in Baltimore. Allan Pinkerton of the Pinkerton National Detective Agency was sure there was a plot to assassinate Lincoln when he passed through Baltimore. Pinkerton proposed that Lincoln should travel alone and incognito through Baltimore to avoid suspicion and arrive unannounced in Washington. Colonel Sumner denounced the plan as a piece of cowardice and suggested a squad of cavalry to cut a path to Washington. Captain Pope, however, supported the Pinkerton plan. Once in Washington Sumner, along with General Winfield Scott and Colonel Charles P. Stone, made arrangements to safeguard the inauguration.[4]

One of Sumner's daughters, Mrs. Sara Sumner Teall, wrote of her experiences at Lincoln's first inauguration. She persuaded her husband to take her to Washington to attend. Along with her father, her sister Mrs. Eugene McLean and her two soon-to-be–Confederate brothers-in-law, she and her husband stayed at Willard's Hotel. The presidential party was at Willard's as well.

Mrs. Teall thought the inauguration ball was "the dullest of all balls." The tent which housed the event was decorated with little taste and was poorly lighted. Senator Stephen Douglas opened the ball with Mrs. Lincoln, who looked "extremely well in a light blue 'Moire' but did not seem to be in good spirits," according to Mrs. Teall's observations. Later that week President Lincoln promoted Sumner to brigadier general. "I remember that I didn't appreciate Mr. Lincoln," Sarah Sumner Teall concluded, "when I could have talked to him every day. I shared the general opinion, that Mr. Seward and Mr. Chase were greater men of the party, Mr. Lincoln, an uncouth Westerner, knowing nothing of statesmanship."[5]

California

Promoted from colonel to brigadier general by President Lincoln on March 16, 1861, General Sumner arrived in San Francisco on April 24, 1861, to replace General Albert Sidney Johnston, commander of the newly-created Department of the Pacific. General Winfield Scott's order to Sumner was brief. It read:

March 22, 1861

Brig. Gen. E.V. Sumner:

Dear General: Prepare to sail from New York the first of next month to relieve Brevet Brigadier-General Johnston, in command of the Pacific Department, say for a tour of some years. The order to sail, &c., will reach you by the next mail, but remain unpublished till you are on the Pacific Ocean, for confidential reasons.

In haste, yours, truly, Winfield Scott[6]

Unsure of Johnston's sympathies and willing to take no chance that Johnston might do as General David Twiggs had done in Texas, surrender Federal posts, Lincoln replaced Johnston with Sumner on March 23. In February 1861, Twiggs, as commander of the Department of Texas, had surrendered nineteen military posts even before the state passed an ordinance of secession. Sumner traveled incognito, his name not appearing on the passenger list. The *New York*

Herald in its April 4, 1861, edition carried a notice from Washington from the day before: "It is believed that General Sumner has been ordered to New York, and perhaps South, to direct the movement of troops, as he left here very suddenly." Johnston himself was unaware of his being replaced until Sumner relieved him of command on April 25.[7] Brevet Brigadier General Albert Sidney Johnston chose to command the Department of the Pacific when it was offered to him by the War Department. He had General Scott's recommendation. The department had been created recently by combining the departments of California and Oregon. The prior commander of the Department of California died, thus leaving a vacancy. Johnston left with his family immediately for his new assignment, his first since his tour in Utah following the Mormon War. On December 21, 1860, the Johnstons left New York on the steamer *North Star* for California via the Isthmus of Panama.[8]

The Democratic Party had dominated California politics since it became a state. The party clung to principles of state sovereignty and white supremacy. Its leaders, the party press and its members sympathized with the South in the coming struggle and wanted the state to form an independent Pacific republic. It is not surprising since the largest number of settlers, particularly in southern California, came from slave states. During the 1850s about 88,000 people arrived whose former homes were south of the Mason-Dixon Line. Of these the bulk had come from Missouri.[9]

The Republican Party was making some progress, however. Republicans elected to the state legislature in the late 1850s supported the right of blacks to testify in courts. In the presidential election of 1860, Lincoln received 38,734 votes to 38,023 for the Northern Democrats and 33,734 for the Southern Democrats.[10] Still, with the strong Southern feelings held by many in the state, it required a show of force tempered with much diplomacy to keep California in the Union. Fortunately, General Johnston and General Sumner who followed him benefited from their past assignments; Johnston from his work in Utah during and after the Mormon War and Sumner from his efforts in trying to keep the peace in Kansas.

As a private person Albert S. Johnston had a love for his adopted state of Texas. He believed in the right of secession. While he supported slavery he sold one slave and freed another before coming to California, a free state. He did not, however, permit his personal feelings and beliefs to conflict with his duties as a soldier. Johnston's first concern upon taking command was for the security of the San Francisco Bay posts, namely forts Point, Alcatraz and Benicia Arsenal. Although in command only from mid–January until the end of April, Johnston began a program to secure posts and to consolidate his resources. It was a sound foundation that his successor General Sumner could build upon. As early as January 19, 1861, Johnston began transferring soldiers from Fort Vancouver to the San Francisco defenses. Later he ordered the transfer of 10,000 rifled muskets, model 1855, with accouterments and 150,000 cartridges from Benicia Arsenal to Fort Alcatraz. The order stated that the cartridges contain "elongated balls." These balls were the Harpers Ferry bullet, an improvement over the older Minié bullet, and developed at Harpers Ferry by armorer James H. Burton. This distinction in the order probably was made because these bullets were new and developed for the model 1855 Springfield. It is also interesting to note that percussion caps were to be supplied rather than the Maynard roll primers for which the model 1855 had been designed. Since they were going to damp Alcatraz Island, Johnston may have believed that caps would be more reliable than the rolled primers, which relied on shellac for a waterproof. On the other hand he may have been of a more conservative frame of mind and suspicious of the new primer. Also of some possible interest is the fact that there were as many as 10,000 1855 rifled muskets at Benicia Arsenal in February 1861. The total number of this arm, manufactured from 1857 to 1861, was but 47,115.[11]

Johnston was not long at his post before rumors began to circulate that he was in league with his fellow Southern officers to take control of key posts, to arm Breckinridge Democrats and to proclaim a Pacific Republic that would be either neutral or worse, side with the Confederacy.[12] Back in Washington, General Scott became concerned about Johnston in California based upon reports from Oregon senator James Nesmith. The senator told Scott of Johnston's involvement with California Disunionists and other groups like the Knights of the Golden Circle. Rumors spread that Johnson was involved with California senators William Gwin and Milton S. Latham along with Oregon senator Joseph Lane to create a western republic. Then too, General David Twiggs' defection in Texas was on everyone's mind.[13]

General Johnston wrote his letter of resignation to the War Department from San Francisco on April 9, 1861. According to Albert Sidney Johnston's biographer Charles P. Roland, the Lincoln administration realized its mistaken judgment of General Johnston even before General Sumner reached San Francisco. Yet on June 3, 1861, over a month after Sumner arrived in California, General Winfield Scott issued two orders to have General A.S. Johnston arrested if he arrived in New York by sea or by overland.[14]

In an attempt to correct their mistake in misjudging Johnston, Secretary of War Simon Cameron through Fitz John Porter sent the following message to Johnston: "I take the greatest pleasure in assuring you, for the Secretary of War, that he has the utmost confidence in you, and will give you the most important command and trust on your arrival here." The telegram message went from New York to St. Louis and then on to San Francisco by pony express. Not until the first of November 1861 would telegraphic service connect the East and West coasts.[15]

Sumner's orders were verbal, so we can only surmise what they may have been. However, the conditions would imply that General Sumner was to keep California and the region in the Union. Three days after having relieved General Johnston of command, he reported on April 28, 1861, "It gives me pleasure to state that the command was turned over to me in good order. General Johnston had forwarded his resignation before I arrived, but he continued to hold the command, and was carrying out the orders of the Government." Sumner went on to state that he was determined to re-enforce the forts in the harbor and see to it that the forces there were to be secure and provided for a duration of six months. He went on to state that there was a strong Union feeling with the majority of the people, strengthened perhaps by news that Fort Sumter had been fired upon. Sumner cautioned, however, "The secessionists are much the most active and zealous party, which gives them more influence than they ought to have from their numbers." Sumner was sure there was "some deep scheming" to draw California into the secession movement. Sumner expressed his belief that the troops on hand would secure all government property unless there was a general uprising of the people. "I think," he added, "the course of events at the East will control events here. So long as the General Government is sustained and holds the capital the secessionists can not carry this State out of the Union."

Perhaps thinking about the line in his orders from General Scott that sent him to California stating that he might be there "say for a tour of some years," Sumner added a caveat. The old dragoon who proposed to lead Lincoln into Washington behind a squad of slashing cavalry could play the diplomat if ordered, as he had been, but at heart he was a soldier and wanted to command on the battlefield, a sentiment that went back as far as his days at Carlisle. So he closed with "I would respectfully say to the General-in-Chief that after my arrangements are completed — and they will be in two weeks — if he should think proper to authorize me to place Colonel Wright here in command of the department everything will be secure; and, if my services should be wanted elsewhere, I could be withdrawn from this department without detriment to the public service." At the end of a report dated June 10, 1861, Sumner again dropped a hint that he would like to come to the East: "I would remind the General-in-Chief that if he needs my services at the East, I can make such arrangements that everything will be secure here. I would not say this unless I knew I could do it."[16]

Before the month of April was out Sumner took action to secure Los Angeles. In his report to Washington dated April 30, 1861, he related that he found it necessary to remove the troops from Fort Mojave and transfer them to Los Angeles. "There is more danger of disaffection at this place than any other in the State." Sumner went on to explain, "There are a number of influential men there who are decided secessionists, and if we should have any difficulty it will commence there." Sumner was learning fast. Of Fort

Mojave he reported that it was an entirely useless post. No hostile Indians were nearby nor was there any travel on the road it was intended to protect.[17] Quartermaster Captain Winfield Scott Hancock was a great help to General Sumner in keeping things generally under control in the Los Angeles area. Hancock had been Sumner's adjutant at Jefferson Barracks in 1855, and despite a disagreement over quarters there, the two worked well together in California.[18] On May 4 Hancock reported the measures he had taken to secure Los Angeles and to outline the political landscape. Although the secessionists' plans never were fruitful, events in southern California remained unsettled even by the time Sumner left the state.

Officials of Santa Barbara County described their fears and outlined their perception of the political climate in a letter of October 18, 1861, to the officer in command of the Forces of the United States at Los Angeles: "The undersigned most respectfully beg leave to represent that in their judgment the safety of loyal citizens of the United States residing in the county of Santa Barbara is in great peril," their letter began. The county officials went on to point out that the bulk of the population of the county was made up of native Californians and Mexicans, "none of whom have ever been supposed to entertain a sincere attachment to the Government of the United States." Confederate successes brought out their support for the Confederacy. "The Americans are not well provided with arms," the letter claimed, and it asked for two companies of soldiers.[19]

General Sumner was sensitive to the importance of seemingly small matters and realized how attention to them would bolster Union support throughout the state. When Major James H. Carleton, First Dragoons, commanding at Los Angeles, wrote on May 22 to ask if his men should take part in the raising of the Union flag at a courthouse ceremony to which they had been invited, Sumner answered yes through his assistant adjutant, General Don Carlos Buell. The next day in General Order No. 9 he changed the name of the quartermaster's brig from *Floyd*, the former secretary of war turned confederate general, to the *General Jesup*, in honor of a long-serving quartermaster-general.[20]

Sumner was more involved with ships than the mere renaming of a brig. On April 29 and again on the 30th Allan McLane, president of the Pacific Mail Steamship Company, wrote to Secretary of War Simon Cameron to instruct the commander of the Department of the Pacific to provide a guard for each steamship sailing between San Francisco and Panama. Later Sumner sent a battery, then followed up with a company of foot artillery to protect Mare Island Navy Yard. The island's commandant asked that Sumner keep him advised of possible disruption to his yard because he believed Sumner had "superior means of gaining information in relation to movements of the day." Sumner then sent two 24-pounder guns to protect the harbor at San

Diego. Sumner issued orders on May 31 to capture or sink any vessels sailing under the secessionist flag. He also supported the idea of chartering a revenue cutter for the port of San Francisco.[21]

California secessionists took heart when they learned of the Confederate success at First Manassas in July 1861. About three hundred Texans under Colonel John Baylor struck the southeastern corner of the New Mexico Territory in late July. Soon after, Fort Fillmore, in what is now New Mexico and just north of El Paso, Texas, surrendered. Its commander, Major Isaac Lynde, Seventh U.S. Infantry, abandoned the fort and later surrendered to Baylor without a fight. For his action he was dropped from the army. On August 1, 1861, Baylor proclaimed all the territory of New Mexico south of the thirty-fourth parallel Confederate territory. Again General Sumner strengthened his forces in southern California. He created a military district there under Colonel George Wright, Ninth Infantry. Wright made military improvements but decided not to weed out and prosecute the disloyal. Colonel Wright was a brother-in-law of General Sumner's and his son, a lieutenant, was killed in 1873 in the Modoc War.[22]

Sumner's instructions to Colonel Wright dated September 30, 1861, were to crush out this disloyalty and to make Fort Yuma, California, perfectly secure. Wright had the discretion to post soldiers where he saw fit. Yet much of the vocal dissent could be cowed by a firm personal stance. Captain John W. Davidson's firm stand in talking down a group of disunionists is an example of vocal dissention and of a bloodless way to not only quiet it but to promote Union support.[23]

Meanwhile General Sumner was trying to avoid conducting an expedition into Texas that General Scott had ordered on August 16, 1861. Sumner was to fit out an expedition of two batteries, ten companies of foot, one regiment of volunteer cavalry and four regiments of volunteer infantry. The expedition was to enter Texas via Mazatlan, Mexico.

Mazatlan, Mexico, is on the west coast just south of the Tropic of Cancer and across the Gulf of California from the southern tip of Lower or Baja California. It would have been quite a march, having to cross the width of Mexico in a northeasterly direction to enter Texas.

Guaymas, also on Mexico's west coast, was far to the north of Mazatlan and about midway in the Gulf of California. It lies about 500 miles north of Mazatlan. The march into the contested area of southeastern New Mexico from Guaymas would have been a march of about 250 to 300 miles.

Sumner replied on August 30, relating the conditions in California. Citing the Confederate success in Virginia in July, he wrote, "I shall get the force authorized to be raised here into my hands as soon as possible; but it will take some time to do this." Sumner explained the difficulty of raising volunteers in a state with a strong party opposed to the government. Next he pointed out that the route through Guaymas would be better than the one through Mazatlan. Sumner then suggested, respectfully of course, that it would be better to transport his command by sea to meet an additional force from the North, "as the commanding general might think necessary." Hoping evidently to convince General Scott to cancel this operation, Sumner closed by pointing out that his revised plan would provide for the necessary ammunition, "which would be impossible for me to carry across the continent." Then as if to twist the knife he had stabbed into the original plan Sumner added, "A march at the usual rate across those deserts would unevitably [sic] unfit volunteers for some time for efficient service in the field."[24]

Back East the *Cincinnati Enquirer* and the *Providence Evening Press* carried the same story on August 15, 1861: "General Sumner has ... informed Flag Officer Montgomery, and also the Government, of a report that Colonel Van Dorn, of the Secession army, has been seen with 1,300 men on the road between El Paso and San Antonio, from which it is believed that an attempt will be made to subjugate Lower California." On August 27, 1861, the *Providence Evening Press* reported: "California — Nine companies of infantry, for service on the plains, have reported to General Sumner, and 1500 cavalry. Nearly all were accepted."

On September 7 Sumner again wrote to Washington expressing his reluctance to conduct an expedition across parts of Mexico and into Texas. While the Union party triumphed in the election, making things safe in San Francisco, in the southern portion of California secessionists were congregating, emboldened by their success in Arizona and New Mexico. They were hoping for support from Texas, Sumner wrote. He then went on to correct his view that Guaymas would be better than Mazatlan as a point of departure. Sumner took the advice of Mr. E.F. Beale, surveyor-general of California, who wrote to him on September 5 and described the difficulty of moving into Texas. Mr. Beale wrote that the road from Mazatlan northward by Durango was impassable for wheeled vehicles. The road from Guaymas, because of the lack of water, would present an almost insurmountable difficulty to an army. Beale's knowledge of Mexico was based upon firsthand experience in the country.

General Sumner recalled times past as he continued to outline the difficulty in the proposed overland campaign into Texas. "I fitted out General [Stephen Watts] Kearny's command of 100 men on the Rio Grande in the fall of 1846," he wrote. "I gave him the best of everything in the regiment, and yet when he arrived on this coast this small force was completely broken down and unable to contend successfully with the Californians who attacked him." Sumner asked the general-in-chief to reconsider. General Scott did so and on September 16, 1861, issued an order through E.D. Townsend to suspend the expedition and to prepare to bring the regular troops, with a few exceptions, to New York by steamship.[25]

Townsend's order ended with instructions for Sumner to order Colonel Wright to relieve Sumner of command of the department and then for Sumner to proceed to army headquarters and report in person. "Brig. Gen. J.W. Denver, U.S. Volunteer service, will be ordered to California to relieve Colonel Wright, who will then proceed to report in person at Army headquarters."[26] Not everyone was happy with the choice of Brigadier-General James W. Denver to command the Department of the Pacific. On September 6, 1861, William C. Kibbe, adjutant-general for the state of California, wrote to Secretary of War Simon Cameron protesting the choice of Denver to the command of the Department of the Pacific. Kibbe claimed that many officers would resign rather than serve under General Denver. They had no confidence in his loyalty. "We are endeavoring to fill up six regiments called for from this State, and I assure you that this report has proved our greatest obstacle," Kibbe wrote.[27]

Perhaps Kibbe's letter did the trick. General Order No. 160 issued at Washington on September 30, 1861, gave command of the Department of the Pacific to Brigadier General Joseph K.F. Mansfield, who would "repair to San Francisco with as little delay as possible." Colonel George Wright, now brigadier-general of volunteers, was to serve under Mansfield in command of the Columbia River. However only two days later on October 2 Mansfield was ordered to go to Fort Monroe, Virginia, and to report to Major General John Wool without delay. Perhaps had Mansfield been able to leave at once for California he might not have been called back and would have avoided his mortal wound a year later at Antietam.[28]

On October 20, 1861, Colonel George Wright, Ninth Infantry, assumed command of the Department of the Pacific. The next day Colonel Wright wrote, "The measures which were taken by General Sumner to secure the quiet and peace of the District of Southern California have thus far produced the most happy results."[29]

Orders issued on September 16, 1861, relieved General Sumner from command of the Department of the Pacific and ordered him to come to army headquarters in person. Along with the general the regulars were to come east as well. It was nearly a month later, on October 14, that Sumner reported he was about to leave on a steamer on the 21st with the Third Artillery, part of the Sixth Infantry and 10,000 muskets. "Colonel Wright ought to remain here in command," Sumner wrote. "The safety of the whole coast may depend upon it."

Not all residents within the Department of the Pacific felt more secure by the government's efforts to bind the state to the Union. In order to protect military posts in and around San Francisco and to suppress any possible insurrection in other parts of the state and nearby territories, General A.S. Johnston as well as General Sumner withdrew soldiers from outlying posts. Settlers living in those areas protested, believing they were vulnerable to Indian attacks.

The commanders of the Department of the Pacific downplayed these fears, perhaps taking a risk with the lives and safety of those residents. Keeping California within the Union was their main concern and responsibility.[30]

To aid the regular troops keep the peace in California, President Lincoln on July 22, 1861, authorized the employment of volunteers. His action resulted in the formation of one regiment of infantry and five companies of cavalry called respectively the First Infantry and First Cavalry, California Volunteers. Among their tasks was to protect the Overland Mail Route between California and the Eastern states by way of Salt Lake City. This force, commanded by Brevet Major James H. Carleton, First U.S. Cavalry, who then became colonel, formed at Oakland, California. By September they had nearly acquired their full complement of men.

The Confederates operating in Texas and the Southwest reacted to the intelligence they had that General Sumner with a 2,500-man army was marching against them. They were reported as being on the march to Fort Bliss coming by way of Guaymas, the route General Sumner considered better than Mazatlan. This news Lieutenant Colonel John R. Baylor reported to General Henry H. Sibley from Dona Ana, Arizona, on October 24 and 25.

This intelligence Baylor got from a man in Santa Fe. Sumner was reported to be coming with eleven companies of U.S. regulars and thirteen companies of New Mexican volunteers. On October 27 Sibley ordered a scout to see if in fact Sumner was coming by way of Guaymas. He was nowhere to be found.

In closing a word of tribute to the men who made up the California Volunteers will not be misplaced. Surgeon McNulty wrote, "The march of this column from the Pacific Ocean to the Rio Grande is somewhat remarkable, from the fact that almost the entire distance is a desert waste, with great scarcity of water and that of the worst quality."

Men marching day after day through burning sands and nearly suffocated with alkali dust required to be made of stern stuff — of such were the men composing this column.[31]

The old dragoon Edwin Sumner knew when to draw his saber and when to keep it sheathed. He approved and supported the formation of home guard companies and suggested that every community form such a company of from eighty to one hundred men. "No Federal troops in the Department of the Pacific will ever surrender to rebels," he ordered. Seizure of arms often was enough to check the actions of secessionists as well as simply talking them down, as First Dragoon captain John W. Davidson had done. As G. Thomas Edwards wrote of Sumner, "This school of 'Bleeding Kansas' had taught him that in an explosive political situation it was the army's duty to uphold the law and that rash deeds created only excitements and enemies. Sumner consistently followed that principle. Not a single partisan was jailed for treasonable utterances." As we have seen, these events in California were of interest in the east; several big-city newspapers reported on events taking place there. The *Cincinnati Daily Enquirer* on October 3, 1861, carried the story of Sumner's "Never Surrender" order.[32]

Just before leaving to come East, General Sumner reviewed some of the home guard companies he recommended communities to form. The *Morning Oregonian,* the newspaper of Portland, Oregon, reported on that review, held on October 17, 1861, at the corner of Sansom and California streets, San Francisco. To appeal to the Irish in the crowd, Sumner told of his long association with the Irish and said he wanted no better soldiers than the Irish. The crowd responded with cheers and laughter to Sumner's many remarks as to the character of the Irish. He concluded his remarks with "Boys, I go to fight for the flag which you, Irishmen, have so nobly upheld. God bless you! Farewell!"[33]

14

Sumner Comes East

The Peninsula

General Edwin V. Sumner left California in late October 1861. He was in Washington by November 18 having supper with General George B. McClellan. During an inspection on Sunday, December 15, Sumner's horse stumbled and fell on him, badly injuring Sumner's chest. He did not return to duty until the latter part of January. This injury to his chest may have contributed to the pneumonia that took his life little more than a year later.[1]

General Oliver O. Howard described General Sumner's accident differently. Not on December 15 but in early January the accident occurred. According to Howard's account the accident was not during an inspection but while Sumner was riding across some fields not far from headquarters, "when his horse stepped into a blind post hole and fell, throwing the general forward to the ground. Injury was done to his shoulder and lungs. He remounted his horse and rode back to camp with difficulty; lame and suffering as he was he sat up in his saddle, as was his custom." Having written earlier that Sumner was remarkable for two military virtues, namely an exact obedience to orders and a rigid enforcement of discipline, it was in his character to return the salute presented to him by the post sentry. "God preserve to our people the remembrance of such a man," Howard concluded. Howard's memory may have failed him.[2]

The *Syracuse Journal* reported on December 16, 1861, that Sumner had been thrown from his horse the day before while reviewing troops. "A rib was broken and other injuries," the paper stated and reported that he would be able to resume his duties in a few days. On the twentieth the same paper stated that he had not broken a rib but had badly bruised his leg. Mrs. Sumner joined him. Then on the 23rd the *Journal* devoted a column to Sumner's fall.

His two daughters, the paper reported, Mrs. Teall and Mrs. Jenkins, were advised by their brother Edwin V. Sumner, Jr., to come Washington. Sumner may have suffered internal injuries when his horse stumbled and fell on top of him, the paper reported.

Finally on December 31 the paper carried a brief notice stating the latest on General Sumner's condition. There was no danger that the disability would prove permanent. He was much better and would soon take over the duties of his division.

Sumner's division, as of early February 1862, was stationed in Virginia at Camp California, so named because of General Sumner's recent service there. Comprising of three brigades under Oliver O. Howard, Thomas F. Meagher and William H. French, it was one of the smaller divisions, with an aggregate of 9,859 officers and men. It had the Eighth Illinois Cavalry Regiment assigned to it and artillery numbering six heavy and twelve field pieces. By March 3, 1862, General Sumner had recovered sufficiently and returned to his division but slept in a house rather than in the Sibley tent he had used prior to his accident. Later that month news came that Centreville, Virginia, had been evacuated, which, according to General Howard, brought forward the peninsular plan.[3]

On March 13, 1862, by General Order No. 101 Headquarters Army of the Potomac, the Second Corps was formed, to be commanded by General Edwin V. Sumner. Three divisions were originally assigned to the Second Corps, those of Israel B. Richardson, Louis Blenker and John Sedgwick. On March 31 Blenker's division was detached, leaving Sumner's Second Corps with but two divisions.[4] The Second Corps would, for all practical purposes, begin its combat role on the peninsula, the neck of land in Virginia between the York and the James rivers. It would assemble with other elements of the Army of the Potomac at Fort Monroe. Some background leading to the decision to attack Richmond, Virginia, from the peninsula, rather than overland, is important.

As the year 1861 faded and the New Year began, President Lincoln believed strongly in renewing the advance upon the enemy. General McClellan gave no hint of a plan. His reticence forced Lincoln to suggest one of his own. A column of 50,000 men would advance, menace and hold the Confederates at their position at Centreville, Virginia. Another 50,000 men would move, some via the Potomac River, some overland, to a point placing them closer to Richmond than were the Confederates at Centreville. Challenged by Lincoln's plan, General McClellan responded with a plan of his own, one that according to Alexander S. Webb "foreshadowed the final move to the Peninsula."[5]

Adding to McClellan's delay was an illness he suffered that confined him to his bed from mid–December 1861 to mid–January 1862. In his absence Lincoln dealt with generals Irvin McDowell, William B. Franklin and Montgomery Meigs. They supported Lincoln's plan to attack the enemy directly overland rather than moving to another base down the Chesapeake as McClellan preferred. After many conferences eight of the twelve division commanders favored General McClellan's plan over the administration's. Those in favor of the administration's plan were Irvin McDowell, Edwin Sumner, Samuel Heintzelman and Chief Engineer John G. Barnard. Those favoring McClellan's plan, known now as the Urbana plan, were Erasmus Keyes, William B. Franklin, Fitz John Porter, William F. Smith, George McCall, Louis Blenker, Andrew Porter and Joseph Hooker.[6] Therefore on March 8, 1862, Lincoln issued orders for McClellan's plan to begin. On March 13 McClellan met with his newly-appointed corps commanders, generals McDowell, Sumner, Heintzelman and Keyes. They agreed to make Fort Monroe the base of operations.[7] The embarkation began March 17. Heintzelman's corps led. Fitz John Porter's corps landed on March 22 and McClellan and his staff on April 2. Ready to move up the peninsula at that time were Heintzelman's corps less Hooker's division, two divisions of General Keyes' Fourth Corps, one division of the Second Corps, George Sykes' regular infantry brigade, Henry Hunt's reserve artillery and three regiments of cavalry. In all there were about 58,000 men and one hundred guns. Still to arrive were Silas Casey's division of the Fourth Corps, Israel Richardson's division of the Second Corps and Joseph Hooker's division of the Third Corps. Another 20,000 men manned the defenses that surrounded Washington.[8]

Major General Edwin Vose Sumner, "Old Bull of the Woods." Massachusetts Commandery Military Order of the Loyal Legion and the U.S. Army Military History Institute.

Among those 58,000, soon to grow to about 130,000, was Warren Lee Goss, a private in Company A of Captain James C. Duane's regular U.S. Engineers. Upon arriving at Old Point Comfort he "looked with open-eyed wonder at Fortress Monroe, huge and frowning." He went on to describe the scene along the shore covered with artillery, baggage-wagons, pontoon trains, boats and crowds of tents and soldiers. "Near at hand," Goss wrote, "was the irrepressible army mule, hitched to and eating out of pontoon boats; those who had eaten their ration of grain and hay were trying their teeth, with promise of success, in eating the boats.

An Army mule was hungrier than a soldier, and would eat anything, especially a pontoon boat or rubber blanket."[9]

The march up the peninsula was slow. The roads were very poor and, according to Private Goss, muddy with recent rains. During his second day's march it rained and the roads, cut up and churned badly by the teams having gone before him, were a semi-fluid filth. When Goss and his mates reached Big Bethel, a hamlet of perhaps a dozen houses, the rain fell in sheets.

On the afternoon of April 5, 1862, elements of McClellan's army reached Yorktown, separated from Gloucester Point and its defensive works by the York River. The Union army settled down for a siege that lasted until May 4, when the army learned the Confederates had abandoned their works. During that time they built another defensive line across the peninsula from the York to the James rivers at Williamsburg.[10]

On the peninsula the Confederates used their equivalent of an I.E.D., an improvised explosive device, known to us today from Iraq and Afghanistan. Private Goss described them: "There was much talk of buried torpedoes in front of the enemy's works, and it was rumored that one officer and several men had been blown to atoms by them; ... We saw a number of sticks stuck in the ground both inside and outside the earthwork, with white rags attached, which were said to indicate the location of the buried torpedoes already discovered."[11]

These mines were also mentioned by the colonel of the 55th New York Regiment, Régis de Trobriand. Here is his description: "The road we followed was sown with murderous snares. There were cylindrical bombs, with percussion fuses carefully concealed, buried so as to leave the capsule level with the ground. The step of a man or horse upon it was sufficient to explode it, and it was always fatal."[12] General James Longstreet and Confederate Secretary of War G.W. Randolph issued orders against their use. If the intention of these buried bombs was to slow the advance of the Army of the Potomac, the Confederates need not to have bothered.

Private Goss' *Recollections of a Private* first appeared as articles in *Century* magazine. Their worth as documentary accounts of life in the Union army is quite high. No less a soldier than Viscount Sir Garnet Wolseley, himself an observer during the Civil War, wrote favorably of Goss' *Recollections* in an article he wrote for the *North American Review*. He had finished reading the second volume of *Battles and Leaders* and wrote, "In particular, I should like those articles by Mr. Warren Lee Goss, the 'Recollections of a Private,' duly studied. For, after all, questions of strategy, of tactics, and of the importance of organization of all kinds turn upon the effect which is ultimately produced on the spirit and well-being and fighting efficiency of the private soldier. Private Goss' *Recollections* have more to say about the battles and the soldiers who struggled, labored and trudged up the miry Virginia Peninsula towards Richmond."[13]

As for General Sumner's Second Corps, only Sedgwick's division landed at Fort Monroe, and it moved up the peninsula under orders of the Third Corps commander, General Samuel P. Heintzelman. By the time the army reached Yorktown General Richardson's division had not yet come up; it did not arrive until April 16. The Third Corps was on the right in front of Yorktown with Sedgwick's division to its left and the Fourth Corps to the left of that division. As of April 6 Sumner was in command of the entire left, all the troops except for the Third Corps.

Francis A. Walker, historian of the Second Corps, wrote: "Just before the date fixed for the bombardment and assault of Yorktown, the enemy, having gained a precious month, evacuated their works.... On May 5, at Williamsburg, twelve miles from Yorktown, was fought the first considerable action of the Army of the Potomac."[14]

Of the siege of Yorktown itself, Alexander S. Webb wrote, "We find the operations were conducted with skill. Batteries were constructed under the supervision of F.J. Porter, W.F. Barry, Chief of Artillery, and J.G. Barnard, Chief of Engineers; ... But the enemy were too shrewd to await our onslaught.... By May 5, they had remained long enough at the Yorktown line for their purpose. A month's time had been gained."[15] The armies marched up the peninsula to their next encounter at Williamsburg.

Not one Second Corps regiment fought at Williamsburg, but Francis A. Walker recognized the battle's importance in the history of the corps. On May 4 Sumner took command of all arms of the corps slogging through the mud to intercept the Confederate withdrawal. Darius Couch, a division commander in the Fourth Corps, would later command the Second Corps. He would be followed in that command by General Winfield Scott Hancock, who, at Williamsburg, was a Fourth Corps brigadier in W.F. "Baldy" Smith's division.

Confederate General Joseph E. Johnston abandoned Yorktown deliberately. Johnston saw but one reason for his remaining on the peninsula: gaining time for the organizing and arming of Confederate troops. He determined to hold his position at Yorktown as long as he could without exposing his men to the fire of powerful artillery. On May 4, 1862, his troops reached Williamsburg.

The Union forces, on the road about noon on May 4, hurried after the retreating Confederates. General George Stoneman's Union cavalry and the infantry of generals Joseph Hooker's and William F. Smith's divisions of the Third and Fourth corps, respectively, were in pursuit. General McClellan, believing there would be no serious fighting for at least several days, remained at Yorktown to meet with General William B. Franklin. General Sumner, second in command to McClellan, directed the divisions moving by land.[16]

A friend of Private Goss in General Hooker's division described his march pursuing the retreating soldiers in General Johnston's army. Their advance over the muddy road came to a halt late in the afternoon of May 4 due to troops stalled ahead of them. They resumed their march, in the rain, about five o'clock, continuing on until near midnight. Having spent the early morning hours of May 5 "bedraggled, wet, tired, and chewing hard tack," they were on the march again before daylight. By daybreak they came out on the edge of a dense wood in front of Fort Magruder and its cordon of redoubts stretching across the peninsula.

Not only the heavy rains but the geology of the peninsula contributed to the viscous quality of the mud. On top of heavy clay subsoil was a bed of equally waterproof shell marl. Above the marl the soil, never more than two feet deep, was light and sandy. The rains sank through the light soil to the marl and, able neither to penetrate it nor to find an outlet, turned the sandy soil into what Colonel Charles S. Wainwright described as having a consistency of soft mortar. An artillery horse, hitched to a gun and harnessed to a dead companion, sank into the mortar-like soil up to its chest and suffocated. When it was discovered, the horse's tail and rump were so deep into the mud as to be out of sight.[17]

While waiting for orders to attack, the men in the ranks had the opportunity to view what lay before them. Fort Magruder was a strong earthwork with bastioned front and a wide ditch. To Goss' friend in Hooker's division Fort Magruder was a "muddy-looking heap of dirt" before which was a level plain sprinkled with smaller earthworks. The forest between Hooker's men and the level plain had been cut down for about a quarter of a mile, and the felled trees formed a "labyrinth of tangled abatis difficult to penetrate. A mile away lay the village of Williamsburg."[18]

In Baldy Smith's division Hancock's brigade was leading, coming up with the cavalry about 5:30 the afternoon of May 4. So Smith's division were the first Union troops on the field; Hooker not arriving until daybreak on the 5th, according to Goss' statement above. General Sumner wished to press the pursuit as fast as possible. Despite the late hour Sumner advanced at once upon the enemy. Smith formed his division in three lines of battle, preparing for a charge through woods and on to the Confederate works. It was 6:30 before they moved, only to find the woods too thick to keep formations or even to get through in the failing daylight. The troops halted in the woods and spent the night there resting on their arms, Sumner among them. Hooker's men would form on their left at daybreak.

"On the following morning the battle of Williamsburg opened — a battle fought without plan, with inadequate numbers, and at a serious sacrifice without compensating result," wrote Alexander Webb. Sumner, Webb continued, seemed to have directed the movements of the day without method. A more recent historian, Robert P. Broadwater, characterized General Sumner as a good soldier more inclined to follow orders than to issue them. "Regrettably," Broadwater wrote, "he [Sumner] neglected to issue any specific orders concerning the assault to either Hooker or Smith."[19]

Hooker began the attack on Fort Magruder on May 5 based upon day-old orders he received from McClellan. Alexander Webb considered this a noteworthy feature of the battle since there were three corps commanders, Sumner, Heintzelman and Keyes, at the front. Hooker was an independent commander in Webb's opinion.

General Johnston left James Longstreet in command at Williamsburg on May 5. Longstreet placed his entire division in front of Hooker.[20] From seven o'clock until about noon on May 5 Hooker alone on the left had been doing all the fighting. Just before noon Hooker sent a note to his corps commander, Heintzelman, for reinforcements. Sumner had already sent word to Phil Kearny to hurry to Hooker's support.

Phil Kearny's biographer described Kearny's actions after receiving Sumner's orders: "In the meantime General Sumner, ... 'had acceded to General Hooker's urgent request for support'; and leaving undisturbed the 30,000 troops within a mile or two of the battlefield, under his personal command, ordered General Kearny, nine miles in the rear, to come forward over the 'impassable' terrain, through the blinding rain, to Hooker's support." Phil Kearny's biographer, Thomas Kearny, must have taken that number of 30,000 from General Hooker's report. Sumner did not have 30,000 troops standing idly by.[21]

Battery commander Captain Thomas W. Osborn in Heintzelman's Third Corps wrote to his older brother Spencer that General Sumner failed to come to Hooker's aid although he had his whole corps next to Hooker. But as Francis A. Walker wrote, not one Second Corps regiment fought at Williamsburg. Osborn also wrote that on the way to Williamsburg Sumner took a wrong road and collided with Heintzelman's corps.[22]

General John J. Peck marched his Second Brigade of General Darius Couch's First Division of General Erasmus D. Keyes' Fourth Corps up with General Silas Casey's Third Division of the Fourth Corps. Casey's men were halted at about 11:00 A.M. when Peck's brigade came upon them. At noon Peck got orders to move his brigade of five regiments to the support of General Hooker, who was fighting on the left. Presumably the orders came from General Keyes. Colonel de Trobriand, in command of the 55th New York, one of the regiments in General Peck's brigade, stated it was about 1:00 P.M. when he went into line. General Peck reported he could not locate General Hooker in spite of several fruitless attempts. Peck, after making a personal examination of the ground, put his brigade into line. Many conflicting reports regarding the enemy reached Peck before the enemy made an attack upon his line. The Confederates hit the 102nd Pennsylvania particularly hard, and Peck had to commit his last regiment, the 98th Pennsylvania, before the Confederates were repulsed.

In General Peck's report he stated, "My thanks are especially due Generals Sumner, Keys and Couch for the lively interest manifested by them, as shown by the liberal supports which they dispatched so soon as at command."[23]

Colonel Régis de Trobriand of the 55th New York Regiment reported that on the morning of May 5 General Philip Kearny's division was marching behind him and came into line. De Trobriand received orders from General Peck to pass by General Silas Casey's division, which had halted in a large open field.

According to de Trobriand's account, in the absence of McClellan generals Sumner and Keyes lost time consulting as to what was to be done. The mud-splattered Prince de Joinville was hurrying to Yorktown in order to bring the general-in-chief to the scene of battle. Sumner was senior in rank, second in command below McClellan, but Keyes alone had troops within reach. With the two generals in consultation nothing was done as far as de Trobriand could see. Meanwhile Hooker lost his position and some of his guns, later recaptured by General Peck's brigade.

As Colonel de Trobriand led that part of his regiment which was on the field "where that idle conference was going on," he met two more of his countrymen. The nephews of the Prince de Joinville, the Count of Paris and the Duke of Chartes, told de Trobriand that everything was going to the devil. "There is nobody here capable of commanding, and McClellan is at Yorktown. As several aids have not been able to induce him to come, my uncle [the Prince de Joinville] has gone himself to look for him, knowing well that without him nothing will be done as it should be," the Duke of Chartes said, according to de Trobriand. The colonel waited until his regiment assembled; many had difficulty keeping up because of the deep mud. By one o'clock his regiment went into action.[24]

In Colonel de Trobriand's opinion, not controlling both rivers made the Williamsburg line untenable for the Confederates, hence their withdrawal. While the ironclad CSS *Virginia* was still straining her boilers to propel her under-powered engines to cruise the James River, the York River was free of Confederate gun boats. In fact McClellan was at Yorktown with General William B. Franklin, planning to send Franklin up the York River to West Point, a community located just where the York River becomes wide and begins to form the peninsula. It was only Union general George Stoneman's cavalry attack that compelled the Confederates to halt and the Southern troops to return to delay the Union pursuit. In doing so they made particularly good use of Fort Magruder, situated at the point where the Yorktown and Warwick roads came together.

Peck's brigade was the first to come to the aid of General Hooker, de

Trobriand's 55th New York on the left of the brigade deployment. The French colonel, solidly in the service of his adopted country, was silent as to who had sent them to Hooker's aid. But from General Peck's report it is implied that the order came from General Keyes after Peck reported to Keyes' headquarters the heavy firing to his front. Hardly had General Peck's brigade deployed when the enemy's line started out of the woods and marched directly at Peck's defenses. Despite volleys fired by the 55th New York and the 102nd Pennsylvania on their right, the Confederates kept advancing.[25]

Some companies of the 55th on the left broke and ran, but de Trobriand's regiment held. The men who broke came back into the line. To his right, in front of the 93rd and 102nd Pennsylvania regiments, the enemy fell back in disorder after having received volleys delivered at a distance of only fifty feet! The engagement lasted about an hour. Kearny's division had arrived. The time then would have been about 2:00 P.M.

Out of ammunition, the 55th New York was replaced in the line by the 62nd New York. By Colonel de Trobriand's watch the last gun from Fort Magruder fired at 5:10 P.M. "A little later," he wrote, "the musketry fire ceased with the day, and the rain only continued to fall on the living and the dead." General Hooker in his report said the guns at Fort Magruder were silenced during the morning but began to fire again that afternoon.[26]

On the Right

General Winfield Scott Hancock, a future commander of the Second Corps, earned his nom de guerre, "Hancock the Superb," at the battle of Williamsburg. His fight in repelling four Confederate regiments under generals Daniel H. Hill and Jubal A. Early was, by Second Corps historian Francis A. Walker's account, "one of the prettiest fights on record." Hancock's action was the result of a plan adopted by the three corps commanders on the field to conduct a flank attack around the enemy's left.[27] Seeming not to know what Hooker proposed to do, they built their plan based upon a report of a local who told of unoccupied Confederate works on the Confederate left. Blacks, questioned by General Keyes and others, confirmed the report. Reconnaissance by engineers supported by four companies of the Fourth Vermont Regiment followed General Smith's orders and reported that a redoubt covering a stream called Cub Dam Creek that emptied into the York River appeared to be abandoned. General Sumner then directed General Hancock with his brigade and part of General Davidson's brigade, also of Smith's division, to take the redoubt. Hancock had the support of the six guns of Andrew Cowan's First New York Battery. In Webb's order of battle the First New York had six three-inch ordnance rifles, guns Hancock referred to at Gettysburg as "pop guns."[28]

Slogging through the rain with Lieutenant George Armstrong Custer, a young officer on General Smith's staff, Hancock moved off about a mile to the right on the Union line, coming in sight of the York River. Cub Dam Creek was on his left, the dam about seventy-five yards wide with a commanding redoubt across from Hancock and his men. Finding the redoubt unoccupied, Hancock saw another one about twelve hundred yards ahead. Reporting his findings to General Smith, Hancock learned he would be supported by four regiments and another battery of artillery. Moving on to the second redoubt, Hancock found it to be unoccupied as well.

Hancock moved still farther forward, deploying skirmishers 1,000 yards ahead of his main body. Two more redoubts were discovered, three hundred and four hundred yards forward, respectively, of Hancock's skirmishers. Hancock's artillery drove the defenders from these works. With things going his way Hancock was surprised to receive orders from General Smith to fall back to his first position at Cub Dam Creek. Hancock was not pleased. After a string of expletives Hancock sent an engineering officer to report the situation to General Sumner, that he, Hancock, held the key to Fort Magruder. To General Smith he wrote that he would wait a reasonable length of time to hear from General Sumner. Hancock was close to insubordination, but the situation required nothing less. At 5:10 P.M. Hancock was about to pull back having received neither reinforcements nor any change in Sumner's orders.[29] But then he saw enemy infantry advancing toward him. Francis Walker's "prettiest fight on record" was about to begin.

Confederate generals Daniel H. Hill and Jubal A. Early convinced General James Longstreet to permit their regiments to drive out Hancock's regiments on the Confederate left. Early commanded the 24th and 38th Virginia regiments; Hill commanded the 5th and 23rd North Carolina regiments. Coming out of thick woods wherein the regiments became disoriented, the Confederates had to wheel to their left to confront Hancock, a maneuver difficult to make on that muddy field. The Confederate "brigade," believing the Yankees to be retreating, continued to move forward. The retreat was a ruse.

General Hancock withdrew his troops behind the crest of a ridge. When the Confederates were within range the Union men fired two effective volleys and then charged the Confederates with the bayonet. The Confederates broke and fled, many having been bayoneted. Early received a bullet wound to his shoulder early in the fight. About six hundred men were casualties and the Fifth North Carolina was annihilated. Hancock lost one hundred twenty-six men. McClellan, in a letter to his wife, wrote, "Hancock was superb yesterday." Division commander Baldy Smith called the engagement brilliant.

McClellan inflated Hancock's success when he talked to the press to obscure what Alexander Webb and others saw as mishandled fighting around Fort Magruder. Other officers in the Army of the Potomac took exception to the excessive praise Hancock received. As David M. Jordon wrote in his biography of Hancock, "The battle was still just a badly managed collision with the rear guard of the retreating Confederates."[30]

General Longstreet had to be persuaded to authorize the attack on Hancock. At first Longstreet ordered the attack not to be made, explaining that they were only fighting for time to draw off their trains. But General Hill argued that he could make the attack and not delay the overall Confederate withdrawal. Longstreet quoted from a letter Hill wrote to him after the war: "The slaughter of the Fifth North Carolina Regiment was one of the most awful things I ever saw, and it was caused by a blunder."[31]

General Hancock received no support because General Sumner was concerned for the troops on his left, those of General Hooker and those supporting him, fighting before Fort Magruder. How concerned was debated among the officers involved. Initially Sumner agreed to reinforce Hancock when Sumner met with Hancock's messenger, Second Lieutenant Francis U. Farquhar at about 3:30 P.M. on May 5. Then, before the reinforcements were barely under way, Sumner countermanded the order. Because of his concern for his left, as Hancock stated in his report, Sumner would not send any troops to Hancock's support until more came up from the rear.[32]

In Sumner's report he claimed to have sent three regiments to reinforce Hancock. He reported too that he ordered General Phil Kearny with his division to support Hooker. "At 3 o'clock P.M.," Sumner wrote in his report, "the enemy made a furious attack upon my center, which was directly in front of their principal work and half a mile distant.... Several of our regiments expended all their ammunition, and I was obliged to interpose fresh regiments between them and the enemy."

On May 16, 1862, four days after the date of his report above, Sumner wrote an addendum to his report of May 12. Again Sumner stated his concern for his center. As soon as his concern for the center was over he sent reinforcements to Hancock, although too late.[33] Though critical of the performance of generals Sumner and Keyes, whose conversation he somehow knew was "idle," de Trobriand's critique of McClellan was scathing. "One need not be very much surprised, then, that, knowing nothing himself of what had happened, but in a hurry to give an account of the battle, he [McClellan] had sent a dispatch at ten o'clock in the evening, the errors of which bordered on the ridiculous," de Trobriand wrote. McClellan claimed to have Johnston — with a force much greater than McClellan's own and strongly entrenched — in front of him, when in fact the enemy was abandoning his position. "I will, at least, try to hold them in check here. The total of my force is, without any doubt, inferior to that of the rebels," de Trobriand quoted McClellan as saying. De Trobriand reported the size of McClellan's army was 112,392. The Confederates had not half that number, he wrote.[34]

De Trobriand also corrected McClellan's boast of Hancock's achievements. "Hancock's success was gained with a loss not exceeding twenty, killed and wounded," were McClellan's final words in his praise of Hancock's fight on the right of the Union line. "This was an error," de Trobriand recorded. "Hancock lost more, 126. But would it not appear from this report that Hancock was the only one who had been engaged? As to Hooker, he hardly mentioned him." McClellan mentioned neither Kearny nor Peck. Hooker fought for six hours and lost seventeen hundred men; Kearny lost about three hundred and de Trobriand's brigade about one hundred twenty-four.[35]

After the battle Colonel de Trobriand talked with a wounded Confederate captain in a makeshift hospital. "What we wanted at Yorktown," the captain said, "was simply to delay your arrival before Richmond until the summer heat. We have succeeded." Then he added, "You did not take Yorktown; we made you a present of it, when it was no longer of use to us."[36]

In his communications with Secretary of War Edwin M. Stanton on May 4 and 5, McClellan was boisterous in his accounts of his success against his enemy Joe Johnston. None of his subordinates received censure. Then on May 6 in a letter to his wife McClellan wrote that when he arrived from Yorktown to Williamsburg he found things in a bad state: "Sumner had proved that he was even a greater fool than I had supposed & had come within an ace of having us defeated.... I saw at once that I could save the day. I immediately reinforced Hancock, & arranged to support Hooker — advanced the whole line across the woods—filled up the gaps & got everything in hand for whatever might occur." The more McClellan wrote the more exuberant he became in his claim of victory: "We have given them a tremendous thrashing." Then McClellan paused to proclaim how much greater the victory would have been had he been on the scene just five hours earlier. His army would have captured 20,000 prisoners from the enemy McClellan believed greatly outnumbered his own; "but the utter stupidity & worthlessness of the Corps Comdrs came near making it a defeat. Heaven alone can help a General with such commanders under him."[37]

Army Politics

For Alexander Webb, Sumner fought the battle of May 5 without a plan, with inadequate numbers and at a serious sacrifice without result. Webb criticized Sumner, perhaps with justification, that when Hooker began his attack on May 5, Sumner, Heintzelman and Keyes had adopted another plan of action, a flank attack around the enemy's left. "There was no concerted action; hence failure," Webb wrote. "In a word, neither Sumner nor any one else had the entire field under his eye and control.... By the time General McClellan arrived on the field, about 5:00 o'clock, the divisions of Hooker, Kearny, Smith, Couch and Casey were well in hand."[38]

McClellan wrote his wife that Sumner was a greater fool than he had imagined and his corps commanders stupid and worthless. But when McClellan met Sumner on the field about 5:30 by Sumner's report, McClellan had nothing to say other than, "There seems to be nothing more doing here," and moved to the right.[39]

The adoption of the other plan that Webb mentioned was a result of reconnaissance made on the enemy's left that found their works unoccupied. When Sumner learned of Hooker's engagement about 11:00 o'clock he ordered General Kearny's division up to Hooker's support and sent Heintzelman to the left, where Hooker was fighting, to take command of the troops in that area. In Heintzelman's report he stated the enemy attacked Hooker at 9:00 A.M. Heintzelman was with Sumner and reported Sumner's reconnaissance, learning by 11:00 that an assault on the enemy's left was practicable. Sumner delayed the attack until provisions came for some of the men in Smith's division. At the same time Heintzelman left for Hooker's position around 11:00 A.M., not arriving until 1:30. It was 2:00 when reinforcements reached Hooker, according to Heintzelman.[40]

The enemy made a furious attack upon the center, and Sumner's report stated that he had not many troops to meet it. At 3:30 Hancock sent an aid to Sumner asking for support, but Sumner at this time was concerned for his center. Sumner sent several officers to the rear to hurry the troops forward — sometime after 3:00 P.M. The leading brigade of Couch's division, General Peck's, came up first.[41]

The time of day reported in the several accounts is confusing. Sumner said it was after 3:00 P.M. when Peck arrived. Yet Colonel de Trobriand, in Peck's brigade, wrote that his regiment went into action at 1:00 P.M. Also de Trobriand wrote that Peck's brigade was the first to come to the aid of General Hooker, possibly because his regiment was on the left of the line deployed by General Peck when his men went into battle. However, Sumner said he used Peck's brigade to reinforce his center.

In General Hooker's report of the battle, he made no entry stating that he asked for support. On the contrary he wrote, albeit indirectly, that his position was tenable for eight hours against three times his numbers.[42] By 9:00 A.M., the time Heintzelman reported the enemy attacked General Hooker, Hooker wrote in his report that every gun in Fort Magruder was silenced by Hooker's own artillery and that the enemy troops on the plain before the fort had been dispersed. At 11:20 Hooker stated he did not despair of success.[43]

About the time Heintzelman left Sumner at 11:00 to go to Hooker, General Hooker sent a note to Heintzelman that failed to reach him. It got to General Sumner instead. Sumner returned it with a message of his own written on the envelope, stating that Sumner had read the message. The envelope, according to Hooker, was destroyed by rain.[44]

Hooker's message to Heintzelman, which Sumner read, did not ask for support. It said, "Batteries, cavalry, and infantry can take post by the side of mine to whip the enemy." In other words, where Hooker was fighting was a good spot to place troops of all arms, a suggestion, nothing more. By this time Sumner and the other corps commanders had decided to concentrate on their right and center. At the conclusion of Hooker's report, which told what a good job Hooker was doing on the Union left and told of Heintzelman and his staff arriving early in the afternoon, he wrote that the men of his division "were permitted to carry on this unequal struggle from morning until night unaided in the presence of more than 30,000 of their comrades with arms in their hands; nevertheless it is true."[45]

Joseph Hooker believed that Sumner had 30,000 men sitting idly by while he and his men fought valiantly. He testified under oath before the Joint Congressional Committee on the Conduct of the War to that fact. It is doubtful that any officer testifying before the committee would tell anything but the truth as he knew it. The committee had a definite political agenda and a bias against military officers, especially those graduated from the military academy; still it was able to compile from that testimony an account of the conduct of the war that supplemented the reports of the officers themselves. Before that committee Hooker stated on March 11, 1863, "General Sumner was in command with a large force, certainly not less than 30,000 men.... If General Sumner had advanced the rebellion would have been buried there. He did not advance at all."[46]

The number 30,000 was used by others and was probably based upon Hooker's estimation of troop strength. But how did he come to believe that Sumner had that number of troops under him? In Sumner's sworn testimony before that same committee on February 18, 1863, a little more than a month before his death, he stated he had no more than 3,000 men, a tenth of what Hooker claimed. When asked by the chairman as to Sumner's response to Hooker's request for support, Sumner stated that he sent staff officers back to hurry forward the troops from the rear: "I did not deem it safe to send any more troops from the centre, and the result showed that it was fortunate that I had not done so." The chairman asked questions to confirm Sumner's testimony, emphasizing that Sumner had complied with the request for support and reinforcements by ordering up troops from the rear "instead of detaching them from your own corps." Sumner explained he had no troops of his own corps; his troops were ten miles in the rear. "I was in command there by virtue of my seniority of rank."

Committee member Moses Odell then asked the number of troops under Sumner's command at the center. Sumner answered that before General Peck arrived there were no more than a brigade and a half or about two thirds of General Baldy Smith's division. When asked by the chairman how many men that was, Sumner replied 3,000. All the rest of the forces under Sumner's control were in the rear coming up. "I had been placed by General McClellan in command of the army as it moved," Sumner testified, "and he had also given a similar order to General Heintzelman." Next he was asked to estimate the number of troops engaged at Williamsburg. "I suppose there were altogether, on the right, centre, and left not more than 10,000 or 12,000 men under fire," Sumner answered.[47]

In the report on the Peninsula Campaign, the committee stated that there seemed to have been great misapprehension in relation to the management of the troops at Williamsburg. "When the pursuit first commenced on Sunday [May 4, 1862], General Heintzelman was instructed by General McClellan to take charge of operations in front. On the morning of Monday orders were sent to General Sumner to take the command," the report found. It ascertained that the heavy rain that fell on Sunday had made the roads "almost impracticable for the passage of troops. The troops of different commands became mingled — divisions and brigades, to some extent, were separated from each other — and it seems to have been difficult to get the troops up in time."[48] So in light of the fact that both Heintzelman and Sumner had orders to take charge, perhaps the conversation between generals Sumner and Keyes was not so idle as Colonel de Trobriand believed.

The flaw in General Sumner's conduct of the fight on May 4 and 5, 1862, was that he was unsure as to whether he was fighting an offensive or a defensive battle. Late in the afternoon of May 4, based upon information from General Stoneman that the woods before Fort Magruder were passable to infantry, Sumner ordered Smith's division into them, preparatory to an attack the Confederate works. The woods, however, proved to be a tangle, nearly impenetrable to troops trying to keep a semblance of organization. The natural abatis of deadfalls on the forest floor coupled with the approaching darkness convinced Sumner to cancel his attack for that day. The soldiers camped in the woods, sleeping on their arms, with their venerable commander spending the night with them, his back propped against a tree.

The next morning Sumner learned the redoubts on the Confederate left might be abandoned; he investigated and sent Hancock to take them. But by the afternoon of May 5 Sumner was back on the defensive, worrying about a Confederate breakthrough on his center. He also was concerned about Hooker's position and sent Kearny's division to Hooker's support, not to take the offensive but to support the defense.

Certainly conditions on the field that day caused the balance between offense and defense to shift. Regiments ran out of ammunition, supply wagons were slow to reach the needy men, some regiments lacked provisions and artillery pieces with their limbers and caissons were frequently up to their axels in mud. Regiments such as Colonel de Trobriand's 55th New York were under-strength at first when they first arrived because of the mud-induced straggling. Although Hancock's troops repulsed the four regiments under Confederates Jubal Early and Daniel Hill, decimating the Fifth North Carolina Regiment, the two-day battle cost the Union a total of over 2,200 casualties.[49]

Politics were never more than just below the surface in the Army of the Potomac. One reason General Ulysses Grant kept General George G. Meade in command of the Eastern Army in 1864, against the advice of some of the western men Grant had brought with him, was Meade's long service with the army and his knowledge of its internals. Not only were the politics that of a group of officers, mostly Democrats, set against a Republican administration and a Radical Republican–dominated Committee on the Conduct of the War, but internal political rivalries smoldered among the officers themselves. Alexander Webb wrote of "an undercurrent of jealousy or unfriendliness" between Sumner and Heintzelman. Sumner amended his Williamsburg report on May 16, 1862, with a rider containing this line: "As to General Keyes' report, so far as it regards myself I consider it unworthy of notice. In reply to General Heintzelman's report and that of others, indirectly charging me with not hav-ing supported Hooker, I would refer to General Kearny's report, in which he states that he received an order from me before 11 o'clock A.M. on the 5th instant to advance with his division and support Hooker."[50]

Although he was not directly involved at Williamsburg, First Corps com-mander General Irvin McDowell was part of the Army of the Potomac. General John Gibbon described General Sumner's attitude and opinion of McDowell's promotion to major general. Sumner was loud in his condemnation of a pro-motion made in that manner. Gibbon was referring to Sumner's belief that McDowell received his promotion before he had done anything to deserve it. Political considerations earned McDowell his second star.[51]

McClellan had no patience with old men and felt saddled and inconve-nienced by the corps organization and the men selected by President Lincoln to command them. Lincoln's General War Order No. 2, issued on March 8, 1862, created five army corps. Major General Irvin McDowell's First Corps consisted of four divisions. Then Sumner's Second Corps, Heintzelman's Third and Keyes' Fourth Corps had three divisions each. The last three corps were commanded by brigadier generals. A fifth corps, not designated as such, was commanded by Major General Nathaniel P. Banks and composed of his division and that of General James Shields.[52]

Lincoln picked old men to command the corps because of their grade and experience with the army. Sumner was born in 1797, Heintzelman in 1805 and Keyes in 1810, all long before McClellan's birth on December 3, 1826. Closer to McClellan's age was Irvin McDowell, born in 1818, but he was still eight years McClellan's senior. Actually there were several other old men who would serve the Union during the Civil War. Commanding at Fort Monroe was John Wool, born in 1788. The chief of engineers, Joseph Totten, was also was born in 1788. The chief of ordnance, General James W. Ripley, first saw the light of day in 1794. Ethan Allen Hitchcock, an old soldier and during the war an advisor to the president, was born in 1798. General Joseph K.F. Mansfield, killed at Antietam, was born in 1803.

McClellan's impatience with old soldiers may have began in 1855, when Secretary of War Jefferson Davis picked McClellan to join majors Richard Delafield and Alfred Mordecai to visit Europe and the Crimea to study the latest developments in arms. Delafield was in the West Point class of 1818, Mordecai in the class of 1823, years before McClellan was born. He expressed his exasperation with his two teammates in a letter in which he wrote, "These damned old fogies!! I hope that I may never be tied to two corpses again — it is hell upon earth." On March 8, 1862, President Lincoln tied him to three.[53]

Commenting on Lincoln's selection of corps commanders, Second Corps historian Francis A. Walker wrote that McClellan should have been allowed to select his corps commanders. If McClellan was not fit to pick his subordinates he could hardly have been fit to command. Walker saw nothing but mischief coming from this decision of the White House.

Walker then went on to explain the weaknesses in the commanders. McDowell was under a cloud following his defeat at First Bull Run. Of Heintzelman and Keyes, Walker wrote, "The unanimity of the consent with which they were 'shelved,' after a short trial, affords a sufficient commentary upon their original selection." Walker agreed that there was merit to the argument that Edwin V. Sumner, advanced in years as he was, should not have been placed in command of twenty thousand new troops. They would face "a resolute and tenacious foe." But no one could dispute Sumner's soldierly qualities. "Jupiter, shining full, clear, and strong in the midnight heavens," Walker wrote, "might be the disembodied soul of Edwin V. Sumner."[54]

Following the battle at Williamsburg and during the march up the peninsula to the Chickahominy River, two new corps were added to the Army of the Potomac. This was General McClellan's attempt to parry President Lincoln's selecting his corps commanders. McClellan reduced the present corps to two divisions and created the Fifth Corps from George Sykes' division that contained the regulars and the division of Fitz John Porter. Porter, McClellan's confidant, was to command it. The Sixth Corps, commanded by William B. Franklin, was formed out of Franklin's division and William F. "Baldy" Smith's division from the Fourth Corps.

15

Fair Oaks and Seven Days

McClellan advanced his army corps up the peninsula following the battle at Williamsburg, establishing his headquarters and supply depot at White House by May 16, 1862. White House was located on the Pamunkey River and on the Richmond and York River Railroad line. The Pamunkey snaked its twisted course through the Virginia tidewater country to meet the Mattapony River at West Point. At this point they come together to form the York River. Bisecting the upper peninsula the Chickahominy river flows, sluggishly much of the time, in a southeasterly direction. Then about nine or ten miles due south of White House the Chickahominy turns south to empty into the James River, about five miles upstream from Jamestown Island. The Union army concentrated between the Pamunkey and the Chickahominy rivers.

About two and a half miles west on the Richmond and York River Railroad from where the line crosses the Chickahominy is Savage's, or Savage Station. Just south of this spot and running roughly parallel with the railroad west to Richmond is the Williamsburg road. Just shy of three miles west of Savage's Station at the intersection of the east/west Williamsburg road and the northwest-to-southeast-running Nine Mile road was Seven Pines. About one mile north of Seven Pines where the railroad ran across Nine Mile road was Fair Oaks Station or simply Fair Oaks. Around the triangle of land formed by these three points, about seven miles east of Richmond in 1862, the Confederate Army of Northern Virginia and the Federal Army of the Potomac clashed in a bloody, hard-fought battle. It was known to the South as Seven Pines; to the North as Fair Oaks.[1]

By May 25 the corps of the Army of the Potomac straddled the Chickahominy. The Fourth Corps took up a position at Seven Pines on the south side of the river and was joined by the Third Corps. The divisions of General Heintzelman's Third Corps moved more to the south; Hooker around White

Oak Swamp; Kearny camped near Savage's Station. On the north side or the left bank of the river the Second Corps and the two new corps, the Fifth and the Sixth, called Provisional Corps at this time, took up their positions. Nearby at Gaines' Mill, between Mechanicsville and New Cold Harbor, McClellan moved his headquarters there, transferring from White House.

Francis A. Walker believed it was the deployment of McClellan's corps that brought on the battle of Seven Pines or Fair Oaks. The corps were divided by the Chickahominy River, although it was little more than a creek when the corps took their positions on either bank. Confederate general Joseph Johnston's plan was to attack McClellan's left wing on the Williamsburg road when, by advancing, "it had sufficiently increased its distance from his, McClellan's, right — north of the Chickahominy."[2]

The Union Fourth Corps, General Erasmus D. Keyes in command, was west of Seven Pines, General Silas Casey's division of three brigades in advance with General Couch's three brigades deployed behind Casey. General Samuel Heintzelman's Third Corps was behind Keyes but not in supporting distance. Both corps were on the south side or right bank of the Chickahominy. "Until the communications across the Chickahominy had been made complete, rapid, and safe, it was the larger and not the smaller half which should have been exposed to the enemy's attack upon the Richmond side of the river," Walker wrote.[3]

General Oliver O. Howard explained McClellan's plans during the later part of May 1862. Situated as he was, between five and seven miles from Richmond, McClellan believed his supply depot at White House on the York River was too far in his rear. The railroad supply line running from White House to his army was too long and vulnerable. Believing he was to gain the support of General McDowell's 40,000-man First Corps, McClellan planned to change his base and be supplied by the James River. Therefore, according to Howard, McClellan and his officers were not pleased at having the army divided by even the narrow Chickahominy, little more than a creek at this time. To make amends they built a series of bridges. Near Bottom Bridge the 50th New York Volunteer Engineers built a bridge of the style of an Austrian Tressle [sic] bridge across the Chickahominy. A trestle bridge refers to the supports for the flooring or roadway and is fixed as opposed to a pontoon bridge or floating supports for the roadway.[4] The New Yorkers moved on to Gaines' Mill. Regular engineers built a bridge in the vicinity of Gaines' Mill and the 50th New York built a crib bridge, the work being very hard because the logs required had to be hauled a considerable distance. Still another bridge, known as the Woodbury Bridge for General Daniel Woodbury of the engineers, was built by the 50th New York under the supervision of Major Wesley Brainerd.

Meanwhile General Sumner had two bridges built for his corps, one for each division. About a mile and a half downstream from the one built by the

50th New York, the First Minnesota Regiment built a bridge for General Sedgwick's division. This was known as the Grapevine Bridge, so called because of the way it resembled a grapevine in its crooked windings across the Chickahominy. In service on May 30, the bridge was held in place by ropes tied to tree stumps on the upstream side.[5] Farther downstream the men of the Fifth New Hampshire Regiment of General Howard's brigade built a bridge for General Israel Richardson's division. It was built from large logs, according to General Howard.

General Sumner, wishing to hurry the bridge construction, gave the Fifth New Hampshire Regiment a barrel of whisky. Temperate General Howard objected. "Yes general, you are right," Sumner replied, "but it is like pitch on fire which gets speed out of an engine though it burns out the boiler," Howard recalled of the incident. He added, "The two structures were named Sumner's upper and Sumner's lower bridge. Our engineers farther up, when the south bank had been seized by us, repaired the old bridges and threw across others till the Chickahominy appeared but a slight obstruction."[6]

On May 30 the two Union corps on the south side of the river were the Fourth Corps of some 12,000 men and the Third Corps of some 20,000. General Silas Casey's division of the Fourth Corps was forward of Seven Pines about a mile and a half while General Couch's division deployed behind Casey. General Samuel Heintzelman's Third Corps was back at Savage's Station with General Philip Kearny's division while General Joseph Hooker's division was to the south at White Oak Swamp and not in easy supporting distance.

Confederate probes tested Casey's strength and position on May 29 and 30. Casey's redoubts and other defensive works were only partially completed. On the 30th, fighting in front of Casey's position became so heavy that at his request part of General Peck's brigade from Couch's division went out to support him. Peck had done the same at Williamsburg. Rain fell in a torrential downpour throughout the night and into the early morning of the 31st. Accounts of the severity of the storm appear in all battle reports. The volumes of water swelled the streams and rivers. The bridges built by the infantry in Sumner's Corps were in jeopardy of being flushed down the Chickahominy all the way to the James River. To Confederate general Joseph Johnston, while the rain hampered his movements somewhat and retarded the advance of his artillery, it proved to benefit his plans by isolating the Fourth Corps. Johnston had five divisions. McClellan could support his left wing—but slowly.

The Confederate attack began on May 31 between 12:30 and 1:00 P.M. (reports differ), General Daniel Hill, under General James Longstreet, making the attack. Hill had at one time taught school and used to test his students in arithmetic with problems dealing with unscrupulous Yankee peddlers who put sand in the sugar and sold wooden nutmegs. Such was Hill's opinion of his foe. Hill's men attacked along the Williamsburg road overlapping Casey's line. A Yankee bayonet countercharge caused the Confederates to recoil momentarily, but they soon drove the Federals back. Next it was Couch's division that became overwhelmed by Daniel Hill's troops.

Heintzelman, in command of all troops on his side of the Chickahominy, was near Savage's Station. He received no word of the condition of the Fourth Corps until it was too late to help Casey. Kearny's division did go forward and worked to stabilize the Union line.[7]

When General Longstreet made his fierce attack down the Williamsburg road he had four brigades under General D.H. Hill and two of his own. Among Casey's troops were some of the newest and least disciplined in the Federal army, and some quickly gave way. They were soon driven back onto the second line of General Darius Couch's division.

General Joseph Johnston was with his left wing, away from Longstreet's front, posted at the junction of the Nine Mile and the New Bridge roads. He was waiting for Longstreet's attack, the sound of the guns being the signal. For some reason the sound never reached Johnston. It was four o'clock before he got word of Longstreet's attack. Johnston then got started with five brigades commanded by his second in command, General Gustavus W. Smith. As this force advanced, Johnston joined it with two more brigades. They brushed aside two regiments General Couch personally brought forward as ordered by Fourth Corps commander General Keyes to hit the Confederates on their left flank. Johnston's movement cut Couch off from his corps and isolated him north of the railroad with only four regiments, General John J. Abercrombie's brigade and a four-gun battery under Captain James Brady.[8]

The Confederate brigades of generals J. Johnston Pettigrew, Robert H. Hatton and Wade Hampton, all under Confederate general G.W. Smith, were approaching Fair Oaks Station. Couch fell back along the Grapevine Bridge road, taking a position on a slight elevation from where he could see the station. Brady's battery began to fire on Pettigrew's brigade. Pettigrew attacked but could make no headway against Couch in his defensive position. General G.W. Smith then sent Hatton's and Hampton's brigades in to support Pettigrew.

Meanwhile five Confederate brigades came on the field to support Longstreet's men. Longstreet's forces, exhausted by several hours of fighting, could go no farther when they hit the assembled troops of Keyes' and Heintzelman's corps. But "Old Pete" Longstreet knew that heavy reinforcements were near at hand.

"As the fresh Confederate troops were coming on cheering and confident," General Howard wrote, "there came from their left front, toward the Chickahominy, a sudden check." Some Union guns opened fire upon them to a degree that Confederate general G.W. Smith could not ignore. He ordered the guns taken. Two of his brigades tried. Then other units that had advanced returned to join in the attack on the Union guns. The artillery fire grew worse. No such stubborn resistance should be coming from that direction, Smith thought. So destructive to the Confederate advance was this Union interruption that not only General Smith but General Johnston as well went to investigate. The source of the Confederate discomfiture was the fruit of action taken by General Edwin Vose Sumner in what may have been his finest hour.[9]

Sumner's corps was deployed along the Chickahominy and opposite the battlefield. That morning, May 31, McClellan ordered Sumner not to move without permission. Hearing the guns that opened the battle, Sumner telegraphed army headquarters for permission to cross on his two hastily built bridges. "He walked up and down like a caged lion. McClellan first telegraphed him to be ready. He was ready," Howard recorded. To save time whenever the order from McClellan came, Sumner sent Sedgwick's division to the upper or Grapevine Bridge and Richardson's division to the lower. Finally at 2:30 that afternoon the order came when the force of the water in the flooded Chickahominy made Sumner's bridges impassible, in the opinion of the engineers.[10]

The only order to be found in the *Official Records* is the one ordering Sumner to cross. Sumner wished to cross on the night of May 30. The order read:

> Headquarters Army of the Potomac
> May 31, 1862
>
> General E.V. Sumner:
>
> You will cross the Chickahominy River with your command and march to the support of General Heintzelman.
> Send out strong reconnaissance to the right towards New Bridge road and Old Town.
>
> R.B. Marcy, Chief of Staff

Brevet Lieutenant Colonel George A. Bruce of the Twentieth Massachusetts Volunteer Infantry, its historian, wrote that at one o'clock with the first sound of battle the Twentieth fell in with sixty rounds of ammunition. Bruce stated that Sumner, "this noble old soldier, marched his men to the bridges and his promptness saved at least an hour.[11]

Colonel W. Raymond Lee of the Twentieth Massachusetts Regiment reported, "On the afternoon of the 31st ultimo I received your orders [from General Dana] to get my regiment under arms for immediate movement in light marching order, with one day's rations and 60 rounds of ammunition per man."[12]

Perhaps Sumner remembered his experience from his Cheyenne campaign of 1857, and the way Percival Lowe crossed the quicksand bottomed South Platte River. At any rate when the weight of the troops and the horses pressed down upon the log roadway of the Grapevine Bridge it became more stable and better resisted the force of the flood waters. Beyond the bridge the rushing water was nearly up to the men's waists. "Our lower bridge was worse," Howard described. "As soon as French's brigade had crossed, the bridge began to break so much that [General] Richardson turned my brigade, followed by [General Thomas] Meagher's, to the upper one."[13]

As difficult as it was for the infantry to cross the Chickahominy on Sumner's risky upper bridge, it was more so for the artillery. Only Lieutenant Edmund Kirby of Battery I, First U.S. Artillery, was able to get his six Napoleons across on the upper bridge in time to take part in the fight. His guns went across following General Willis A. Gorman's brigade, the first brigade of Sedgwick's division to cross. It was about 3:30 P.M. when Lieutenant Kirby made his crossing. "The roads were almost impassable for artillery," he wrote in his official report, "and I experienced great difficulty in getting my guns along. I was obliged at times to unlimber and use the prolonge, the cannoneers being up to their waists in water."[14]

The remaining batteries of Sedgwick's division followed the third brigade, that of General Napoleon J.T. Dana. Coming across the open field leading to the bridge after Kirby had gone before and cut up the roadway, the remaining batteries had to corduroy a large portion of it. In spite of the artillery horses sinking to their girths and the guns and caissons sunk in over their axle-trees, they got on the bridge, with few exceptions, without unharnessing the artillery horses. Still Captain Charles H. Tompkins' battery did not arrive on the battlefield until the close of the engagement, and Captain Walter O. Bartlett managed to get but one of his guns on the field at the close of the action. Part of the bridge over a ditch broke through, making it necessary to unhitch the horses and bring part of Bartlett's battery and all of Captain Charles D. Owen's battery across by hand. One hundred men of the Forty-second New York Regiment of General Dana's brigade helped in this unpleasant, fatiguing endeavor.[15]

Sumner's own report was brief and modest. Once across the swollen Chickahominy on a bridge of questionable stability, Sumner arrived on the field to find General Couch with four regiments plus two companies of infantry and Captain James Brady's Battery H, First Pennsylvania Light Artillery. Colonel Alfred Sully, son of the portrait painter Thomas Sully, with his First Minnesota Regiment of General Willis A. Gorman's brigade, was the first of Sedgwick's regiments to come onto the field. Sully went to the right to protect that flank along with Edmund Kirby's battery of six Napoleons. Sedgwick's troops were formed into a line of battle as soon as they crossed the Chickahominy and came onto the field. Sumner sent one of Couch's regiment to open communications with General Kearny's division on the left, and the remainder of Couch's troops formed on the left of Sully's regiment.

"These arrangements were hardly completed when the enemy advanced upon us in great force and opened fire," Sumner reported. "Our men received it with remarkable coolness and returned it rapidly, Kirby's battery playing with extraordinary rapidity and accuracy." After firing for some time Sumner ordered five regiments, three from General Gorman's brigade and two from General Dana's, the last of Sedgwick's brigades to arrive, to move forward to the front and charge with the bayonet. Although two fence rows intervened and had to be pulled down or jumped over, the Federals attacked and the Confederate troops broke and fled. This action ended the fighting on that part of the line for the day.

The next day, June 1, 1862, the battle resumed at 6:30 A.M. The brunt now fell on General Israel B. Richardson's division of the Second Corps. It had been placed the night before parallel to the railroad. "This was a most obstinate contest, continuing for four hours, in which our troops showed the greatest gallantry and determination, and drove the enemy from the field," Sumner wrote.[16]

In concluding his report he mentioned his staff, among whom were his son, Lieutenant S.S. Sumner, and Lieutenant A.H. Cushing. Lieutenant Cushing was killed at Gettysburg fighting his guns of Battery A, Fourth U.S. Artillery, at the height of Pickett's Charge.

There was more emotion in General Darius Couch's battle report. Couch and four regiments plus Captain James Brady's battery were cut off from the rest of the Fourth Corps by the advance of the enemy. Before General Sumner and Sedgwick's division came to Couch's support he had been trying to make contact with the bulk of his corps. "After making demonstrations to cut through and rejoin the main body it was abandoned as suicidal," Couch reported. Mistaking Confederate troops for those of the Union, Couch allowed men of the Confederate Hampton Legion to get close to Brady's guns before the mistake was discovered. Brady, firing canister, forced the Confederates to lie down or seek shelter behind trees.

Learning that General Sumner was at hand, Couch sent word to generals Keyes and Heintzelman that he would hold until Sumner's troops arrived. "This noble soldier came on rapidly with Sedgwick's division, and when the head of his column was seen a half mile distant I felt that God was with us and victory ours," Couch confided in his report.[17]

At 4:30 P.M. when General Couch saw Sumner's troops coming up with reinforcements, he put the 65th New York and the 82nd Pennsylvania regiments close in front of the woods on the right of the road to Fair Oaks Station and the 62nd New York and the Seventh Massachusetts Regiments in the open field on the left of the road in support of the guns. Colonel Sully's First Minnesota Regiment, the first of Sumner's troops to arrive, was sent to the right to extend the line.

Colonel David H. Williams of the 82nd Pennsylvania Regiment reported that his men were well positioned behind a low rail fence and were next to the 65th New York. The enemy was met with a withering fire. The Confederates charged repeatedly and got to within twenty yards of Colonel Williams' lines, but as he wrote, "no valor or impetuosity could withstand the steady and well-directed fire of our men." This conflict lasted for about two hours.[18]

General Couch stated that Sumner assumed command upon coming on the field and distributed the regiments as Sumner reported. Couch had praise for the work done by the artillery, that of Lieutenant Kirby and of his own artillery under Captain James Brady and Lieutenant Andrew Fagan, who commanded a section of Brady's battery. Couch went on in his report to state, "At 2:30 A.M. General Sumner called around him his generals and gave them their orders. At daylight the extended woods were to be cleared of rebels by a sweeping charge."[19]

The artillerists' reports provide us with a vivid description of the fury of the artillery defense. Captain Brady reported on the manner in which Lieutenant Andrew Fagan fought his two-gun section: "This section, after exhausting canister played upon the enemy's lines with spherical case and shell without fuse, bursting the shell as it left the gun, as determined by the yellow sulphurous smoke, sweeping its broken fragments before it, eliciting the remark from the enemy that nothing could stand up before such 'rotten shot.'" Brady too, in support of Colonel Alfred Sully's First Minnesota Regiment on the right of the line, reported his gunners shot spherical case without fuse, "exploding in the enemy's lines and crushing his flank, causing them to retire."[20]

Spherical case shot was one of several kinds of artillery projectiles used by Civil War artillery units and was anti-personnel. The case was a hollow cast-iron shot forming a hollow sphere that was filled with balls. Melted sulphur or resin was poured in to fill up the space between the balls and keep them in place. The walls of spherical case shot were thinner than those of shells. The balls inside weighed seventeen to the pound, or just under an ounce for each one. Artillerist Tully McCrea wrote of a friend killed by such a shell at Fredericksburg: "Lieutenant Dickenson of the Fourth Artillery, with whom I was well acquainted was killed by a bullet from a spherical case shot, which went into his brain."[21]

Couch's other battery commanders wrote of the severity of the cannonade in their reports. Captain Jeremiah McCarthy, Battery C, First Pennsylvania Light Artillery, wrote, "My men by this time [about 5:15 to 5:30 P.M.] were greatly fatigued, nearly all hands working in their shirt sleeves ... the guns being so hot that they burned the thumb-stalls while on the men's thumbs. Several cartridges were also singed whilst they were being put in the pieces."[22]

The thumb-stall Captain McCarthy wrote about was a protective leather covering for the thumb of the number-three man of the artillery crew. One of his jobs was to cover the vent or touch hole with his thumb while the bore of the gun was being swabbed after firing. Covering the vent prevented air from entering the gun barrel. The swab would act like a bellows, expelling air from the tube through the vent as the swab was pushed from the muzzle to the breach and sucking air back in as the swab was withdrawn. Should there be a smoldering bit of cartridge bag in the breach from the last shot and the vent be uncovered, air would be sucked into the tube and ignite the bit of rag. That flame would prematurely set off the next cartridge rammed into the gun. The cartridge was a flannel bag of powder attached to the projectile by a wooden plug called the sabot. The very hot cannon barrel could scorch the flannel bag. That was how the cartridge could be singed as Captain McCarthy stated.

Captain Theodore Miller, Battery E, First Pennsylvania Light Artillery, and one of Couch's artillery commanders had this to report. He began firing about 2:00 o'clock,

> using spherical case-shot, the distance about 900 yards, elevating the piece 2½°.... I ordered my left section to load with canister, which was barely done when a large body of rebel infantry came pressing out of the woods. The canister was poured into them at about 350 yards from my battery, and when the smoke cleared away I perceived that besides the canister doing its usual work not a single rebel could be seen in that direction.... I was joined ... by [Captain Edward H.] Flood's and [Captain Jeremiah] McCarthy's batteries, and our united fire continued for upwards of one hour; the distance at 750 yards ... using spherical case-shot and shell. During the last part of the fight I was compelled to use solid shot.

Captain Miller retired from the field around 6:00 P.M. He reported that his wheels and axle-trees were shot up by musket balls.[23]

General Couch, who wrote his report on June 7, 1862, may have incorrectly remembered the time of day that General Sumner ordered the charge of the five regiments to clear the woods. Couch reported it took place at daylight on June 1.[24] Sumner wrote that he ordered the attack at the close of fighting on May 31. Second Corps historian Francis A. Walker's account of the fight supports Sumner's statement of the time. To clear the woods on the far side of the road between Sumner's upper bridge and Fair Oaks station, Walker stated that Sumner ordered up the 34th and 82nd New York regiments, the Fifteenth Massachusetts Regiment from General Gorman's brigade, and the Seventh Michigan Regiment and Twentieth Massachusetts Regiment from General Dana's brigade. They charged as soon as the line was formed. "Two fences intervened between them and the foe; but these were hastily torn down or pushed over," Walker recorded. "Our men at first advanced firing; but they gathered inspiration as they went, and when within fifty yards of the position where the foe still sullenly held the ground, outside the woods, they spontaneously broke into a cheer; a sharp clatter along the line told that bayonets were fixed, and the five regiments, in one long line, sprang forward. It was enough."[25] Prior to this attack large Confederate brigades massed in these woods. For an hour and a half they withstood the left oblique fire from the First Minnesota Regiment, direct fire from the 82nd and the 65th New York regiments and right oblique artillery fire. In killed and wounded the Confederates took 1,174 casualties including three generals. General Robert Hopkins Hatton was killed, General J. Johnson Pettigrew was wounded and captured and General Wade Hampton was wounded but remained in the fight.[26]

The Twentieth Massachusetts Regiment, part of General Dana's brigade, came in sight of the field at 5:45 P.M. and hurried to the left of the line.[27] The Twentieth Massachusetts' historian wrote,

> After a few minutes of heavy firing, the rebels attempted to capture the guns by assault. Some of them got within fifteen yards of the guns, but could not stand the fire. As they fell back, General Sumner gave the order for the whole line to charge, and it moved forward on double-quick with fixed bayonets, tore down the fences on both sides of the road, and charged into the woods. Our part of the line had to charge over a soft and muddy plowed field into which the men actually sank up to their knees at every step. The enemy fled.[28]

Colonel James A. Suiter of the 34th New York Infantry Regiment described the bayonet charge. His regiment received orders about 7:45 P.M. to charge the enemy positioned in the woods with the bayonet. He preceded the charge by "pouring into them a withering fire." Still the Confederates held their ground until the men of the 34th New York mounted the fence on the skirt of the woods, when they broke and ran "in great confusion."

Lieutenant Colonel Henry W. Hudson of the 82nd New York Regiment made this brief comment on the bayonet charge in his official report: "In company with the Thirty-fourth New York Volunteers and the Fifteenth Massachusetts we pressed forward, firing as we advanced and finally drove him from the field at the point of the bayonet, and darkness closing about us, we rested on our arms."[29]

Colonel Lee wrote in his report, "I am happy to record that the men of my regiment cheerfully gave up their blankets and rations to these wounded unfortunates who had thus come under our care."[30]

From Silver Spring, Maryland, the politically astute daughter of Andrew Jackson's old crony Frank Blair, Elizabeth Blair Lee, wrote to her sailor husband Samuel Phillips Lee of the Federal navy on June 9, 1862, telling him of recent events: "The fight of the Oaks this day a week ago was very like the Pittsburg Landing Affair Casey a fussy political general got posted in advance — with troops which he had never drilled & got routed — Couches brigade saved us until Heintzelman & Sumner came to the rescue."[31]

The Seven Days

Among the Confederate wounded in the battle of Seven Pines was the commanding general, Joseph E. Johnston. On May 31 at Fair Oaks about sundown Johnston received a bullet wound in his shoulder and then was hit in the chest by a shell fragment. These two wounds took him out of the fight.[32] His wounds were responsible for the emergence of General Robert E. Lee and began Lee's remarkable association with and leadership of the Army of Northern Virginia. Although it came at a high price in casualties, the victory from a series of battles known as the Seven Days that Lee initiated between June 25 and July 1, 1862, pushed Union general George B. McClellan and his Army of the Potomac off the peninsula, thus saving Richmond until the end of the war.

June 1862 began with a lessening of the fighting but with the continuation of heavy rainfall. The bridges now were washed away and were not rebuilt until the rain ended about June 8. Until they were replaced the men were on short rations. The Twentieth Massachusetts Regiment, for example, had to wait until June 11 before they had a chance to change into clean uniforms. To correct scurvy that was beginning to break out, the men received some lemons and potatoes, both raw and mashed, in vinegar.[33]

As early as June 5 General Robert E. Lee had determined what he believed was McClellan's plan and how to deal with it. Writing to President Jefferson Davis on that date, Lee stated that McClellan would make this a battle of posts, taking position from position under cover of his heavy guns. Lee estimated it would take 100,000 men to resist a siege on Richmond. "I am preparing a line that I can hold with part of our forces in front, while with the rest I will endeavor to make a diversion to bring McClellan out," he wrote. Lee believed McClellan was obliged to stick to the railroad to provision his army unless he could change his base to the James River. Lee wrote to Confederate chief of ordnance Colonel Josiah Gorgas to have an iron-plated battery mounted on a railroad car to travel on the York River Railroad "to sweep the country in our front. The enemy cannot move his heavy guns except on the railroad."[34]

Stonewall Jackson's spectacular movements in the Shenandoah Valley prevented the Lincoln administration from sending General McDowell's corps to support McClellan. McClellan did receive General George McCall's division that had been assigned to General Fitz John Porter's Fifth Corps. McCall's division was made up of the thirteen regiments of the Pennsylvania Reserves, regiments Thirty through Forty-two of the Pennsylvania Volunteers, also known as the First through the Thirteenth Reserves. The Reserves came by their undistinguished title as a result of their being formed and then ordered by Washington to be disbanded as they could not be readily absorbed into the

Union forces. There was not enough equipment to arm them. Pennsylvania governor Andrew Curtin did not disband the regiments, realizing their possible need considering the long border his state shared with questionable Maryland. The term "Reserve Volunteer Corps of the Commonwealth" was given to the units by the state legislature.[35] Drawn from all parts of the state, no finer group of soldiers was to be found on either side. One brigade commander was General John F. Reynolds, who was killed at Gettysburg on July 1, 1863, while in command of the Union First Corps. He would be captured along with General George McCall at Glendale on the peninsula. A second brigade had as its commander General George G. Meade, commander of the Army of the Potomac at Gettysburg, who would retain that position throughout the war. He was to receive two wounds at Glendale. The third brigade commander was General Truman Seymour. Somewhat resented by his men for not being a Pennsylvanian, Seymour was competent, had an ordnance background and was at Fort Sumter with Major Robert Anderson when it was fired upon and surrendered.

The Seven Days series of battles began on June 25, 1862, with the battle of Oak Grove. This was followed on June 26 with the battle of Beaver Dam Creek. June 27 witnessed the battle of Gaines' Mill. As McClellan withdrew towards the James River he fought at Golding's Farm and Savage's Station on June 28 and 29. On June 30 Lee tried to split the Army of the Potomac at Glendale while General William B. Franklin's Sixth Corps held Stonewall Jackson at White Oak Swamp. The last battle, fought on July 1, 1862, was at Malvern Hill.[36]

After the battle of Fair Oaks the Union line stretched from Bottom's Bridge on the left to Mechanicsville on the right. General Silas Casey's division was turned over to General Peck, who protected Bottom's Bridge as well as the numerous crossings at White Oak swamp. General Samuel Heintzelman's Third Corps was in advance of Seven Pines, supported by Couch's division. The Second Corps rested on Fair Oaks and connected on its left with the Third Corps. General Franklin's Sixth Corps, now on the Richmond side of the Chickahominy River, extended the line from the right of General Sumner's Second Corps to the Chickahominy River at a place called Golding's. General Porter was alone with his Fifth Corps on the north bank of the river and extended so that his right was at Mechanicsville. The distance between Mechanicsville and Bottom's Bridge was about twelve to fifteen miles as the crow flies.[37]

General Sumner wrote no reports of his corps' involvement in the Seven Days series of battles until June 29. (The reports were dated July 4, 1862.) However, he did send the brigades of generals French and Meagher to the aid of the Fifth Corps late in the day of June 27 at the battle of Gaines' Mill. They came too late to be of service. Of this offering of support Alexander S. Webb wrote, "Sumner sent French and Meagher, but, in announcing the fact, adds, 'Everything is so uncertain, that I think it would be hazardous to do it.'" Webb provides no documentation for the source of this remark and it certainly is not in Sumner's reports.[38]

Writing to his brother Abraham from Arlington Heights, Virginia, on September 5, 1862, Captain Thomas W. Osborn, commanding Battery D, First New York Light Artillery, described the battle of Savage Station fought on June 29. General William F. "Baldy" Smith, commanding the Second Division of General William B. Franklin's Sixth Corps, requested two batteries from General Heintzelman; they were to report to Smith at Savage Station. When Osborn arrived and reported to Smith, Smith had no orders for him and told Osborn to report back to General Heintzelman. "For a Division Commander to borrow two batteries to aid him in a fight," Osborn wrote, "and then moving off without giving them orders is as good an example of first class stupidity as one can often see."

On his way back to join Heintzelman's Third Corps, Osborn got mixed in with General Sumner's Second Corps. Here Osborn observed the railway gun Lee asked Ordnance Chief Gorgas to construct — "The Railroad Merrimac," Osborn called it. According to Osborn it was of no account whatever. Osborn noted that when he first encountered Sumner the old general was excited and spoke in a loud voice, but he wrote that the grand tactics displayed by General Sumner in fighting this battle were very fine. Learning that Heintzelman was not between Sumner and the enemy as Sumner believed was the cause of his excitement. Once Sumner calmed down he conducted the battle with remarkable coolness, in Osborn's opinion. When Sumner's skirmish line made contact with that of the enemy, Sumner ordered forward a full line of battle. "This first full line had a very serious collision with the enemy's line in position," Osborn explained to his brother, "but of course, broke it. The General knew this would be the result, and another full line was half across the field when the first line gave way." Osborn continued:

> The first line permitted the second to pass through it, and when it came into collision with the enemy the same result followed. A third line of battle was again half across the field and this same passing by the third, of the second line. This third line dislodged the enemy from their position and had them on the move. But before the third line had reached the enemy, General [Thomas F.] Meagher's brigade (Irish) was well on its way towards the enemy's line. As soon as the enemy began to give way, General Sumner ordered General Meagher to give them the bayonet and drive them from the field. This order was carried out literally, and the enemy were driven off the field.[39]

Sumner stated that on the morning of June 29 he left his works at Fair Oaks at daylight and went to the principal depot at Orchard Station. There all government property was destroyed by order of the commanding general.

Orchard Station was on the railroad line about a half mile east of Fair Oaks Station. It served as a supply depot out of range of Confederate artillery.

Private Warren Lee Goss described the destruction and the subsequent march to Allen's Farm: "Details were made to destroy such stores as could not easily be removed in wagons, and some of our officers, high in rank, set an unselfish example by destroying their personal baggage." He went on to relate that tents were slashed with knives, canteens were punctured with bayonets, and clothing was cut to shreds. Sugar was dumped on the ground and whiskey barrels were overturned. "Some of our men stealthily imitated mother earth as regards the whiskey," Goss declared. He went on to say how hot the day became and that the dust rose in clouds to nearly suffocate the marching men. They arrived near a spot named Allen's farm around 9:00 A.M. and formed a line of battle: "The enemy had opened from the woods south of the railroad, with great vigor and precision. This attack was, after some sharp fighting, repelled, and slinging our knapsacks, the march was resumed over the dusty roads. It was scorching hot when we arrived at Savage's Station, and there again we formed line of battle."[40]

Captain Osborn described the destruction of army supplies in the same long letter to his brother dated September 5. The destruction was in progress when Osborn first reported to General Smith. "Great piles of ammunition and of quartermasters and commissary stores were burning," Osborn wrote. "The explosion of loaded shells and small ammunition sounded like a heavy battle. Long lines of freight cars were on fire. A train loaded with blank cartridges was run a little way east of us and set on fire. The smoke from the explosion of this powder was wonderfully beautiful."[41]

From Orchard Station the Second Corps marched to Allen's farm, where they engaged the enemy at 9:00 A.M. Allen's farm was a short distance southwest of Savage's Station and just below the Williamsburg Road. The action was described as sharp and continued until 11:00 A.M. The batteries of Kirby, Pettit and Hazzard did the bulk of the fighting there.[42]

At noon that day Sumner learned that a large force was advancing on him. Sumner concentrated his corps along with the Third and Sixth corps at Savage's Station. The battle began around 4:00 P.M. The enemy shelled Sumner "with remarkable precision from the railroad." At this battle General Heintzelman seems to have been delinquent. His action here was one of a number of actions that were argued for years after the war ended by advocates on either side of the feud. However, they will not be fought in any detail in these pages. Of Heintzelman's suspected defection Sumner wrote,

> When the enemy appeared on the Williamsburg road I could not imagine why General Heintzelman did not attack him, and not till some time afterward did I learn, to my utter amazement, that General Heintzelman had left the field and retreated with his whole corps (about 15,000 men) before the action commenced.

This defection might have been attended with the most disastrous consequences, and although we beat the enemy signally and drove him from the field, we should certainly have given him a more crushing blow if General Heintzelman had been there with his corps.[43]

After the battle Sumner received orders from McClellan to fall back and cross the White Oak Swamp, which he did.

On the morning of June 30, 1862, Sumner received orders to advance his command to Glendale and halt until he received further orders. Glendale was a wide open area south of White Oak Swamp. At noon General Franklin requested reinforcements, as he was preventing Stonewall Jackson's troops from passing through the swamp primarily at White Oak Bridge. Sumner sent two brigades, retaining one brigade and two batteries. At 3:00 P.M. the enemy made a determined assault on General George McCall's division, located some distance from Sumner's right and front. Sumner reported that many of McCall's division came flying into his lines, closely followed by the enemy. Here began another famous feud, did McCall's men break or did they hold and fight determinedly? Sumner reported that he got back his two brigades just as the fugitives from McCall's division were streaming through his lines: "The battle of Glendale was the most severe action since the battle of Fair Oaks, and it gives me great pleasure to state that the troops engaged in it, with the exception of McCall's division, behaved most nobly." Those who fought at Gaines' Mill, including the men in McCall's division that Sumner chose to disparage, a division that suffered 1,603 casualties, would hardly concur. Nearly one-fifth of the casualties suffered by the Army of the Potomac during the Seven Days fell to the Pennsylvania Reserves. What made General Sumner an accurate judge of the performance of General McCall's division? It was located some distance from him by his own account. Sumner may have been influenced by General Hooker's report. Hooker observed some of McCall's men ushering prisoners to the rear and believed McCall's men were retreating.[44]

Perhaps the best judge of McCall's division and its performance at Glendale was that of the enemy, General James Longstreet. That evening after the battle Longstreet spoke to a captured Union surgeon who elected to remain with the Union wounded. "If McCall's division had not offered the stubborn resistance it did," General Longstreet told the surgeon, "we would have captured your whole army."[45] At 9:00 P.M. that evening, upon intelligence that General Franklin had retreated and that General Heintzelman was about to do so, Sumner did likewise, but not before he received orders to withdraw. Sumner reached the lines near the James River at daylight.

On the morning of July 1 Sumner got orders to put his corps near the center on Malvern Hill. The action took place on the left of the line, but two of Sumner's brigades (those of generals Meagher and Caldwell) and Sumner's artillery were engaged. Sumner's report was short. "As the commanding general came onto the field during this battle I ceased to be in command, and therefore do not make a detailed report of the action," Sumner reported.[46]

Confederate General D.H. Hill's artillery fire, although directed entirely at the Union batteries, had its effect upon the infantry. Because of it Sumner withdrew his whole corps and took refuge under the crest of the hills nearest the river. Sumner ordered Fitz John Porter to withdraw as well, but Porter protested. Sumner's withdrawal was seen by the enemy as a retreat, and they launched an infantry attack. Porter wrote, "At about 5:30 o'clock, the enemy opened upon both [General George W.] Morell and [General Darius N.] Couch with artillery from nearly the whole of his front, and soon after pressed forward in columns of infantry, first on one, then on the other, or on both." Porter continued to say that brigade after Confederate brigade charged the Union batteries, but all were mowed down by canister and shrapnel. The Union infantry withheld their fire until the Confederates were in close range. Many Confederate infantrymen were captured after being scattered by the Union infantry volleys. Fitz John Porter, according to E. Porter Alexander, "was, perhaps, the hardest opponent to fight in the Federal army."[47]

Although McClellan may have called General Sumner a greater fool than he had imagined in his letter to his wife, he nevertheless promoted Sumner to brevet major general in the regular army and major general of volunteers on July 5, 1862.[48]

Second Bull Run

General Sumner's Second Corps played only a minor part when the Federal government pinned its hopes on General John Pope. His bluster made him the butt of many jokes, some concerning that very part of his anatomy, when he declared that his headquarters would be in the saddle. General Samuel D. Sturgis, an old campaigner with General Sumner, remarked he didn't care for John Pope "one pinch of owl dung."[49]

Not quite so colorful as Strugis' remark but every bit as concise is Frank J. Welcher's summary of the Second Corps' activities during the Second Bull Run period. The Second Corps remained at Harrison's Landing on the James River until the latter part of August. It went to Alexandria, Virginia, and then on to Centerville, Virginia, on August 30, 1862, too late to take part in the battle of Second Bull Run. It was located near Chantilly but again was not engaged in the fighting there on September 1, fighting that claimed the life of General Philip Kearny. The Second Corps, still under the command of General Sumner, covered the retreat. When the corps reached Washington it took position on the Virginia side of the Potomac River. On September 5 Sumner's corps and the Second Corps of General Pope's Army of Virginia (which later became the Twelfth Corps of the Army of the Potomac) formed the center of the Army of the Potomac, now under the command of the restored General George B. McClellan.[50]

Concerning the death of Phil Kearny, on October 4, 1862, General Robert E. Lee wrote to General George B. McClellan. Lee sent Phil Kearny's horse and sword to McClellan to be forwarded to Kearny's widow. She had written to Lee asking for their return if possible. These items fell into Confederate hands when Kearny was killed at Chantilly on September 1, 1862.[51]

On the same day Lee wrote the above letter to McClellan and sent Kearny's sword and horse to him, he wrote a letter to Confederate secretary of war George W. Randolph, essentially asking permission to do so. The horse and sword, Lee told Randolph, had been turned over to the quartermaster and chief of ordnance respectively. "I would send them at once," Lee wrote, "as an evidence of the sympathy felt for her bereavement and as a testimony of the appreciation of a gallant soldier, but I have looked upon such articles as public property, and that I had no right to dispose of them except for the benefit of the service." Lee ended his letter by saying the decision was Randolph's and requesting an early reply.

Two days later on October 6, Lee wrote again to Randolph telling him that because of troop movements Lee had taken it upon himself to send Kearny's items into the Union lines. Lee stated he had had the items appraised and sent the value to the quartermaster. Where the money came from he did not stipulate. Lee described Kearny's sword and leather scabbard as a light one suitable for a disabled person. (Kearny had lost an arm in Mexico.) Lee wrote that he considered the sword private property "and as such proper to be returned to his family, in accordance with approved usage under such circumstances." Then Lee added, probably knowing full well that Randolph could not possible object, "Its [the sword's] value will also be paid to the ordnance department should you not approve of its return."[52]

16

Antietam

The bloody battle of Antietam, which "turned the landscape red," climaxed the 1862 Maryland Campaign, a campaign General Robert E. Lee initiated in early September. Lee outlined his reasons for invading Maryland in a letter to Confederate president Jefferson Davis dated September 3. "The present seems to be the most propitious time since the commencement of the war," Lee opined to Davis, "for the Confederate army to enter Maryland." Lee pointed out that the two armies he had defeated at Second Manassas were now united but were much weakened by the recent battles. Although they were to be supplemented by some 60,000 new troops, they would be unorganized, and it would take time for these new troops to be trained and prepared for the field. Lee represented his own army to President Davis as being "feeble in transportation," lacking in animals and the men poorly provided with clothing, especially shoes; "Still," Lee emphasized, "we cannot afford to be idle." If Lee's army was not capable of destroying the enemy's army it was able to harass it.

Lee confided in Davis that his greatest fear was running out of ammunition. He asked Davis to lean on the ordnance department, so to speak, to ensure Lee had a sufficient amount of the best kind of ammunition. Specifically, Lee asked for three times as much long-range artillery ammunition as for his smooth-bore, short-range guns. What General Lee may have meant by "long range artillery ammunition" was ammunition for his rifled field pieces. Jennings C. Wise wrote that interest in rifled artillery grew among Confederate artillery officers during the early months of the war. Wise's statistics on Confederate field pieces at the battle of Antietam lists 47 3-inch rifles, 41 ten-pounder Parrotts and four 20-pounder Parrotts.[1]

Antietam was the last battlefield on which Major General Edwin V. Sumner actively commanded troops. On September 14 Union forces pushed Confederate soldiers defending three gaps in South Mountain off their high-ground perch and onto the farm land around the town of Sharpsburg, Maryland, with the Potomac River at their backs.

On the night of September 15 General Sumner sent out a party to cross the Antietam Creek to learn if the Confederates had abandoned their position. Lieutenant Colonel Nelson A. Miles of General Israel B. Richardson's division led the reconnaissance. Nelson A. Miles should not be confused with Dixon Miles, who surrendered Harpers Ferry. Miles, crossing the creek over the Middle Bridge, determined the enemy was still in position on the morning of the 16th.[2]

General Joseph Hooker received orders from General George B. McClellan during the day of September 16 to cross the Antietam Creek with his First Corps and prepare the way for an attack on General Robert E. Lee's left flank. Fog delayed his start. McClellan's report stated that on the afternoon of the 16th Hooker crossed; his corps contained the divisions of generals James B. Ricketts, Abner Doubleday and George G. Meade. Meade, at the head of Hooker's corps with the Pennsylvania Reserves, became engaged with the enemy and the fighting lasted until after dark. At daylight on the 17th the contest continued.

On the evening of September 16, 1862, General Sumner, in command of both the Second and Twelfth corps, received orders to send the Twelfth Corps to support Hooker and to keep his own Second Corps in readiness to march for the same purpose an hour before daylight. Sumner's corps was at Keedysville, just northeast of Sharpsburg and due east of the battlefield located on the site of present day route 34. Stephen Sears believed the idea behind the order to send the Twelfth Corps to General Hooker was to take troops away from Sumner, on whom Sears says McClellan wished to keep a tight rein. Now the Twelfth Corps would be fighting under Joseph Hooker rather than under General Sumner. General Jacob D. Cox believed, however, that Hooker wanted an independent command and insisted that all troops sent to him be placed under his command. The order McClellan sent to Sumner ordering him to move Mansfield's Corps across the Antietam Creek, along with all the artillery and ammunition, was issued from army headquarters at 5:50 P.M. The wording of the order indicates that Sumner was in command of two corps. The order refers to the Second Corps not by name but as "the other corps of your command." If McClellan was working to ease control away from General Sumner, headquarters was careful not to tip McClellan's hand. On the surface at least, McClellan's order to Sumner reads as if Sumner commanded two corps. It was not until 11:30 P.M. on September 16 that Mansfield was ready to move.[3]

No guides were available to usher General Mansfield's corps to his position. In fact General Hooker did not indicate what position the Twelfth Corps should take once it arrived at the front. As a result it went into bivouac a mile and a half in Hooker's rear instead of moving due west after crossing the Antietam Creek and falling in on the left flank of the First Corps.[4]

The extent and the object of that attack were unclear to McClellan's corps commanders, in the opinion of historian Marion V. Armstrong Jr. McClellan possessed no clear, firm plan in his own mind, as his description of his troop deployment and the orders he would give them make clear. McClellan stated, "The design was to make the main attack upon the enemy's left — at least to create a diversion in favor of the main attack, with the hope of something more by assailing the enemy's right — and, as soon as one or both of the flank movements were fully successful, to attack the center with any reserve I might then have on hand."[5]

Was the attack upon the enemy's left the main attack or a diversion? If a diversion in favor of the main attack, then what was the main attack to be and where was it to fall? The attack on the center, according to McClellan, was conditional upon the success of an attack on either or both flanks and only if he had any reserves. Hoping for something more is hardly a plan. McClellan's approach to the coming battle was highly conditional upon events on the ground. What if an attack on one of General Lee's flanks was successful but McClellan had no reserves on hand to attack Lee's center? Sending three corps as he did, although one at a time, against Lee's left, and then sending General William B. Franklin's Sixth Corps there as well when he arrived from Pleasant Valley, would imply that an attack by McClellan's right was the main attack.

Still McClellan's plan, although its final form would be shaped by events on the field and therefore reactionary, was not without merit. Imprecise as it was, it grew out of McClellan's assessment of the conditions confronting him. He was uncertain as to the strength of Lee's army. Lee used the terrain to mask his troops and kept many of them out of sight of Federal observers. Nothing in the way of intelligence gave him reason to alter his belief, incorrect though it was, that Lee had between 80,000 and 120,000 men. McClellan knew Harpers Ferry had fallen and Stonewall Jackson's troops would be joining Lee. McClellan realized that Lee's position, so close to the Potomac, gave Lee the river onto which he could anchor his flanks.

An attack on Lee's right would yield a large benefit to McClellan if he was successful. It would cut Lee off from the only ford available to him to cross the river. But to attack Lee's right required the Antietam Creek to be crossed where it was the widest and deepest. It became a formidable obstacle below Sharpsburg, widening as it flowed to its junction with the Potomac. Another disadvantage was created by the heights above the stream. They provided Lee with an excellent defensive position.

On the other hand, attacking Lee on his left gave the Federals the advantage of an easier crossing of the Antietam Creek, although men in Sumner's corps found the stream where they crossed to be waist-deep. There was more room to attack with a larger force on that part of the field. But an attack on that flank may have resulted in an operation much like the World War II campaign in Sicily where the enemy evacuated the island across the Straights of Messina. Like squeezing a tube of paste, an attack on Lee's left could push Lee's army across the Potomac at Boteler's Ford and towards safety.

Seeing advantages in McClellan's chosen plan, historian Ethan S. Rafuse understood it as giving McClellan "maximum flexibility as the fighting developed" so he could "avoid committing himself to a course of action that circumstances might prove unwise." This argument seems to be a bit of a stretch. If maximum flexibility was desired then why have any plan at all? The price of flexibility was to give Lee the initiative. A plan is made to try to control circumstances. Rafuse believed McClellan intended to start the attack with General Hooker's First Corps pressing Lee's left flank and holding the rest of the Union army intact while he monitored Hooker's progress.[6]

The Army of the Potomac was situated on September 16 as follows: Hooker's First Corps was west of the Antietam Creek and north of Sharpsburg. Burnside was on the east bank of the Antietam Creek and south; generals Fitz John Porter's and Edwin Sumner's corps were in the center; and General Joseph K.F. Mansfield's Twelfth Corps was held in reserve at Keedysville. Finally General William B. Franklin's Sixth Corps would remain in its present position until the Union army learned there was no danger in Pleasant Valley.[7]

Sumner knew little of this plan. He knew Hooker had crossed the Antietam Creek and that General Mansfield's Twelfth Corps had marched to Hooker's support at 11:30 P.M. on the 16th. Sumner's men could sleep until 2:00 A.M. so long as they were ready to march by daybreak. Sumner received these orders on the 16th at 5:50 P.M.

Ready to march his three divisions to the front at first light, Sumner received no orders to advance. The men in the ranks carried a double allotment of ammunition, forty cartridges in their cartridge boxes and an additional forty rounds on their persons. Hopefully the men did not carry them in their pockets, as the Antietam Creek where they crossed was up to their waists. In addition to their arms the men carried only a canteen and haversack.[8]

Sumner must have heard the fighting that opened the battle that day around 5:30 A.M. between the men of Union general Truman Seymour's First Corps brigade and the Confederate forces of Isaac Trimble. By 6:00 A.M. Sumner, along with his son Samuel, a captain and an aide-de-camp, rode to McClellan's headquarters at the Pry House. During the time the Sumners, father and son, waited for orders, about two miles away to the west fighting on a 500-yard front, five thousand Confederates and eighty-seven hundred Yankees were locked in mortal combat. Of the total men engaged, 4,368 were casualties well before Sumner got his orders to advance to the support of the First and Twelfth corps. As Joseph L. Harsh wrote, "[Stonewall] Jackson's two divisions had temporarily ceased to exist, and the skeleton that remained of the [Union] First Corps had not only lost all offensive punch, but it was incapable of withstanding another serious attack from its foe."[9]

Sumner was made to wait at army headquarters, where he received word that all was going well. The gunfire they heard was interpreted by McClellan's staff as that of the Confederate rearguard, and the Union staff passed that on to Sumner. More likely it was Confederate artillery posted on Nicodemus Hill, high ground Hooker had not bothered to secure the day before, firing into the right flank of Union First Corps troops; or it may have been the guns of Confederate Stephen D. Lee, posted near the Dunker Church. Staff officers also told Sumner that McClellan was sleeping after having been up all night attending to details of his plan. What those details may have been would be interesting to know since McClellan's plan, as it has been described, was contingent on the progress of the battle. Then too, who was General Sumner to think he could interrupt McClellan's sleep? McClellan had kept better men than Sumner, President Lincoln for one, waiting while he went to bed.[10]

Strained feelings between McClellan and several of his generals did nothing to contribute to Union success. McClellan had placed General Ambrose Burnside in an embarrassing position when he essentially took General Hooker's corps away from Burnside after the battle of South Mountain and put Hooker on the opposite flank from Burnside. The same was true in McClellan's dealings with General Sumner. Sending General Mansfield's corps to work under Hooker was an affront. At South Mountain on September 14 Burnside commanded the First and Ninth corps, Sumner the Second and Twelfth, and Franklin the Sixth and the Fourth corps. With Sumner, McClellan took halfway measures. According to Charles Russell Lowell, a staff officer who carried messages during the battle, McClellan should have relieved Sumner if he lacked faith in him. Sumner was not so obtuse not to have known he was to be subordinated to Hooker, his junior.[11]

McClellan apparently awoke from his nap and received reports of General Joseph Hooker's early success. This news, historian Joseph Harsh believed, "seduced" McClellan into making a major revision in his battle plan. Believing he could achieve a victory by continuing to hit General Lee on his left flank, McClellan ordered Sumner and his Second Corps to press the gains made by Hooker. "The change in plans," Harsh wrote, "led to unforeseen complications." At 7:20 A.M. Sumner got his orders to move to the front and support both Hooker and Mansfield. But he could not take Richardson's division until the Fifth Corps division of General George W. Morell came up to replace it.

Richardson's position indicated to Joseph Harsh that McClellan's original plan for the Second Corps was to hit the Confederate center when success on either or both flanks justified an attack.[12] Ordering Sumner's corps to attack Lee's left is another example of how McClellan's plan was conditioned upon battlefield developments. Here again one wonders at McClellan's mindset to order Sumner forward with one boot off, so to speak. What was so vulnerable at Keedysville that Richardson had to postpone his advance until General Morell arrived to take his place?

Sumner's 7:20 A.M. order read:

> The Comdg. General directs that you move Sedgwick and French across the creek by the fords which Capt. Custer will point out to you. You will cross in as solid a mass as possible and communicate with Genl. Hooker immediately. Genl. Richardson's Division will not cross till further orders. You will cross your artillery over the bridge and halt after you cross until you ascertain if Genl. Hooker wants assistance.[13]

In this order it appears that headquarters believed the Second Corps had its artillery. But Sumner interpreted his order from late afternoon on the 16 to mean that he was to send the artillery of both his and Mansfield's corps over the Antietam Creek, which he did. Sumner's understanding of McClellan's 5:50 P.M. order left Richardson's division bereft of artillery. The word *corps* is both singular and plural. So when Sumner read the line in his order "that all of the artillery, ammunition, and everything else appertaining to the corps, be gotten over without fail tonight, ready for action in the morning," Sumner read "corps" as plural.

Hardly more than fifteen minutes after Sumner's 7:20 A.M. order to move his two divisions to support the First and Twelfth corps, General Joseph K.F. Mansfield received his mortal wound. The two corps Sumner was to support were quickly melting away.

Sedgwick's division started first; William French's division, comprising of new troops, took longer to get into the marching position of three brigades parallel to each other and marching in columns of regiments. Having two miles to go, they wasted no time following country lanes but marched due west cross country. From what Sumner learned at headquarters, Hooker and Mansfield began their attack at 6:00 A.M. going south along the Hagerstown Pike towards Sharpsburg. Sumner would arrive on the left flank of the two corps and a simple command of "Front!" would bring his men on their left. But the First and Twelfth corps did not attack together, as headquarters told Sumner. The Twelfth did not come to support the First Corps until 7:00 A.M., when Hooker's men were pretty well battered.[14]

Upon drawing closer to the battlefield Sumner began to suspect things were not going as headquarters had led him to believe. Instead of moving south the battle seemed to be directly ahead of him in the East Woods and possibly moving north. So Sumner had to make a judgment and act accordingly. As a precaution Sumner directed Sedgwick to deploy his division from columns of regiments to columns of brigades. This was the formation Sumner's critics found so vulnerable. Sumner ordered Sedgwick to go into line while he was in open country between the Antietam Creek and the East Woods. The line was a standard formation that Civil War commanders emphasized. As Brent Nosworthy wrote, "It would take several seasons for even the most perspicacious of officers to really appreciate the new weaponry and the changes in tactics that were demanded. Until then reliance upon the older methods seemed to remain the most reasonable choice."[15]

It is at this point in the battle that Sumner's critics fault him. Writing to his daughters on September 22, 1862, five days after the battle, General Alpheus Williams implied that Sumner was idle and delayed his march to the battlefield. It was 9:30 before Sedgwick's division of Sumner's corps arrived, Williams wrote, "although he was to be on the ground at daylight."[16] Actually Sumner was on the western edge of the East Woods at about 8:50 A.M. He had been at McClellan's headquarters at 7:20 that morning when he got his orders to move. His Second Corps divisions were a few miles away at Keedysville, to which place Sumner and his aid had to return. Sumner got his men to the battle site in reasonably good time.

Williams' letters say Sumner had done no reconnaissance.[17] That charge is incorrect, as Sumner personally rode over the ground and made observations.[18] Stephen Sears wrote, "With characteristic obtuseness Sumner ignored what George Meade of the First Corps and Alpheus Williams of the Twelfth tried to tell him of the situation at the front, and instead rushed forward incautiously at the head of Sedgwick's division."[19] This judgment by Sears is based most likely on Williams' letter to "Lew" dated September 24, 1862. While Williams may have been angry on that date and vented to "Lew," his report of the battle, dated September 29, makes no mention of Sumner's indifference to his advice. Williams reported that it was nearly 9:00 A.M. when Sumner arrived, not 9:30 as he wrote to his daughters. Williams apparently did not talk directly to Sumner but, as he stated in his report, sent a staff officer "to appraise him of our position and the situation of affairs." When he saw Sedgwick approaching, Williams withdrew his first division in order to replenish their cartridge boxes and to rest. "General Sedgwick's gallant division and the veteran commander of the Second Corps [General Edwin Vose Sumner] were received by hearty cheers of our men," Williams wrote in his report. "This division pushed forward without a halt, and dashed against the strong position of the enemy."[20] This is quite a different account of Sumner's arrival from "generals who would come up with their commands and pitch in at the first point without consultation with those who knew the ground or without reconnoitering,"[21] as Williams wrote in his report on September 29, some days after his letters cited above. Williams may have had a better understanding of events when he wrote his report than when he wrote his letters.

Only Captain Samuel Sumner made any mention of a meeting between his father and General George G. Meade, and that was in his 1917 address before the Massachusetts Military Historical Society. Over time Sumner may have confused General Meade with whomever it was he met. There is no evidence in the reports in the Official Records or in Meade's letters that Sumner ever met with or talked with General Meade. Testifying before the Committee on the Conduct of the War on February 18, 1863, General Sumner replied to a question, "I sent one my own staff-officers to find where they [the First Corps] were; and General Ricketts, the only officer we could find, said that he could not raise 300 men in the corps."[22] There was no mention of having met with General Meade.

After the repulse of Hooker's First Corps and Hooker's being wounded, Meade, placed in command of the First Corps, was occupied with its consolidation well to the north of Sumner. All Samuel Sumner said about meeting Meade was that it was after Sedgwick crossed the Antietam Creek and that he told of Hooker's repulse.[23] General Sumner had a brief talk with Hooker as he was being carried off the field wounded. He also spoke with General James B. Ricketts and General John Gibbon, both from the First Corps. None offered much information about the location or disposition of the enemy.

As General Sumner testified under oath, the only First Corps general that Sumner's staff could locate was James B. Ricketts, who reported that he could not raise more than 300 men from his second division. Losses for Ricketts' division, as listed in *Battles and Leaders*, totaled 1,180. There is some uncertainty among the several accounts and the documentation concerning with whom and at what time Sumner met First and Twelfth corps officers. However, after these consultations Sumner must have known that neither of the two corps he was ordered to support was able to take part in any advance. After General Sumner's brief contact with the wounded General Hooker he received another message from army headquarters. Back at the Pry House, where McClellan had his headquarters, they believed Hooker was driving the enemy. If Hooker did not require Sumner's support on his right, the orders stated, then Sumner was to push up on Hooker's left, get possession of the woods to the right and push on towards Sharpsburg and a little to its rear. Headquarters also sent a message to Hooker which said that Sumner was directed to move on Hooker's left and push forward to Sharpsburg if Hooker did not need Sumner's support on Hooker's right.[24]

What intelligence Sumner received from these interviews with Hooker, the member of William's staff and General Ricketts may not have been too accurate, if General Cox's account of the battle is correct. Union officers on this part of the field were deceived in part, Cox wrote, as to the extent and direction of the enemy line because of the effective use Jeb Stuart made of his artillery. Cox also believed that, though brief, Sumner's talk with Hooker was enough to make him believe haste was essential. The Second Corps had been ordered to support Hooker's and Mansfield's corps and to continue the assault. Adding to the confusion was the fact that the Twelfth Corps made its advance on an oblique line to the axis of attack made by the First Corps. Hooker attacked primarily due south from his position above the North Woods. Mansfield made his in a more northeast-to-southwest direction, understandable from the position where he bivouacked the night before.[25] However, the western woods—into which Sumner saw Federal troops advancing and driving the Confederates—were the key to winning on this part of the field. The Second Corps' capturing the West Woods, as they came to be known, would deny the Confederates a defensive line north of Sharpsburg. From what Sumner could see, the southern end of these strategic woods around the Dunker Church was in Federal hands. Fighting died down at the northern end. Sumner believed if Sedgwick's troops could fill the gap they would be to the right of the men around the white church and on the left of those at the north end of the West Woods.[26]

A Matter of Fifteen Minutes

Around 9:00 o'clock that morning, about the time Sedgwick's division was preparing to cross to the West Woods, General Sumner saw that General French's division was too far to the left to be able to connect with Sedgwick. Sumner sent an urgent message to French to make a vigorous attack so as to be able to come to the aid of Sedgwick. The messenger was none other than young Captain Samuel Sumner.[27] The order made somewhat sentimental news back home in Syracuse, New York. On October 1, 1862, the *Syracuse Journal* reported that General Sumner had sent his son to carry a message through shot and shell knowing full well he might never see his son alive again. The young captain returned unharmed and the paper reported, "The scene was touching to those around." Captain Sumner found that French was engaged with the enemy at the Sunken Road and was committed to that part of the field during the entire battle.

Later on that day when General Lee was making plans for a counterattack upon the Union right he came across the Rockbridge Artillery, where his own son Rob Jr. served. The grimy-faced youth asked his father if he planned to send them in again "in our crippled condition." "Yes my son," Lee replied, and pointed across the Hagerstown Pike. "You all must do what you can to help drive those people back."[28]

While Captain Sumner was in route to general French, generals Robert

E. Lee, James Longstreet and Daniel H. Hill were making observations on a knoll in the center of the Confederate line. Lee anticipated an attack upon his center. While both Lee and Longstreet were on foot, Hill, ignoring Longstreet's advice, remained on horseback. Longstreet, observing the Federal line about a mile away through binoculars, saw a puff of white smoke from a single Union gun and remarked, "There is a shot for you." Seconds later a cannon shot tore the front legs from Hill's unfortunate horse, making it difficult for Hill to dismount. To Longstreet it was the second best artillery shot he witnessed up to that time.[29]

Union artillerist Captain Stephen H. Weed, Fifth U.S. Artillery, was part of the artillery assigned to General George Sykes' Second Division of General Fitz John Porter's Fifth Corps. Weed made the shot that killed Hill's horse, one of three of Hill's horses killed before the battle ended.[30]

As Sedgwick's division proceeded across the open field to the woods, Sumner rode close behind the leading brigade of General Willis A. Gorman. Looking back, Sumner was surprised not to see General Napoleon J.T. Dana's brigade following. At this point General John B. Gibbon, an old artillerist and brigade commander in the First Corps, offered his services to Sumner. Gibbon was conversing with General George H. Gordon, a brigade commander in General Alpheus Williams' division of the Twelfth Corps. "Whilst seated here on our horses, talking, we observed a line of battle coming out of the woods behind us (the East woods) and as it advanced across the open space extending to the Hagerstown pike, I soon recognized the old veteran, Gen. Sumner as in command of it," Gibbon wrote. Gibbon offered his services, and Sumner asked if Gibbon would assist Sumner's chief of artillery and help him place some batteries. Gibbon complied and placed some guns on high ground near the Dunker Church. Gibbon later witnessed the men of Sedgwick's division streaming from the woods and tried to help rally them.

Sumner's meeting with Gibbon was a bit curious. He could see where Sedgwick was heading but gave no warning, something he surely would have done had he known of danger ahead. But what was Gibbon doing so far away from his own men as a "looker on"? Surely General Meade could have used his services in trying to assemble the fragmented First Corps. Also a bit curious is the name of Gibbon's favorite horse, "Sugar Plum," an unusually delicate name for a war horse. Gibbon, however, had two young daughters, and it is quite possible the loving father had allowed his youngsters to name his horse.[31]

Sumner's guns were not the first General Gibbon served that day. Gibbon, author of *The Artillerist's Manual*, helped the men of his old Battery B, Fourth U.S. Artillery, earlier that day on the western side of the Hagerstown Turnpike near the Miller barn. Lieutenant James B. Stewart's two-gun section had been battling men of the Fourth Texas, Eighteenth Georgia, and Hampton's Legion when the other four Napoleons of Battery B came to their aid. Some infantry men were assisting the gunners. Gibbon, who was nearby, saw that the elevating screw on one of the guns had been run down, causing the gun to shoot high over the heads of the enemy. In the fury of the battle the cannoneers had not noticed. Gibbon quickly jumped from his horse and ran the screw up, causing the muzzle to point low. When the gun fired the canister tore away the fence and, in Gibbon's own words, "produced great destruction in the enemy's ranks as did subsequent discharges."[32]

The Second Corps batteries, assisted by General Gibbon, were joined by those of the First and Twelfth corps in supporting Sedgwick's initial success in accompanying the infantry to the very front lines. The artillery men fought at distances as close as 300 yards. "The contest here was prolonged and bitter in the extreme, but the Confederates succeeded in containing what at first threatened to become a clean breakthrough by Sedgwick, and before 1:00 P.M. had forced their assailants back to the edge of the East Woods."[33]

After his brief conversation with General Gibbon, Sumner rode to the right flank of Gorman's brigade. There was virtually no resistance to Gorman's advance at this time. As Sumner caught up to the men on the right flank of Gorman's line, men of Colonel Alfred Sully's First Minnesota, General Sumner saw their colors were cased.

"In God's name, what are you fighting for? Unfurl those colors," he roared in a voice heard by the entire regiment. To Sumner it was mandatory to advance against the enemy with flags flying to inspire the men.[34] Sumner rode on the right of his line in order to observe the situation in the northern portion of the West Woods. He needed to know if the enemy there might pose a threat to Sedgwick's right flank.

Certain events delayed the movement of Dana's and Howard's brigades, but as Howard, who had lost an arm at Fair Oaks, was crossing the fields west of the East Woods, he was ordered to send the 71st Pennsylvania Regiment to the support of the troops in the northern end of the West Woods, where Sumner went to make his observation. At this point, sometime around 9:30 A.M., the sound of heavy small-arms fire was heard from deep in the West Woods, indicating Gorman's brigade had made contact with the enemy. Sedgwick ordered Howard to close up with his whole brigade, and the 71st Regiment was recalled. Howard halted his brigade until the 71st resumed its place in the line.

Concern for the fighting at the northern end of the West Woods had already caused the 71st Pennsylvania to be sent there, only to be recalled. In order to connect with those troops General Gorman, whose brigade was well into the West Woods and in advance of the other two brigades of Dana and Howard, ordered his regiments to move at a right oblique in order to shift his brigade more to the north. But his left-most regiment, the 34th New York, did not get the message and continued moving forward and came upon the 125th Pennsylvania near the Dunker Church.

So far Gorman's brigade had cleared the woods of Confederates and was fighting them in a ravine. Both sides took advantage of the cover provided by haystacks, hedgerows, fences, boulders and orchard trees on the farm of Alfred Poffenberger.[35] General Gorman reported that the First Company of Andrew Sharpshooters under Captain J. Saunders, part of Colonel John W. Kimball's Fifteenth Massachusetts Regiment, along with the left wing of that regiment silenced one Confederate battery by driving the cannoneers from the gun each time they tried to reload the piece. Armed with target rifles with telescopic sights attached, the sharpshooters were well equipped to shoot at long range. But at close range the specialty arms were of little use. The regiment as a whole fought at a range of from fifteen to twenty yards, "each partly sheltering themselves behind fences, large rocks, and strawstacks." Colonel Kimball, in his report, confirmed the distance between the warring parties as being fifteen yards; however, the artillery battery that the Andrew Sharpshooters were shooting at was reported to be 600 yards away.[36]

General Gorman's report went on to state that after his men had fired from forty to fifty rounds at the enemy it became evident the enemy were moving in large force on his left. "On our left, in the woods, there was a force that told me they belonged to General [Samuel W.] Crawford's brigade [125th PA], that were posted there when we first entered it. They fought handsomely until the heavy force of the enemy turned their left, when they retired rapidly, and by this movement in five minutes the enemy's fire came pouring hotly on our left flank and rear."[37]

The troops who charged into the flank of the 125th Pennsylvania and the 34th New York regiments were from Confederate General Joseph Kershaw's brigade. Colonel James A. Suiter of the 34th New York, a part of Gorman's brigade, stated, "From some cause to me unknown, I had become detached from my brigade, the One hundred and twenty-fifth Regiment Pennsylvania Volunteers being on my right."[38] Kershaw saw that Confederate troops of General Lafayette McLaws were about to cross his front, and to avoid firing into them Kershaw moved his men east of the Hagerstown Pike, where they were shattered by a super-battery of Union artillery — guns from the Union First, Second and Twelfth corps. The Confederates who hit Sedgwick's left flank and devastated it were 400 Mississippians and 600 Georgians under Confederate George T. Anderson. At the same time, 700 men under General Paul Semmes fired into Sedgwick's men from the front.[39]

Even before this disaster struck, severe problems developed in Sedgwick's division caused by the three lines of battle in brigade fronts. This formation was taken based upon Sumner's earlier concept of his coming in on the flank of the First and Twelfth corps; he would front on their left and move south towards Sharpsburg. But now having to fight their way forward, they failed to maintain the fifty- to seventy-yard interval between brigades and the lines began to bunch up. When men of the 59th New York, a regiment in General Dana's brigade, coming behind Gorman's leading brigade, began to fire at the enemy through the left wing of Colonel Kimball's Fifteenth Massachusetts Regiment, they shot the Bay State men in the back. Colonel Kimball's efforts to have them cease fire were to no avail until he met General Sumner, who got the New Yorkers to cease firing and to retire, "which order was executed in considerable confusion," Kimball wrote. So desperate did things become that an order was issued forbidding the carrying of wounded men to the rear. It was obeyed to the very letter, Colonel Kimball reported.[40]

As the 59th New York began to move to the rear, General Gorman reported to General Sumner that the left flank regiments of his and Dana's brigades had been broken and the men were streaming back, the enemy in pursuit. The division had to withdraw, and Sumner rode to General Howard's brigade, the one farthest back, to start the retreat. This time Sumner's loud "Bull of the Woods" voice could not carry above the roar of combat. Sumner resorted to hand signals to tell Howard to withdraw.[41]

In General Howard's Philadelphia Brigade, men in the 69th Pennsylvania Regiment were ordered to lie down, so destructive was the enemy's fire. Sumner, coming up to the front and waving his hat, got their attention and indicated to them to retire. The 71st Pennsylvania Regiment's account of its part at Antietam, a regiment in that same brigade as the 69th, stated that General Sumner rode over every part of the field and ordered General Howard to change front and lead his command against the enemy on his left. But the man who recorded the part played there by the 72nd Pennsylvania Regiment of the Philadelphia Brigade was more critical: "Had the Philadelphia Brigade been faced to the left to have met this attack when it was first made, the line might have been preserved intact. But its commander [General Howard] moved on without heeding the dangers upon his flank until it was too late."[42]

In his autobiography Howard wrote that his first indication that there were no troops covering the left flank came when General Sumner ordered him to face about. Like the men in the 69th Pennsylvania Regiment, Howard could not hear even Sumner's loud voice above the roar of combat and only through his motions and arm waving could Howard understand his orders.[43]

After his pantomime with General Howard, Sumner rode back among Sedgwick's disintegrating division to try to rally the broken regiments. One soldier of the 59th New York remembered his regiment being completely flanked on the left and rear when Sumner personally rode in through a terrific fire and brought them out. Colonel Joshua T. Owen of the 69th Pennsylvania wrote, "General Sumner appeared in person in the midst of a most deadly shower of shot and shell, and an order was received to fall back." Stephen

Sears wrote, "Sumner was at his best now, the fearless old warrior riding slowly back and forth encouraging his men by calm example."[44]

Extricating Sedgwick's division was in historian Rafuse's opinion "a tactical success of the first order and attributable to sheer luck, rather than design." He went on to write, "Had McLaws arrived in the West Woods fifteen minutes earlier, Sumner would have no doubt overwhelmed his exhausted men, had they arrived fifteen minutes later, Sumner would have already made his turn south and been rolling up the Confederate left."[45]

General Howard managed to get the 106th Pennsylvania Regiment to hold a position behind a rail fence to stall the Confederate advance. Colonel Alfred Sully of the First Minnesota had been on the far right of Gorman's line. He managed to move his regiment to the north, where he was joined by the 82nd New York and the Nineteenth Massachusetts regiments. But even Sully's regiment took heavy casualties. He lost 147 men out of 500. The fighting was so terrific that his horse became gun shy. Sully planned to put him out to pasture as soon as he could find one.[46]

The Confederate counterattack began when it hit the Seventh Michigan and the 42nd New York regiments of General Dana's brigade. As historian Marion V. Armstrong Jr. wrote, "Just as these two regiments were about to take up a position that would have plugged the gap between the left of Sedgwick's line and the 125th Pennsylvania, they were subjected to a terrible concentration of fire from enemy units advancing up the ravine."[47]

The counterattack lost momentum finally to Federal resistance, but not until they reached several hundred yards beyond the north end of the West Woods. It was Sumner's artillery, the work of some fifty guns, that halted the Confederates as they poured out of the West Woods and across the corn field. General John Sedgwick stood behind Lieutenant George A. Woodruff's Battery I, First U.S. Artillery, when he was hit twice and his horse killed. His nephew and aide, Major William D. Sedgwick, was mortally wounded.[48]

General Sumner now began to assess and appreciate the scope of the disaster to Sedgwick's division. Seriously wounded, Sedgwick and his brigade commander Dana were out of action. General John Sedgwick had been a loyal subordinate to Sumner, as we have seen, since the formation of the First Cavalry Regiment in 1855. The division lost a tremendous number of men as casualties, over 2,200 or about forty percent.[49] As senior officer present, Sumner began to build a defensive line from the fragments of the regiments of his corps plus those effectives from the First and the Twelfth corps. The defensive line Sumner built ran from the southwestern edge of the East Woods to the southeastern edge of the North Woods, then north along the Hagerstown Pike. It was crowded with artillery.[50]

Ethan S. Rafuse wrote that what happened in the West Woods did not inspire McClellan with confidence in Sumner and McClellan did not trust

Sumner with an independent command. Yet Rafuse admitted fifteen minutes had made all the difference. Sumner's experience at seeing Sedgwick's division shattered seemed to have badly shaken this usually combative general, Rafuse wrote. However, he managed to create a defensive line and rally the remnants of Sedgwick's division to form it.[51]

Sumner received reinforcements in the form of General William F. "Baldy" Smith's division of General William B. Franklin's Sixth Corps. Smith's division comprised the brigades of General Winfield S. Hancock, Colonel William H. Irwin and General William T.H. Brooks. Fighting broke out again in the early afternoon on Hancock's front.

General Hancock arrived on the field as a brigade commander in the Sixth Corps. By the end of the day he was a division commander in the Second Corps, once again serving under General Sumner. Upon General Richardson's wounding General McClellan personally appointed Hancock to division commander.[52]

General George S. Greene, a Twelfth Corps division commander, began to fall back from his position in the woods around the Dunker Church. Perhaps until now he had not known how far forward he was. He was pursued by two separate columns of Confederate infantry. Then the Confederates in turn retreated to a position west of the Hagerstown Pike and south of the West Woods, driven by several regiments of General Israel B. Richardson's division coming out of the Sunken Road and by General Irwin's brigade as it was coming into the position assigned to it. Just minutes before, Richardson's men had cleared the Sunken Road of enemy.

Generals Sumner and Franklin held opposite views concerning the ability of the troops to attack the enemy successfully. They expressed their differences so heatedly that an aide rode to McClellan's headquarters to report. Sometime between 2:30 and 3:00 P.M. McClellan rode to a spot behind the East Woods where Franklin and Sumner were in deep disagreement. Franklin wished to attack but with less than his entire corps. Sumner believed a corps was insufficient to attack Lee's left successfully and that the men he had on the field were too worn out to take part in an offensive operation. After all, three corps, the First, Twelfth and Second, had attacked individually and had been beaten back. The heart of Sumner's argument was this: there was no reason to believe Franklin's 9,000 men could do what 30,000 had failed to accomplish. Sumner also argued that there was a chance of a Confederate counterattack. Sumner was not prescient, but a counterattack was exactly what General Lee was planning. However, it was cancelled.[53]

General Sumner, the man McClellan accused of being a greater fool than he had imagined, argued quite convincingly as to the thin Union line that ran from the North Woods to the Sunken Road. But perhaps it was the carnage McClellan witnessed for himself along the way to this impromptu conference that was as convincing as Sumner's arguments. McClellan sided with Sumner. The commanding general stripped his center of half its defenders and sent them to General Franklin's support.

General Marsena R. Patrick, a brigade commander in the First Corps who fought most of September 17 north of the West Woods, agreed that an attack of the Sixth Corps would have been foolish. In his diary entry for the 18th he recorded, "We were not attacked last night & this morning Sumner told me that McClellan's orders were not to attack.... It seems to be fairly understood, that only Madcaps, of the Hooker stripe, would have pushed our troops into action again without very strong reinforcements." General Patrick's last entry for September 15 was "Can't say that I like to serve under Hooker."[54]

Stephen Sears cited a message sent to Sumner at 9:10 on the morning of the 17th, a message Sumner never got, cautioning him as to how to make his advance. "Impatient of any further delay," Sears wrote, "Sumner pushed ahead with Sedgwick's division." What would advancing cautiously have done to avoid the contact with the enemy that struck Sedgwick? It seems that Sears fell into the trap Joseph Harsh cautioned historians to avoid. That is believing that if one thing fails its opposite would have succeeded. Seeing that Sumner moved quickly to occupy the gap beyond the Dunker Church and was severely repulsed, Sears implied that had an order to proceed cautiously reached Sumner it might have prevented disaster.[55]

If Sumner, with his characteristic obtuseness, rushed forward incautiously with Sedgwick's division as Stephen Sears wrote, then what about General Joseph Hooker, "one of the most aggressive generals in the Potomac army," as Sears described him? His attack the morning of September 17 wrecked his corps and possibly shattered the nerve and will of his men. Straggling and temporary desertion became widespread among the survivors of the First Corps. Hooker charged ahead from his position above the North Woods at the J. Poffenberger farm, the Dunker Church and the high ground on which it sat being his goal. He made his attack with little reconnaissance and little knowledge of what was ahead. Just as General William French's division marched away from Sedgwick, the right of General Gibbon's brigade, because of the standing corn, marched ahead of the left and received heavy volleys from the West Woods. The First Corps suffered nearly 2,500 casualties. Straggling too after the corps was repulsed reduced the efficiency of the corps.[56]

McClellan received reinforcements on September 18 but postponed an attack until the next day. During the night of September 18, 1862, General Robert E. Lee withdrew his army over the Potomac at Boteler's Ford and the Maryland Campaign, for all purposes, came to an end.

Historian Marion V. Armstrong Jr. in his essay "A Failure of Command?"

argues that the West Woods was the key piece of the terrain in that area of the battlefield. Only 2,000 yards separated the village of Sharpsburg from the Potomac River. Boteler's Ford was the only suitable crossing open to Lee's army, and it was two miles southwest of Sharpsburg. There was little possibility of crossing that river north of town. "This body of woods was on the western edge of the crown of land between Antietam Creek and the Potomac River, situated at least in part on some of the highest terrain in the area," Armstrong stated.

At the time of Sedgwick's assault Confederate forces in the vicinity of the West Woods were inadequate to defend against an attack by a division the size of Sedgwick's. Confederate troops there, under General Thomas J. "Stonewall" Jackson, were thin after defending against the attack of the Union First and Twelfth Corps. What troops were there were fighting the brigade of First Corps general Marsena R. Patrick. Armstrong credits Sumner for correctly surmising that the West Woods, south of where General Patrick and General Jubal A. Early with Colonel Andrew Grigsby fought, did not hold any significant body of troops. The gap between Patrick to the north and the troops south around Dunker Church had to be filled, and Sedgwick's division was the only available body of troops to do the job. The gap had to be plugged, and quickly. But as it turned out and as Joseph Harsh wrote, "fortune did not always favor the bold."[57] The astute and humorous Private Warren Lee Goss had this to say about armchair, after-the-fact judges of military campaigns:

> McClellan had been criticized [sic], perhaps justly, for not making the attack at an earlier hour, while yet Lee's force consisted only of Longstreet's and D.H. Hill's corps. A general, to be judged fairly should be criticised [sic] by the facts known, or obtainable by him, before and during the battle, rather than those gained by investigation from the safe distance of after years. Those who fight battles long after their issues are decided have more time to deliberate than the actors on the actual field.

Goss believed Hooker's advance was ill-timed. Because of the fog it could not have been made earlier, so Goss believed it should have been postponed until the next day. All Hooker did on the 16th was to telegraph his punch and gave Lee time to strengthen his left flank.[58]

As for alerting Lee to McClellan's intentions, Lee could have understood the terrain as well as McClellan. He could have seen the advantage to the Federals to attack Lee's left and the disadvantages of the Federals hitting him on his right. It is doubtful that Lee was unsure of where McClellan would attack.

Confederate E. Porter Alexander saw things pretty much the same way: "The times of these orders [to Mansfield at 5:50 P.M. and Sumner at 7:20 A.M.] is much more suggestive of a gradually developed plan, than of one formulated beforehand, and it resulted in four extensive combats instead of one great battle."[59]

General Jacob D. Cox was much of the same opinion. "Could Hooker and Mansfield have attacked together," Cox wrote, "or, still better, could Sumner's Second Corps have marched before day and united with the first onset, — Lee's left must inevitably have been crushed long before the Confederate divisions of [Lafayette] McLaws, [General John G.] Walker and A.P. Hill could have reached the field."[60]

From a frame of mind embittered by his wounds and capture at Antietam, Francis W. Palfrey in 1882 published *The Antietam and Fredericksburg* for the Charles Scribner's Sons series Campaigns of the Civil War. He was a severe critic not only of General Edwin V. Sumner's tactics at the battle of Antietam the morning of September 17, but of nearly everyone above his rank of lieutenant colonel. He blamed General McClellan, the entire military and the Lincoln administration for what he saw as the mismanagement of the war. He never would have taken up arms, he declared, had he known how things were to be managed. He found little consolation at home, becoming angry at how people continued to see the dead as noble.[61]

Palfrey served in the famous Twentieth Massachusetts Regiment, part of General Napoleon Dana's Third Brigade in Sedgwick's division. In Palfrey's opinion what General Sumner had attempted to do with General John Sedgwick's Second Division of the Second Corps was madness. Both Palfrey and Second Corps historian Francis A. Walker advanced the dubious claim that Sumner's cavalry background gave him the idea he could cut his way in and cut his way out of a difficult spot.[62]

George A. Bruce, historian of the Twentieth Massachusetts, believed Sumner suffered from a nervous state of mind brought on by the long delay in being ordered to attack, "but it may well have been that under such circumstances [mental nervousness] he was not in condition to exercise that self-control and cool judgment which the situation required."[63] Why Sumner wasn't afflicted with mental nervousness at Fair Oaks while he stood with Sedgwick's division at his Grapevine Bridge waiting for McClellan's order to cross that frail structure against the advice of his engineers, Bruce didn't say.

Artillerist Colonel Charles S. Wainwright, a frequent critic of General Sumner's tactics but not of the man himself, was ignorant of many of the facts that governed Sumner's movements on September 17. Wainwright wrote that Sumner was ordered to move at 3:00 A.M. but did not get underway until after daylight and then moved slowly. Not only did Wainwright not know the original starting time, he was uninformed that Sumner received no order to move until 7:20 A.M. That Sumner moved slowly is entirely incorrect. So based upon Wainwright's faulty understanding of Sumner's orders, he concluded, "This is the second time 'Old Bull' has allowed the rebs to escape by his stupidity or pigheadedness, and it is queer to me that he is kept in command. Still one cannot forget how splendidly he behaved at Fair Oaks."

In 1956 on the eve of the Civil War centennial, Bruce Catton published *This Hallowed Ground*. His account of General Sumner at Antietam was kindly though condescending. It also was factually undernourished. "This morning," Catton wrote, meaning September 17, "Sumner was to take his three divisions and crush the Rebel left." According to Catton, Sumner rode with General Sedgwick's division and "forgot about the other two." More accurate accounts of the battle have been written since Bruce Catton undertook to tell the story.

Stephen W. Sears in his books *Landscape Turned Red* and *George B. McClellan, the Young Napoleon* characterized General Sumner as obtuse, rash, hasty and incautious.[64] Sears relied on the letters of General Alpheus Williams of the Twelfth Corps to bolster his opinion and believed the letters were an apt summary of Sumner's actions.

Author Jeffery D. Wert asserted that the primary reasons for the destruction of General Sedgwick's fine division was corps commander Sumner's misreading of the situation on the field, neglecting to reconnoiter and selecting a formation for Sedgwick's brigades that blunted its firepower and maneuverability. Sumner, according to Wert, led his men into a Confederate "trap."[65]

Historian and essayist Robert K. Krick understood that luck had a major part to play in the Confederate success against Sedgwick's left flank. "The apparently beautifully orchestrated Confederate execution," Krick wrote, "included more of good fortune than deft forethought." Acknowledging Federal tactical mistakes, Krick added, "Fragments of four Southern divisions popped up in the right place around the West Woods at the right time."[66]

If it had been happenstance to a large degree that brought the Confederate forces against Sedgwick's left flank, then no matter how much reconnaissance Sumner may have made — and he did make some, despite claims to the contrary — he would not have discovered the enemy force that destroyed much of Sedgwick's division.[67]

It is true that Sumner misunderstood some of the actual conditions on the field, but he early realized that what he had been told at headquarters did not square with what he saw before him. His selection of a formation was based not upon the unforeseen and unfortunate circumstances he encountered but upon what he planned to do: fall in on the left of the Twelfth Corps and support General Hooker's men as he had been instructed to do at McClellan's headquarters and by orders he received later that morning on the field. The claim that he failed to reconnoiter is not right, but what would more reconnaissance at that time have told him concerning the attack on Sedgwick's left flank? General Jacob D. Cox wrote that there were absolutely no Confederate troops in the West Woods when Sedgwick's men entered them.[68]

As for a "trap," Jeffery Wert may have used the wrong word. A trap implies something set and waiting for its prey. There were no Confederate troops waiting to ambush Sedgwick's division. The Confederates happened to come up upon Sedgwick's men when they were opposed by a thin line of Confederates under General Jubal A. Early.

Joseph L. Harsh wrote possibly the best history of the Maryland Campaign to date. His *Taken at the Flood* is grounded on impressive research. "Sumner did not, as has been sometimes alleged, march his lead division into a trap," Harsh wrote. "He did, however, advance so far to the west that Sedgwick's entire left flank was in the air." Hearing that the Confederates had retreated in disorder to the west across the Hagerstown Pike, Sumner believed he had a great opportunity if it was quickly seized upon. Then about 9:20 A.M., two hours after Sumner began his advance, Sedgwick was hit from the front and the left flank. In twenty minutes nearly forty percent of his division were casualties. "Yet, withal," Harsh wrote, "the execution of the Confederate assault on Sedgwick was so sloppy and inefficient as to attest that luck is as important in war as intelligence."[69]

17

Fredericksburg

On September 21, 1862, General Sumner received orders to proceed to Harpers Ferry and to hold until reinforcements arrived. On October 7 Sumner's request for a leave of absence was granted, and he turned the Second Corps over to General Darius N. Couch. Sumner made it known to McClellan that he desired to be reassigned to command a military department before he returned to his home in Syracuse, New York. During the summer of 1862, reports appeared in the Syracuse newspapers of General Sumner being captured and held as a prisoner in Richmond. On July 14, 1862, the *Syracuse Journal* stated such reports were untrue. In its issue of September 18, 1862, that paper reported that he had passed through the recent battles in Maryland unharmed.

On October 13, 1862, the *Journal* reported that General Sumner was home in Syracuse looking worn and thin but in good health. On October 20 the same paper noted that General Sumner had received as guests at his home a number of citizens on Saturday evening and was serenaded by Dresher's Band. On the 30th the *Journal* reported that Sumner had left Syracuse to resume his command and that Lieutenant Colonel William Teall, his son-in-law, was to leave on Sunday to take his place on General Sumner's staff. The next day the *Syracuse Standard* reported that fact as well. Finally on November 5 the *Journal* noted that Maj. Gen. Sumner had left Washington on Tuesday morning to resume command in the Army of the Potomac.

William W. Teall was born on April 23, 1818, in Onondaga County, New York. He received a fine education and graduated from Yale, having studied law. He was active in New York State government and business. Teall married Sarah Montgomery Sumner on May 14, 1850. His letters, written to his wife in Syracuse almost daily from the front, reveal traits of General Sumner during his last command with the Army of the Potomac at Fredericksburg.

Teall held the beliefs and attitudes of the patrician that he truly was. By today's standards his social views may seem patronizing, but they may have been a sincere expression of noblesse oblige. In one of his first letters to his wife he wrote: "For the first time on the route a new made grave marks the last resting place of some poor soldier who made his last march & the mind unavoidably turns to loved ones at home — in the humble walks of life to be sure, but none the less dear & none the less heart rending the separation, than if he had mingled with the gifted in the land."[1]

When General Ambrose E. Burnside replaced McClellan to command the Army of the Potomac, Sumner was to take command of the Right Grand Division, one of three grand divisions into which the Army of the Potomac was newly organized. Sumner's Grand Division comprised the Second and the Ninth corps. The other two grand

Major General Edwin Vose Sumner. Massachusetts Commandery Military Order of the Loyal Legion and the U.S. Army Military History Institute.

divisions were General William B. Franklin's Left Grand Division, First and Sixth corps, and General Joseph Hooker's Center Grand Division, Third and Fifth corps. Sumner took command on November 14.[2]

Sumner's Right Grand Division led off, starting out on November 15, 1862. He arrived across from Fredericksburg sometime during the late afternoon or evening of the 17th. Pontoons were to have been available for Sumner to cross the Rappahannock River, but through administrative fumbling the first bridge train did not leave Washington until November 19, the same day that Burnside arrived. Sumner, anxious to cross while Fredericksburg was still lightly defended, asked permission to cross at an upstream ford, but Burnside declined to issue such an order. Burnside believed the ford was impassible for infantry and artillery. A cavalry force might have been able to swim across but might then become stranded. Without pontoon bridges it would be impossible to supply any forces across the Rappahannock, Burnside argued. Hence General Sumner, who had managed to build two bridges across

General Sumner and his staff before the Battle of Fredericksburg. From left to right ascending the stairs are First Lieutenant William G. Jones; Major Laurence Kip; Lt. Col. Joseph H. Taylor; General Edwin V. Sumner, on porch landing; Captain J.M. Garland, next to post, only head visible; Captain Samuel S. Sumner, against the post and standing on two steps, General Sumner's youngest child; unidentified officer, possibly Second Lieutenant Ranald S. McKenzie; and Lt. Col. William W. Teall, General Sumner's son-in-law. Massachusetts Commandery Military order of the Loyal Legion and the U.S. Army Military History Institute.

the Chickahominy six months earlier, was not permitted even to try to make a crossing.[3]

Still Sumner was criticized for remaining across the river from the virtually undefended city. The criticism shows how contemporary opinions oftentimes were based upon incomplete data. Artillerist Colonel Charles S. Wainwright faulted Sumner for the Union army's not being in possession of Fredericksburg. "From what I can learn," Wainwright wrote, "we are again indebted to the incapacity of General Sumner for not being in possession of Fredericksburg and the heights above it." Wainwright admitted Sumner had no pontoons, but believe that with an army of 30,000 he could have built a temporary bridge. "Sumner is very much blamed for his not acting at once as the possession of the heights would have saved us a fight at this point," Wainwright concluded.[4]

From New York on November 13, 1865, Ambrose E. Burnside wrote his report of the operations of the Army of the Potomac during the time of his command. Concerning General Sumner's wish to cross the Rappahannock before the pontoons arrived, Burnside wrote: "General Sumner, on arriving at Falmouth on the 17th, suggested crossing a portion of his force over the fords at that place, with a view to taking Fredericksburg; but from information in my possession as to the condition of the ford, I decided that it was impracticable to cross large bodies of troops at that place. It was afterwards ascertained that they could not have crossed."[5]

After the war Sumner's son-in-law Armistead L. Long wrote *Memoirs of Robert E. Lee: His Military and Personal History*, published in 1886. Long stated that it was General Burnside who ruled against Sumner's crossing the Rappahannock River: "On the 17th, Sumner's corps reached Fredericksburg. This energetic officer would probably have immediately crossed the Rappahannock by the fords above the town and thus have saved much delay. He was, however, restrained by Burnside, who directed him to await the arrival of the pontoons." Earlier Long had recorded the surprise among Confederate officers upon their learning that Burnside had been elevated to the command of the Army of the Potomac above "the distinguished merit of Sumner, Sedgwick, Meade, and others."[6]

General Sumner was dealing with the civil authorities of Fredericksburg, threatening to shell the town in retaliation for his troops being shelled from the city. Sumner demanded a reply by 5:00 P.M. that day, November 21, or he would begin shelling the town at 9:00 A.M. the next morning, the hours in between allowed for the evacuation of the townsfolk. The mayor replied that the time was insufficient, as was the 5:00 P.M. deadline for his reply. Based upon assurances from the mayor, Sumner replied that he would not fire on the town next morning.[7]

Colonel Teall, as was his habit, wrote to his wife and told the story from the Union side. General Patrick finally arrived around 7:00 P.M. and told his story. He crossed the river in a boat that morning about 10:30 under a flag of truce and was kept in a guard house. Patrick reported that the civil authorities were willing to comply with the Federal demands but General James Longstreet had arrived, assumed command, and forbidden the surrender. Teall wrote his wife the next day that a time extension had been granted to permit proper evacuation of the town.[8]

General Patrick recorded in his diary for Saturday night, November 22, that he had met generals Sumner and Burnside, who drew up a summons that the town was to surrender by 5:00 P.M., otherwise it would be shelled sixteen hours later. Patrick waved a white towel at the river bank and waited a long time before someone rowed across to ferry him to Fredericksburg. His summons was addressed to the mayor and council. It was not until 7:30 P.M. that Patrick got a reply, having seen Major G. Moxley Sorrel of Longstreet's staff in the meantime. When Patrick finally returned to the Union lines and reported, he learned that an agreement had been made and that Patrick should be at the Lacy house next morning at 9:00 to meet with the mayor and city authorities. The final agreement, as Patrick recorded in his diary, was to grant an extension until 11 o'clock the next day (which must have been Sunday, November 23, according to the dates in Patrick's diary) and "that the town will not be shelled until *she* fires etc, etc."[9]

The missing pontoons were a source of concern for Burnside. Even had they arrived as late as November 20, the army could have crossed with little opposition. Sumner would have had 33,000 men at Fredericksburg. But Confederate General James Longstreet arrived and took possession of the city before the pontoon trains arrived.[10]

Burnside and his generals considered various plans for placing pontoon bridges once they arrived. With General Lee's forces occupying the high-ground ridge beyond Fredericksburg, the proper placement of the bridges was critical. At last, almost in desperation, Burnside decided to place the bridges and construct crossings right in front of Fredericksburg proper.[11]

Not knowing it was General Burnside's order to place the pontoons in front of the town, Captain Thomas W. Osborn wrote to his brother Abraham, thinking it was General Sumner's decision. On December 11, 1862, Osborn wrote, "I cannot satisfactorily explain to myself why General Sumner laid his bridges just in front of the city where of necessity he must suffer from the fire of many sharpshooters and lose a good many men."[12]

Historian Frank O'Reilly wrote, "Burnside relied on Sumner as his confidant. Unfortunately, Sumner had limited mental capacity and an overwhelming desire to accommodate his superior."[13] Sumner's desire to accommodate and to follow the orders of his commanding general was well known. His crossing the Chickahominy on his wobbly bridge because he was ordered to is perhaps the clearest example of his commitment to following orders. Second Corps commander General Darius Couch noted how Sumner wanted to carry out everything Burnside suggested even when those suggestions went against his own judgment.[14]

Yet Sumner had reservations about Burnside's plan to lay pontoon bridges directly in front of the town. The engineers would be vulnerable to Confederate marksmen posted in the riverfront houses. Instead Sumner considered crossing below the town, guarding the bridgehead with artillery, and turning General Robert E. Lee's right flank by marching the entire army to fall on Lee's right flank. Attacking a flank with the entire army may have been an idea sparked in Sumner's "limited mental capacity" by his experience at Antietam. After all, Sumner knew something about being hit on the flank. Hitting the enemy's flank was Sumner's advice to Sedgwick back on the western plains.

There was serious dissension among General Burnside's subordinates against the plan to attack the enemy through the town of Fredericksburg. General Joseph Hooker denounced the plan, and there was almost unanimous disapproval among the corps and division commanders in Sumner's Right Grand Division.

By various means did Burnside and his staff work to obtain intelligence on Lee's operations across the Rappahannock River. Professor Thadeus S.C. Lowe used a balloon to ascend up to about 900 feet to make observations. General Sumner's son-in-law, Lieutenant Colonel William W. Teall, was assigned a special duty to find a spy willing to cross the river. Teall was authorized to spend the princely sum of $5,000 to encourage someone to take the risk. His efforts were in vain.[15]

On the night of December 9, 1862, General Sumner called a meeting of the commanders in his grand division down to the brigade level. The discussion was frank. When the commanding general, Burnside, learned of the meeting he called the same officers together the next evening at his headquarters. General Burnside was angry and particularly severe with General Winfield S. Hancock, a newly appointed division commander in the Second Corps. Hancock told Burnside he meant no discourtesy but thought it would be difficult to take the line of fortified heights across the river. Burnside said he had made his plan and all he wanted was for it to be carried out loyally. That plan was to cross in two columns, one at Fredericksburg and the other just below the town. One column would attack Marye's Heights and the other, crossing below the town, would attack the Confederate right. Burnside's meeting on December 10 enhanced no one's confidence in General Ambrose E. Burnside.[16]

Colonel Teall described the meeting in his letter of December 10:

> The morning was full of preparations for the advance. Three days' rations for the troops have been cooked and placed in their knapsacks. During the evening Genl Burnside came and met the genl officers of our Right Grand Division, the meeting lasting until 10:15.... Your father has determined to cross immediately in rear of his advanced guard, and his staff all feel that they are to march into the jaws of death itself. Time can never efface the impression they all gave me of their almost sure and certain destruction. But manfully they held up under it. Their gray-haired chieftain has spoken the word and like all true soldiers they are prepared to meet their approaching doom without murmur.[17]

General George G. Meade, a division commander in the First Corps of General Franklin's Left Grand Division, thought Burnside's problem with his subordinate generals was of his own making. It resulted from Burnside's frequent expressions of self-doubt. While Meade had genuine regard for Burnside, he told his wife he could not turn a blind eye to the fact that Burnside was not equal to the job. He was, Meade thought, "deficient in that enlarged mental capacity which is essential in a commander."[18]

Newspaperman Henry Villard remarked that despite Burnside's genial, frank, honest and sincere nature, he found nothing in the general that indicated intellectual eminence or executive ability. No experienced or judicious person, Villard believed, would take Burnside for a great man.[19]

When several of the engineer officers learned where the bridges were to be constructed, they concluded the time had come for them to write their last wills and testaments. The enemy was strongly posted on the opposite side of a river 400 feet wide where the bridges were to be placed. To attempt to lay a pontoon bridge right in their very faces seemed like madness, Wesley Brainerd of the 50th New York Volunteer Engineers Regiment thought.

Still these were the orders, and the orders had to be obeyed. Just before dark on December 10 the pontoon train began moving down to within a mile of the crossing sites and concealed themselves in a ravine out of sight of the Confederates.[20]

Wesley Brainerd described his interview with General Sumner the evening before the construction began and stated he had met Sumner at the Phillips House. It was after dark that Brainerd with Ira Spaulding visited Sumner. Colonel Teall's letter of November 20 states that General Sumner and his staff occupied the Phillips mansion. Sumner moved to the Lacy house on December 12, and it served as Sumner's headquarters during the battle.

Along with Major Ira Spaulding, Brainerd examined the crossing site, taking note of the landmarks so as not to be mistaken when the moon went down. Then they went to the Phillips House to see if General Sumner had any special orders for them. General Sumner received the two engineers "with a smile on his dear, frank old face and a hearty hand shake." Brainerd said the room from which Sumner came to address them was filled with officers receiving their final orders. "This was the last time my eyes ever beheld glorious old General Sumner."[21]

Clara Barton camped outside on the grounds of the Lacy House. She could hear "Bull" Sumner bellowing on December 11, because of the order from General Burnside forbidding him to cross the river. She spent much of that day in the Lacy House which the Second Corps medical director designated as a branch hospital.[22]

The engineers began the hard work of constructing the bridges Burnside's plan required by dragging the heavy pontoons, built like large flat-ended canoes, to the bank of the Rappahannock River as early as 3:00 A.M. the morning of December 11, 1862. The volunteer engineers of the 50th New York Regiment worked on the bridge opposite the town while the regular engineers built theirs more than a mile downstream. At 4:00 A.M. Burnside began writing attack orders for the grand divisions. Sumner and Hooker would cross into the city with the bulk of the army and attack Marye's Heights. Franklin would cross on the lower bridge to engage General Lee's right wing so those troops could not be shifted to add to the defenses on Marye's Heights. General Franklin was also to employ his men to turn the Confederate right, a maneuver Sumner suggested.[23]

The engineers who built the pontoon bridges played an important part in the battle of Fredericksburg. About 6:00 A.M. the ghostly forms of the engineers working on the bridges crossing the fog-shrouded Rappahannock River were distinct enough to be targets for Confederate general William Barksdale's Mississippi riflemen shooting from the riverfront houses. Major Ira Spaulding called it a "galling fire." A captain and two men were killed plus several others wounded.[24] To silence these marksmen Union artillery men moved their batteries to the river's edge and shelled the houses harboring the snipers. Captain Thomas W. Osborn described the shelling:

> The firing from 147 guns commenced this morning [December 11, 1862] at six o'clock, the immediate occasion being the enemy opening with musketry upon our men putting down the bridges. The enemy had taken shelter in the houses or were covered by the streets or other obstructions forming temporary shelter.
> When the enemy fired on our men, our batteries opened on the position held by the men and on the city. The firing was very rapid and continued until considerably after noon. It has been the most severe artillery fire I have seen. Judging from the fires in the city and its general appearance together with the number of shells thrown into it, the city must be nearly or quite ruined. Late in the afternoon by the aid of the partly finished bridges and the assistance of boats, a considerable force was put over the river and now occupies the city. It is said at Division Headquarters that General Hooker's Grand Division is crossing tonight. I presume this report is correct.
> It is possible a battle will be in progress tomorrow. At all events we may expect one very soon, and just now it looks as though heavy fighting was in the very near future.[25]

But sniping continued from the basements of the riverfront houses; the debris only adding to the snipers' defenses. They halted and interrupted the completion of the bridges. Finally Henry Hunt, although an artillery man himself, sent Union infantry across the river in pontoons as if they were war canoes to drive the Mississippians from their protective cellars in the bombarded houses. They were successful after numerous sharp encounters. Chasing away the troublesome snipers allowed the engineers to finish the bridges, and as evening approached, troops from two corps of Sumner's Right Grand Division crossed over and into the town, abandoned by its citizens.[26]

The failure of the Union artillery to silence the snipers was but one example of the limits of some of the batteries. The smoothbore cannons lacked the range and the elevation in some cases to reach the targets on Marye's Heights. The smoothbores in Lieutenant Edmund Kirby's Battery I, First U.S. Artillery, and Captain John D. Frank's Battery G, First New York Light Artillery, for example, achieved very little and made no impact. Frank's battery could not get sufficient elevation to reach the top of Marye's Heights and suffered from the Confederate rifled guns placed atop the heights. Artillery officer Tully McCrea wrote:

> On Saturday morning [December 13] the battle began and continued all day — the hardest fought, bloodiest, and most hotly contested of the war. We were kept back in one of the streets near the river until twelve o'clock, when we were ordered to the front. I supposed we were going to have a hand in the fight, but there was no suitable place for smooth-bore guns. We were placed at a street crossing to protect the retreat of our troops if it became necessary, which seemed probable several times.[27]

The day before, December 12, 1862, more troops had crossed on both of the bridges; Sumner's men went into town, Franklin's into the plain below the town. In fact the entire day of December 12 was used to cross these two grand divisions. The men carried three days' rations and sixty rounds of ammunition. They were backed up with a wagon train carrying twelve days' rations.[28]

The Yankees in town amused themselves by looting and vandalizing the unoccupied houses. Despite provost guards stationed at the bridges to prevent looters from carrying their ill-gotten booty back to camp, much personal property was stolen. What could not be stolen successfully was wantonly destroyed. Provost Marshal Marsena R. Patrick found some officers guilty of pillaging.[29]

Towards the end of September, Captain James Wren of Company B, 48th Pennsylvania Volunteers, received a promotion to major in the regiment. A coal miner before the war, he was a diamond in the rough and he spelled the way he pronounced the words he spoke. He kept a diary.

On December 12, 1862, at the "Frunt of Fredericksburg, Va.," Major Wren crossed with his division over the pontoon bridge that morning about 9:30. They were shelled but the rounds went over their heads. Everything in town was riddled with bullet holes, the fences were knocked down and there were few inhabitants. "Things in genrel looked bad in Appearance," Wren wrote. A chimney fell and wounded one man. Another died from his wounds when a second chimney fell on him. "He was Bruised all over, His Leg was broken in 2 places. We buried him in the rear of the Baptist Church near whear we war Quartered in the town," Major Wren recorded. His entry for the next day told of his part in the battle:

We suffered Considerable in going into Battle line owing to us having to Cross a plain, open field & right in range of the enemy guns. We war shelled fearfully.... Richard Brown, belonging to my old Co. B, 48th Lost one arm & Michael Divine was Cut right in 2 pieces with a shell & his insides Lay on the grass alongside him.... Ebey Thompson of Co. H 48th Pa. Vols. Shot with a Minie Ball in the mouth.[30]

The battle began on December 13, 1862. The initial assault was made by General George G. Meade's division of Franklin's Left Grand Division, supported on the right by John Gibbon's division. By taking advantage of a wooded swale the Confederates thought too difficult to get through and therefore left lightly defended, Meade's Pennsylvania Reserves penetrated the Confederate line as Meade had predicted. But as he also had said, his division would not be strong enough to hold his position, and the Pennsylvanians were forced to retreat as Confederate forces rallied. General Sumner's men waited until General Lee's troops on his right were fully engaged before advancing against Marye's Heights. From the Union perspective looking out towards the heights, it appeared to be an uninterrupted incline. What they could not see was a sunken road that ran at the base and for the length of the heights. A stone retaining wall held back the bank of earth on either side. The sunken road proved to be a perfect defensive position for Confederate infantry, and many Union soldiers would be killed and wounded as they attacked this formidable position. Twenty-five hundred men of General James Longstreet's infantry stood along this sunken road entrenchment. When Union general William French's men attacked they fell by the score, and no one got to within one hundred feet of it.[31]

"No men could have fought better or shown more bravery than did ours in these repeated charges," Captain Osborn wrote to his brother Spencer as he described the repeated attempts to attack the stone wall at the foot of Marye's Heights. Osborn believed the order for "such violent tactics" must have come directly from General Burnside. "We have no Grand Division, corps, or division commander, who would voluntarily slaughter his men as was done here. As rash as General Sumner is, he would not have continued this hopeless assault without specific instructions to do so."[32]

General Burnside had forbidden General Sumner from crossing the river himself. Sumner wanted to take control of the battle and worried about his men pinned down in front of the heights. To keep informed of the progress he had to rely on the messages provided by the telegraphs operated by the signal officers and from balloon observations. Operating the balloon was Thaddeus Lowe. His brother Percival G. Lowe had provided Sumner with invaluable service on the Cheyenne Expedition five years before. By noon on the 13th the wind became too strong for a long ascent, and Lowe had trouble controlling his airborne observation platform.

The stout-hearted Colonel Teall made several trips in Lowe's balloons. Unfortunately no experienced battlefield officer went up who was able to interpret what could be seen from 800 to 900 feet in the air. Sumner declared going up in Lowe's balloon to be more of a hazard than to march in front of the cannon's mouth. Teall also recorded in his December 13 letter about one of his trips with Professor Lowe, "The atmosphere was somewhat smoky but the view was beautiful. At 12:10 your father left for the Lacy house, designated by Genl Burnside as his headquarters during the battle, with all his staff except [Lt. Col. Charles G.] Sawtelle and myself."[33]

A witness recalled Sumner's impatience with his restriction on crossing the river personally to observe the battlefield firsthand. He habitually removed his false teeth when barking orders with his spectacles on his forehead. He paced to and fro in front of the Lacy House with one arm thrown around the neck of his son, Samuel, his face haggard with sorrow and anxiety.

General Burnside planned a renewed attack on General Lee's defensive positions for the next day, December 14. Sumner was instrumental in convincing General Burnside to call it off. In letters to both his wife and his father, General Orlando Willcox told of his meeting with Sumner, Burnside and others. Sumner requested Burnside to suspend the movement until the grand division and corps commanders could be consulted: "The boldest men, such as Sumner, deemed the case too critical for experiment."[34]

General John Gibbon was hit on his wrist by a shell fragment as his division supported General Meade's assault. After having his wound dressed he was taken to the Philips House where both generals Burnside and Sumner had their headquarters. "As I left the field," Gibbon wrote, "I could not help noticing the great number of unemployed troops in sight, and reflected how useful they *might* have been to us in the fight. But a subordinate seldom knows in battle anything beyond his own immediate orders." Gibbon went on to write that he had been placed in General Sumner's own room, "where the brave old soldier treated me with the gentleness of a woman."[35]

December 15 sparked renewed activity along the battle lines. The skirmishers were active, and both sides were constructing defensive earthworks. The artillery traded shots. General Burnside went to Sumner's headquarters very dejected. He had little appetite for breakfast. Sumner bolstered him with enough encouragement for Burnside to ride into Fredericksburg for a conference with his generals. No one suggested that the attack be renewed. A truce to recover the wounded that were still on the battlefield took hours to arrange. Representing the Federals during the truce was Captain Edwin V. Sumner, Jr. His Confederate counterpart was Lieutenant James Power Smith. The two men got along amiably, with Powers being the more reserved of the two. Though cautioned by their officers not to fraternize, relations between Billy Yank and Johnnie Reb were cooperative and in some cases even friendly.

It provided an opportunity for trading, and the Yanks got tobacco for coffee and sugar. When the truce ended both sides returned to their positions and resumed their warlike postures. A Carolina soldier reflected, "What a strange thing is war."[36]

Another truce was established, and the Union crossed in sufficient strength for a burial party on December 17 and 18. At the end all Union dead had been "buried" one way or another. The ground was frozen now and some graves were but a shallow trench.[37]

From a camp near Potomac Run, Virginia, Charles Francis Adams, Jr., an officer in the First Massachusetts Cavalry, wrote to his ambassador father on January 28, 1863. Of the aftermath from Fredericksburg he wrote, "The New York Herald may say what it pleases, but the Army of the Potomac is at present fearfully demoralized. Even I can see that, small means of observation as I have."[38]

Elizabeth Blair Lee was more hopeful that General Joseph Hooker might become the general the Union so sorely needed. In her letter to her husband, "Dear Phil," from her vantage point at Silver Spring, Maryland, on January 28, 1863, she penned: "Hookers appointment is the theme on the topis today — I find consolations in it — one is that — although Sumner & Franklin are both brave & good they are good soldiers— but are not poets or generals— so a turn in the wheel may as in lotteries turn up a General."[39]

Lieutenant Colonel Teall made several crossings to Fredericksburg under a flag of truce. On January 8, 1863, he escorted the Confederate widow of Captain Edward P. Lawton and Lawton's remains to the Confederate side of the Rappahannock. Lawton was mortally wounded on December 13. Teall won high acclaim from the Confederates for his conduct. On February 3 he wrote and told his wife of a conversation he had with two Confederate officers upon such a crossing:

> They said finally, "When, in God's name, will you let us go home? We are tired of this war and wish it were ended."
> "But," I replied, "how can we do that? The stability of the Northern government depends on our successfully repudiating the doctrine of secession. We must have no North, no South, no East or West — only one country. Nothing but your power to revolutionize our government, or your submission, can ever induce us to abandon the contest. There can be no compromise."[40]

Fredericksburg was the last campaign for General Sumner, the rugged old soldier. He was relieved of command along with Burnside with the statement in the order, "at his own request." Author Frank O'Reilly wrote that in fact neither Burnside nor Sumner asked to be relieved. But the order relieved Sumner from duty with the Army of the Potomac and Sumner was looking forward to commanding a military department.[41]

Captain Thomas Osborn believed General Hooker was behind it. Osborn believed Hooker had never forgiven Sumner for not helping him at Williamsburg. Once again rumors factored into Osborn's opinion. "There [at Williamsburg], he let General Hooker's division be cut to pieces while he was in easy helping distance with about 30,000 men," Osborn wrote. Again, that 30,000-men idea that was so commonly held by the Third Corps continued to cloud Sumner's reputation in some circles. Then Osborn went on with another unfounded accusation: "I am told by officers here that General Sumner was unnecessarily slow in going to General Hooker's assistance at the battle of Antietam."[42]

President Abraham Lincoln's General Order Number 20, which relieved General Sumner from the command of the Army of the Potomac, was issued on January 25, 1863. The next day the *Syracuse Journal* printed a brief statement that General Sumner having been relieved of his command was on his way home. The following day it printed the same news, adding that he had a leave for thirty days. On January 28 and again on January 31 the newspaper printed accounts of Sumner's relief from duty with the Army of the Potomac, his return to Syracuse and the group of his friends who met him at the station to escort him to his residence on Fayette Park. The *Syracuse Courier* carried the same item.

Between February 2 and March 14 the *Syracuse Journal* published brief items on Sumner's itinerary while at home in Syracuse. A dinner was held in his honor; his farewell address to his Right Grand Division was published. Announcements of his assuming command in the west were reported. Incidents of his character appeared in the press during his stay in Syracuse. On February 18 the *Journal* reported that Sumner had been called to Washington to preside at the trial of John S. Powell, an alleged spy.

On March 16 the paper reported that Sumner was about to start for St. Louis and that he had a severe cold and high fever. Still he was determined to leave that evening. The next day the paper reported on his condition, stating he had not left and continued to be suffering from a severe cold and fever. He would try to leave that evening, as he was anxious to return to duty, the paper noted. His condition did not improve and was so reported on March 18 in the *Journal.* On March 20, the day before he died, the paper reported on his condition: "The sickness of Gen. Sumner has developed into a severe attack of congestion of his lungs. He is closely confined to his room, and unable to sit up for any length of time."

News of General Edwin V. Sumner's death on March 21, 1863, along with testimonials to his forty-some years of service, appeared in all major Eastern newspapers. The *Syracuse Journal* published the details of the funeral and reprinted items from other newspapers as well. Sumner's remains lay in state at the Syracuse City Hall. Thousands came to pay their respects, the paper reported. Syracuse businesses were closed during the funeral hours and schools closed for the day. While the war prevented many of his fellow officers from attending the service, they sent their regrets and condolences. Two who did come were John C. Frémont and General Henry W. Slocum. John Sedgwick, Sumner's old and faithful lieutenant, participated in some of the ceremonies held throughout the Army of the Potomac in honor of General Sumner.[43]

The *Syracuse Journal* reported in its March 24 edition:

> The remains are enclosed in one of the Barstow metallic caskets. The body is dressed in the full uniform of a Major General. The features of the lamented dead are very natural, and all beholders are deeply impressed by their manly dignity and nobleness.
>
> The silver plate upon the casket bears the following inscription: "Major-General Edwin V. Sumner, U.S.A. Died March 21, 1863, Aged 67 years, 1 month and 23 days."

It is possible the paper got his age incorrect. He was born in 1797, so his years should have been 66 not 67. He was, however, in his sixty-seventh year. If the inscription was engraved exactly as the paper reported, then the error was buried and out of sight forever. The *Journal* went on to report that an elaborate canopy was erected over the remains composed of national flags, white and black cloth and evergreens. An American eagle surmounted the canopy and from its talons was suspended the last words of the patriot soldier, "God Save My Country, the United States of America!"

Epilogue

General Sumner's widow died at the home of her daughter Mrs. A.L. Long in Charlottesville, Virginia, on December 9, 1880, at seventy-five years of age. She was visiting her daughter, the postmistress of Charlottesville, for her health. Her remains were returned to Syracuse, New York, and buried with those of her husband.[1]

General Sumner's two sons, Edwin V. Sumner, Jr., and Samuel S. Sumner, survived the Civil War and had careers in the army. However, General Sumner's grandson was killed. An item in the *Syracuse Journal* dated May 2, 1863, announced the "at large" appointment by the president to the West Point Academy of one George Sumner Jenkins, a grandson of the late Major General Sumner. George may not have accepted the appointment. On November 3, 1864, the same *Journal* carried news of young Jenkins' death. Only seventeen, he may never have known his father, Leonidas Jenkins, who died of yellow fever in Mexico in 1847, the year George was born. Young Jenkins died on October 19, 1864, at New Bern, North Carolina, just one month after he joined the Third New York Artillery. As no fighting was reported at New Bern at the time of his death, it may have been accidental.[2]

Edwin V. Sumner, Jr., attained the rank of brigadier general. Born August 16, 1835, he died in San Francisco on August 25, 1912. During the Civil War he was appointed from the state of New York a second lieutenant in the First U.S. Cavalry. Later, in September 1864, he was appointed colonel of the First New York Mounted Rifles.

Following the Civil War, Sumner participated in the Indian wars against the Modocs, Nez Perce and Bannock tribes. He was a major in the Fifth U.S. Cavalry, lieutenant colonel in the Eighth Cavalry and colonel in the Seventh Cavalry to 1894. At the outbreak of the Spanish American War he was appointed brigadier general of volunteers. He retired from the army on March 30, 1899.

Sumner married Margaret Forster of Harrisburg, Pennsylvania, in 1866. He was survived by his brother Samuel S. Sumner and two daughters, Mrs. Edward King and Mrs. Carson.[3]

Samuel Storrow Sumner died at the age of ninety-five at his home in Brookline, Massachusetts, on July 26, 1937. He was a veteran of the Civil War, the Spanish American War, the Philippine Insurrection, the Boxer Rebellion and campaigns against the Indians. He was a former military attaché to Great Britain.

Samuel Sumner was born in Carlisle, Pennsylvania, on February 6, 1842. Privately educated, he received an appointment as second lieutenant in the Second Cavalry shortly after the outbreak of the Civil War. He married Frederika Bennett, who predeceased him on March 6, 1932.[4]

Following the Civil War, Samuel S. Sumner commanded Camp Bowie, Arizona, from 1873 to 1875. He took part in the Big Horn and Yellowstone Expedition. He received promotions to major, Eighth Cavalry, and lieutenant colonel, Sixth Cavalry. He retired for age on February 6, 1906.[5]

It was Brigadier General Samuel S. Sumner, acting as temporary replacement for General Joseph Wheeler, who marched the Rough Riders out to their charge on Kettle, better known as San Juan, Hill.[6]

Appendix

Item 1.

Secretary of War Jefferson Davis' instructions to Sumner in Kansas from Tony R. Mullis, "The Dispersal of the Topeka Legislature," in *Kansas History: A Journal of the Central Plains* 27 (Spring–Summer 2004): 65–66:

> If, therefore, the governor of the territory, finding the ordinary course of judicial proceedings and powers vested in the United States marshals inadequate for the suppression of insurrectionary combinations or armed resistance to the execution of the laws, should make requisition upon you to furnish a military force to aid him in the performance of that official duty, you are hereby directed to employ for that purpose such part of your command as may in your judgment consistently be detached from their ordinary duty.
>
> The question as to where the men may come from, or whether armed or unarmed, is not one for the inquiry or consideration of the commanding officer. It is only when armed resistance is offered to the laws and against peace and quiet of the territory, and when under such circumstances, a requisition for military force is made upon the commanding officer by the authority specified in his instructions, that he is empowered to act.

Item 2.

Private Robert M. Peck's description of the buffalo stampede from Robert Morris Peck, "Recollections of Early Times in Kansas Territory," in *Kansas State Historical Society*, KHC 8 (March 21, 1901): 488:

> As we approached the Big Bend, crossing the level stretch of eight miles between the Plum Buttes and the Arkansas river, with our beef herd and a train of about fifty six-mule teams strung out behind us, we had an exciting bit of experience in a buffalo stampede, a description of which may assist the reader to realize the immensity of the herds of these animals near the center of their range. This stampede might have resulted in a direful calamity to us but for the prompt

action of Captain Sturgis, who, having been in such a predicament before many times, knew just what to do and how to do it.

Item 3.

Stuart's letter to his wife Flora of June 1, 1857, a description of his wounding and recovery, in Stuart, James Ewell Brown Papers, 1850–1908, Mss 1 ST 923c2:

I found [Lunsford] Lomax in imminent danger from an Indian who was on foot & in the act of shooting him. I rushed to the rescue & succeeded in firing at him in time wounding him in his thigh he fired at me in return with an Allen's revolver but missed.

My shots were now exhausted, & I called on some men approaching to rush up with their pistols & kill him, they rushed up fired without hitting. About this time I observed [1st Lt. David S.] Stanley and [1st Lt. James B.] McIntyre close by, the former said, "Wait — I'll fetch him," dismounting from his horse so as to aim deliberately but in dismounting his pistol accidentally discharged the last load he had, he began however to snap the empty barrels at the Indian, who was walking deliberately up to him with his revolver pointed, I could not stand that but drawing my sabre rushed on the monster inflicting a severe wound across his hand that I think would have severed any other man's but simultaneous with that he fired his last barrel within a foot of me the ball taking effect in the center of the breast but by the mercy of God glancing to the left lodging near my left nipple but so far inside that it cannot be [felt?]

Here below is an excerpt from his letter of August 14.

A heavy fog envelopes us this morning and to our utter amazement & despair we find on starting that the *Pawnees are gone*, the rascals our sole dependence for guidance have deserted us in this thick fog when most needed. And all this is due to that stupid numbskull Foote who is no more fit for a separate command than a child six months old. He has been bullyragging & tormenting these Indians for the last week with his absurd notions getting mad with them because they cant [sic] understand English — mounting them one day & dismounting them the next — till they are completely disgusted & have cleared out. But by *his folly* we *all* suffer & the wounded particularly First Sergt McKeown are in great jeopardy.

Item 4.

General Winfield Scott's letter about guarding supply trains:

Head-Quarters of the Army

West Point, N.Y.
August 19, 1857

Sir: In forwarding, yesterday, the communication of General Harney respecting the loss of a large number of beef cattle for the Utah Expedition — on which paper I endorsed my remarks— I omitted to refer you to my instructions issued June 29th to the commander of that Expedition.

I now beg your attention to the extract, given below, from my letter, of that date, to General Harney, from which it will be seen that the loss in question has resulted from a neglect of my orders in the case.

(Extract) A small but sufficient, force must, however, move separately from the main column, guarding the beef cattle and such other supplies as you may think would too much encumber the march of the main body. The cattle may require to be moved more slowly than the troops, so as to arrive in Salt Lake Valley in good condition. Or they may not survive the inclemency or scanty sustenance of the winter.

This detachment, though afterwards to become the rear guard, may, it is hoped be put in route before the main body, to gain as much time as possible before the latter passes it.

Item 5.

General William S. Harney's letter criticizing Sumner's Cheyenne Expedition:

Head Quarters, Army for Utah

Fort Leavenworth, August 22nd, 1857

Colonel: I have the honor to enclose a copy of a communication from Colonel Sumner to the Commanding officer of Fort Kearney [sic] reporting an affair with the Cheyenne Indians on the 29th ultimo near Solomon's Fork of the Kansas River.

Also, a copy of a communication from Lieutenant Marshall of the 6th Infantry Commanding Fort Kearney reporting the loss, on the 2nd instant, of 824, head of beef cattle intended for the Army of Utah, in consequence of an attack of 150 Cheyenne Indians upon the party in charge.

Colonel Sumner's action took place some sixty or seventy miles south of Fort Kearney on the 29th of July — and the fact, that in four days after, 150 of these Indians attacked this cattle party within twenty-eight miles of Fort Kearney, shows they not only had no fear for their families from Colonel Sumner's Command, but that his action was not attended by any moral consequences. Colonel Sumner makes no mention of the number of killed & wounded of the Indians in his Engagement, which I judge to be small from the above facts & from private reports of the affair.

Colonel Sumner should have sent at least two companies of his mounted force to Fort Kearney, immediately after his action, to protect the millions of both public and private property upon that road, which is without a single mounted soldier from this to Fort Laramie; as I have stated before, Infantry is useless to pursue mounted Indians.

I am, Colonel, very respectfully, Your Obt Sevt,

> Wm S. Harney
> Colonel 2nd Dragoons & Bvt. Brig. General Commanding
> Lieut. Colonel L. Thomas
> Assistant Adjutant General Hd. Quarters of the Army
> West Point, New York

Item 6.

Sumner's order for expedition, 1860:

Expedition Ordered Against the Kiowas and Comanches
Saint Louis, Mo. April 3d, 1860

The four companies of the 1st Cavalry, at Fort Riley, under Major Sedgwick, and two companies of the 2nd Dragoons, at Fort Kearny, to be designated by the commanding officer of that post, will compose an expedition to operate against hostile Kiowas and Comanches. The Cavalry will march from Fort Riley on the 15th and the Dragoons from Fort Kearny on the 8th of May, for Pawnee Fork. They will marched well armed and carry with them an abundant supply of ammunition, a few necessary articles of clothing, and the equipment for the additional horses they will require. Besides two wagons to each company (including the company wagons) each command will be furnished with transportation for thirty days provisions—five-sevenths (5/7) of the meat rations to be fresh beef on the hoof.

Instructions for the conduct of the Expedition, beyond the Arkansas, will be furnished hereafter.

By order of Colonel E.V. Sumner

Item 7.

Lieutenant James W. Abert's description of butchering a buffalo, in Abert, *Expedition to the Southwest*, p. 58.

In shooting cows the hunter always selects the fattest in the band. In butchering them the skin is cut open on the back, and the meat on each side of the long spines of the vertebral column, termed the "fleece," is then removed, and the spines themselves, broken off close to the vertebra, form that part called the "hump ribs," a favorite part; then comes the "bass," just back of the neck, the side ribs, and tongue. The remainder is generally left to the wolves. Sometimes the large bones of the legs are brought in for the marrow, which, when roasted, is delicious; much resembling butter, and of a deep yellow color.

Item 8.

Recruiting Service for the Dragoons
Captain E.V. Sumner, First Dragoons, Superintendent,
stationed at Carlisle, PA.

	1839	1840	1841	1842
Boston, MA	15	0	58	88
New York, NY	220	329	264	149
Philadelphia, PA	1	87	60	0
Lancaster, PA	13	0	0	0
Carlisle, PA	38	48	21	20
Harrisburg, PA	10	19	0	0

	1839	1840	1841	1842
York, PA	6	3	0	0
Baltimore, MD	79	10	50	0

In 1842 the superintendent at Carlisle Barracks was listed as Major C. Werton, First Regiment of Dragoons. There is no listing for this officer in Heitman's Register. Statistics come from the Secretary of War Reports for 1839, p. 75; 1840, p. 48; 1841, p. 79; and 1842, p. 211.

Chapter Notes

Introduction

1. Crumb and Dhalle, *No Middle Ground*, 133–34; Crumb and Dhalle, *The Eleventh Corps*, 36; U.S. War Department, *The War of the Rebellion: A Compilation of the Official Records* (hereafter cited as *O.R.*), series 1, vol. 27, part 1, 375.

2. *O.R.*, series 1, vol. 48, part 1, 521, 524.

3. Palfrey, *Antietam and Fredericksburg*, 54; Harsh, *Taken at the Flood*, 3, 6–7.

4. O'Reilly, *Fredericksburg Campaign*, 24; Sears, *Landscape Turned Red*, 239; Hennessy, *Return to Bull Run*, 101.

5. Sears, *George B. McClellan*, 178.

6. Sears, *Landscape Turned Red*, 112.

7. Sears, *George B. McClellan*, 183.

8. Nevins, *A Diary of Battle*, 68.

9. Marvel, *Burnside*, 197–98.

10. Nevins, 84.

Chapter 1

1. Stuart, *Papers, 1850–1908*, Mss 1ST 923c2, letter March 21, 1863.

2. *O.R.*, series 2, part 5, 540.

3. A.L. Long, *Memoirs of Robert E. Lee*, 5; Heitman, *Historical Register*, vol. 1, 639.

4. Woodward, *Mary Chestnut*, 17n3, 59, 104–05; Laas, *Wartime Washington*, 232.

5. *O.R.*, s. 1, vol. 11, part 1, 763.

6. Malles, ed., *Bridge Building*, 69, 356n12; William J. Miller, "I Only Wait for the River," 52–53.

7. Howard, *Autobiography of Oliver Otis Howard*, vol. 1, 237.

8. Nevins, *A Diary of Battle*, 174.

9. Donald, *Charles Sumner*, 5; Vose, ed.,

Robert Vose and His Descendants, 75; Boatner, *Encyclopedia*, 1157.

10. Hale, *Milton Academy*, 217–18.

11. Storrow, "The North-West in 1817," 169–81; Morris, *Sword of the Border*, 12, 167, 217, 273; Heitman, *Historical Register*, vol. 1, 930; Ganoe, *The History of the United States Army*, 537.

12. Morris, *Sword of the Border*, 6, 15, 70, 169, 177, 262–63.

13. Bundy, *The Nature of Sacrifice*, 36–57.

14. Wilentz and Earle, eds., *Major Problems*, 284.

15. Paul E. Johnson, *The Early American Republic*, 143–44; Edwin Vose Sumner to Charles P. Sumner, January 11, 1833, Charles Pinckney Sumner Papers, Massachusetts Historical Society.

16. Hagan and Roberts, eds., *Against All Enemies*, 95.

17. Ibid., 87, 92, 93.

18. Eckert, *In War and Peace*, 95; Niven, *John C. Calhoun*, 90–91; Coit, *John C. Calhoun*, 91; Hagan and Roberts, eds., *Against All Enemies*, 92; Morris, *Sword of the Border*, 225.

19. Gallagher and Pigeon, eds., *Infantry Regiments*, 15; Elting, *Amateurs to Arms*, 285; Morris, *Sword of the Border*, 198.

20. Morris, *Sword of the Border*, 13–15, 26; Beach, *The United States Navy*, 117; T. Harry Williams, *The History of American Wars*, 109.

21. *Syracuse Journal*, December 10, 1880.

22. Appleton, *Record of the Descendants of William Sumner*, 102, entry 338.

Chapter 2

1. T. Williams, *The History of American Wars*, 140–41.

2. Elliott, *Winfield Scott*, 261.

3. Stanley, *E.V. Sumner*, 43, 47.

4. Donald, *Charles Sumner*, 5–6, 11.

5. Edwin Vose Sumner to Charles P. Sumner, January 11, 1833, Charles Pinckney Sumner Papers, Massachusetts Historical Society.

6. Ibid., April 2, 1836.

7. Donald, *Charles Sumner*, 8, 92n6; Blanchard, *Margaret Fuller*, 331, 332, 335; *The International Magazine of Literature, Arts and Science*, August 5, 1850, 174; Longfellow, *The Letters of Henry Wadsworth Longfellow*, vol. 3, 342.

8. Heitman, *Historical Register*, vol. 1, 344.

9. Gluckman, *United States Muskets*, 364–66.

10. William W. Long, *A Biography*, 7–11; Kearny, *General Philip Kearny*, 44.

11. *Daily National Intelligencer*, Washington, D.C., April 1, 1835, p. 3.

12. Appleton, *Record of Descendants of William Sumner*, 102; W. Long, *A Biography*, 14–17.

13. W. Long, *A Biography*, 20–22.

Chapter 3

1. Edwin Vose Sumner to Charles P. Sumner, May 13, 1838, Charles Pinckney Sumner Papers, Massachusetts Historical Society; Zuver, *A Short History of Carlisle Barracks*, 71; Tousey, *Military History of Carlisle*, 185.

2. Zuver, *A Short History*, 71; Pfanz, *Richard S. Ewell*, 29.

3. Wells, *Diary*, vol. 1, pp. 73, 87, 110; F. Williams, *Matthew Fontaine Maury*, 116, 144.

4. Wilkes, *Autobiography of Rear Admiral Charles Wilkes, U.S. Navy 1798–1877*, 554–56.

5. Wade, ed., *The Journals of Francis Parkman*, vol. 2, 406.

6. Edwin Vose Sumner to Charles P. Sumner, July 9, 1838, Charles Pinckney Sumner Papers, Massachusetts Historical Society.

7. Teall, *Papers, 1862–1864*, Nov. 9, 1862.

8. Elliott, *Winfield Scott*, 363–66.

9. Secretary of War Report, 1839, 62–63.

10. Kearny, *General Philip Kearny*, 45.

11. Pfanz, *Richard S. Ewell*, 28–30.

12. Stanley, *E.V. Sumner*, 101; Utley, *Frontiersmen in Blue*, 121n18.

13. Hamlin, *The Making of a Soldier*, 60–61; Pfanz, *Richard S. Ewell*, 50–52; Wilcox, *History of the Mexican War*, 296.

14. Tousey, *Military History of Carlisle*, 184.

15. Tousey, 187–88; Zuver, *A Short History*, 76.

16. Tousey, 187, 189.

17. Benét, *A Collection of Annual Reports*, vol. 1, 435–36, vol. 2, 380.

18. Benét, vol. 1, pp. 2, 5, 9, 380; Butler, *United States Firearms*, 141–42; Stockbridge, *Digest of U.S. Patents*, 40; Gluckman, *United States Muskets*, 260; Houze, *Colt*, 26–29; W.B. Edwards, *Civil War Guns*, 97.

19. Spiller et al., ed., *Dictionary of American Military Biography*, vol. 3, 914–15; Birkhimer, *Historical Sketches*, 55.

20. Secretary of War Report, 1839, 49; Secretary of War Report, 1840, 22; Hughes, *General William J. Hardee* 19.

21. "Carlisle Papers," Zuver, *A Short History*, 71.

Chapter 4

1. T. Williams, *History of American Wars*, 145; Merk, *Manifest Destiny and Mission in American History*, 24–25; Schlesinger, *The Age of Jackson*, 427–28.

2. Merk, 31, 46–47, 60.

3. T. Williams, *The History of American Wars*, 149; Remini, *Henry Clay*, 633–34; Borneman, *Polk*, xiii.

4. Borneman, xiii–xiv.

5. Robert R. Miller, *The Mexican War Journal and Letters of Ralph W. Kirkham*, xvi–xvii.

6. T. Williams, 173; Eisenhower, *Agent of Destiny*, 223, and *So Far from God*, map, inside book cover.

7. Kearny, *General Philip Kearny*, 113.

8. Bauer, *The Mexican War, 1846–1848*, 128–31; W. Long, *A Biography*, 39–41; Dawson, *Doniphan's Epic March*, 55.

9. Wilcox, *Mexican War*, 141–42.

10. Bauer, 138–39; Borneman, 240–41; Fleek, "The Mormon Battalion," 21–25.

11. Wilcox, 618; Elliott, *Winfield Scott*, 449–50; Eisenhower, *Agent of Destiny*, 235–36, 218–19, 227–29; Borneman, 255–56; Hutton, *Soldiers West*, 47.

12. Wilcox, 248–49; McCaffrey, "Surrounded by Dangers of All Kinds," 39.

13. Semmes, *Memoirs of Service Afloat*, 276–78.

14. Patterson, *From Blue to Gray*, 1; Wilcox, 634.

15. Wilcox, 117.

16. Ibid., 61–62.

17. Ibid., 62, 68.

18. Eisenhower, *So Far from God*, 253–54; Elliott, *Winfield Scott*, 452.

19. Elliott, 458–59; Eisenhower, *So Far from God*, 263–65; Wilcox, 255.

20. Wilcox, 255–57.

21. Ibid., 257.

22. W. Long, *A Biography*, 51, 53–54; Wilcox, 271.

23. Wilcox, 276.

24. Ibid., 284.

25. Utley, *Frontiersmen in Blue*, 121n18, photo caption 176; Woodworth, *Manifest Destinies*, 251; Timothy D. Johnson, *A Gallant Little Army*, 80.

26. George W. Curtis, ed., *Correspondence of John Sedgwick*, 88; Cress, *Dispatches from the Mexican War*, 211–12, 216, 234; *Scientific American*, June 5, 1847, 1; *New London Democrat*, New London, Connecticut, May 15, 1847, p. 1; *Daily National Intelligencer*, Washington, D.C., May 8, 1847, p. 3.

27. Maury, *Recollections of a Virginian*, 37; T. Johnson, *A Gallant Little Army*, 80–81.

28. Eckert and Amato, *Ten Years in the Saddle*, 68; F.L. Williams, *Matthew Fontaine Maury*, 87, 107, 166.

29. Wilcox, 297, 303, 313.

30. Ibid., 333–37.

31. Ibid., 338–39.

32. Ibid., 341.

33. Ibid., 358, 374.

34. R.R. Miller, *Mexican War Journal*, 47; T. Johnson, *A Gallant Little Army*, 158–59.

35. Wilcox, 380.

36. Freeman, *R.E. Lee*, vol. 1, 269.

37. Wilcox, 392; Pfanz, *Richard S. Ewell*, 55–56; Kearny, *General Philip Kearny*, 97–98.

38. Wilcox, 429–31.

39. Ibid., 431–32.

40. Ibid., 434–35; *Augusta Chronicle*, Augusta, Georgia, November 25, 1847, p. 1.

41. Wilcox, 434n440.

42. T. Johnson, *A Gallant Little Army*, 207.

43. Wilcox, 449.

44. Ibid., 446–47, 452.

45. Ibid., 514.

46. W. Long, *A Biography*, 64–67.

47. Ibid., 68–71.

Chapter 5

1. Utley, *Frontiersmen*, 28–30.

2. Ganoe, *History*, 230–31.

3. William C. Davis, *Jefferson Davis*, 235.

4. Utley, 54–57; Abert, *Expedition to the Southwest*, 16n23, 59.

5. Greiner, "Private Letters," May 12, 1851.

6. Ibid., 543.

7. Utley, 86–87; Faulk, *Crimson Desert*, 53; *New York Tribune*, May 6, 1851.

8. Greiner, 546.

9. Ibid., 549.

10. Ibid., 552–53.

11. Wetherington, "Cantonment Burgwin," 392–94.

12. "Preserved Meats and Meat Biscuit," *Scientific American*, March 20, 1852, 1; Kane, *Arctic Exploration*, 9.

13. Utley, 21n8, 89–90; *Alexandria Gazette*, Alexandria, Virginia, January 15, 1853, p. 2; *New York Tribune*, Jan. 10, 1853.

14. Dawson, *Doniphan's Epic March*, 101.

15. Utley, 86–88; Faulk, 56–57; Trafzer, "Politicos and Navajos," 11–12.

16. Trafzer, 10; Faulk, 54–55.

17. Wooster, *The Military and United States Indian Policy 1865–1903*, 7; Faulk, 148–49.

Chapter 6

1. McLaughlin, *Lewis Cass*, 238; Etcheson, *Bleeding Kansas*, 15; Goodwin, *Team of Rivals*, 123.

2. McLaughlin, 238; Etcheson, 15.

3. McLaughlin, 239; Remini, *At the Edge*, 7–8.

4. Etcheson, 14; William C. Davis, *Jefferson Davis*, 246.

5. Etcheson, 4, 18–19, 52; Bundy, *The Nature of Sacrifice*, 115–16.

6. Etcheson, 51–52; William C. Davis, 249.

7. W. Long, *A Biography*, 114.

8. Ibid., 121.

9. Field, *Memories*, 243–46.

10. Niven, *Salmon P. Chase*, 365; Hart, *Salmon P. Chase*, 315. Maunsell B. Field (1822–1875) was the assistant to the secretary of the treasury from 1861 to 1865. His failure to be appointed to a position endorsed by Treasury Secretary Salmon P. Chase was a cause of Chase's departure from Lincoln's Cabinet.

11. Etcheson, 69; Holt, *Franklin Pierce*, 107.

12. D. Ball, "Scapegoat?" 164–83; *Daily National Intelligencer*, Washington, D.C., Feb. 20, 1856, p. 2.

13. Mullis, "The Dispersal of the Topeka Legislature," 65; *Syracuse Daily Journal*, Feb. 21, 1856.

14. *Alexandria Gazette*, Alexandria, Va., Feb. 20, 1856, p. 2.

15. Mullis, 66.

16. Nichols, *Franklin Pierce*, 473.

17. D. Ball, 175; *New York Tribune*, July 10, 1856.

18. Mullis, 69; Govan and Livingwood, *Joseph E. Johnston, C.S.A.*, 21.

19. D. Ball, 184; Villard, *John Brown*, 217–19; Stampp, *America in 1857*, 4–5.

20. D. Ball, 180–81; Crist et al., *The Papers of Jefferson Davis*, vol. 6, 43–44; Nichols, 478.

21. D. Ball, 183; Crist et al., vol. 6, 170–71; Hughes, *General William J. Hardee*, 60n40; William C. Davis, *Jefferson Davis*, 54, 241, 261.

22. D. Ball, 170.

23. Six White Horses, "J.E.B. Stuart Papers," http://6whitehorses.com/cw/jebs/letters_lizzie peirce_june6_1856.html.

24. Etcheson, 107–111; Oates, *To Purge This Land with Blood*, 133–37; Villard, 148–188.

25. Villard, 169.

26. Ibid., 170.

27. Villard, 170; Meyer, *The Magnificent Activist*, 23.

28. Villard, 170–71; *Alexandria (Virginia) Gazette*, June 16, 1856, p. 2.

29. Oates, *Purge*, 155–56; Etcheson, 115; *Cleveland (Ohio) Plain Dealer*, June 16, 1856, p. 2.

30. Villard, 208–09.

31. *Cleveland Plain Dealer*, June 16, 1856, p. 2.

32. Villard, 209.

33. Ellicott and Andrews, "The Chronology," 86.

Chapter 7

1. Herr and Wallace, *The Story of the U.S. Cavalry 1775–1942*, 73–76; Weigley, *History of the United States Army*, 190; Freeman, *R.E. Lee*, vol. 1, 360–61; Roland, *Albert Sidney Johnston*, 170–71; Heitman, *Historical Register*, vol. 1, 405; Davis, *Jefferson Davis*, 359.

2. Lee, *General Lee*, 63.

3. Appleton, *Record of Descendants*, 102; Heitman, *Historical Register* 572; Wilcox, *Mexican War*, 617. Appleton's report of the location of Fort Atkinson as being in Iowa is incorrect. The fort was in what would become Wisconsin. Sumner was stationed there when his daughter married (see chapter 3).

4. W. Long, *A Biography*, 123–24; Livingston, *War Horse*, 15, 43–44.

5. Crist et al., *Papers*, vol. 6, 55–56; Tate, *From Under Iron Eyelids*, 41–47, 74–75; Tate, *Col. Frank Huger, C.S.A.*, 23.

6. Utley, *Frontiersmen*, 113.

7. Utley, 113–14; Finerty, *Warpath and Bivouac*, xviii.

8. Utley, 114–15.

9. Phipps and Peterson, "The Devil's To Pay," 15–16; Utley, *Frontiersmen*, 116–17; Taylor, *Gouverneur Kemble Warren*, 21–26.

10. W. Long, *A Biography*, 132–34.

Chapter 8

1. Chalfant, *Cheyennes and Horse Soldiers*, 12–14; Finerty, *Warpath*, xvii.

2. Chalfant, 25–26.

3. Ibid., 59–62.

4. Seabrook, "Expedition of Col. E.V. Sumner," 309.

5. Chalfant, 62–63; Peck, "Recollections," 486.

6. Schaff, *The Spirit of Old West Point*, 121–23.

7. Chalfant, 320.

8. Gluckman, *United States Muskets*, 390–91; W.B. Edwards, *Civil War Guns*, 119.

9. Peck, 485; Chalfant, 318–322; Heitman, *Historical Register*, vol. 1, 922.

10. Chalfant, 66.

11. Ibid., 323.

12. Peck, 484.

13. Chalfant, 164.

14. Peck, 485–86.

15. Rafuse, *McClellan's War*, 61; Sears, *George B. McClellan*, 44; Crist et al., *Papers*, vol. 5, 125n3.

16. Chalfant, 66–67; Peck, 486.

17. Chalfant, 72, 172; *Syracuse Daily Journal*, July 17, 1861.

18. Chalfant, 64–65.

Chapter 9

1. Chalfant, *Cheyennes*, 71–72; E. Long, "Journals of the Cheyenne Expedition"; *New York Tribune*, June 12 and 16, 1857.

2. Chalfant, 72–73; E. Long, "Journals," May 27.

3. Peck, "Recollections," 487.

4. Chalfant, 104–05; Lowe, *Five Years a Dragoon*,185–86.

5. Chalfant, *Cheyennes*, 103.

Chapter 10

1. Lowe, *Five Years a Dragoon*, 167–68.

2. Stuart, *Papers*, June 1, 1857.

3. Chalfant, 110–11.

4. E. Long, "Journals," May 29; Schlissel, *Women's Diaries of the Western Journey*, 177; Bandel, *Frontier Life in the Army*, 228; Abert, *Expedition*, 96.

5. Gibbon, *Adventures on the Western Frontier*, 13–14.

6. Custer, *My Life on the Plains*, 82; Scott, ed., *The Memoirs, Journals, and Civil War Letters of Orlando B. Willcox*, 145.

7. Scott, 63; Abert, *Expedition*, 77.

8. Abert, *Expedition*, 58–59.

9. E. Long, May 29.

10. Peck, "Recollections," 488.

11. Chalfant, 79–80.

12. E. Long, May 30.

13. Dodge, *The Plains of North America*, 147; Russell, *Firearms, Traps and Tools of the Mountain Man*, 214; Fehrenbach, *Commanches: The Destruction of a People*, 104–05; Hebard and

Brininstool, *The Bozeman Trail*, vol. 2, 260; Holmes, *Covered Wagon Women*, 262.

14. Wade, ed., *The Journals of Francis Parkman*, vol. 2, 434, 476–77.

15. Scott, 163.

16. Schlissel, *Women's Diaries*, 167, 176.

17. Schlissel, 177; Abert, *Expedition*, 58.

18. Peck, "Recollections," 488.

19. E. Long, May 31–June 6.

20. Peck, 488–89; Faulk, *Crimson Desert*, 161; Wooster, *Military*, 139.

21. Bandel, 79, 201–02; Abert, *Expedition*, 58.

22. Lowe, 185–87.

23. Ibid., 44–45.

24. Ibid., 187–89.

25. Lowe, 189–90; Schlissel, 223.

26. E. Long, June 20, 21.

27. Lowe, 197–99; Chalfant, 124–26; Peck, 493.

28. Rhea, *The Battle for Spotsylvania Court House*, 260–61.

29. Grinnell, *The Fighting Cheyennes*, 107–09; Hyde, *The Life of George Bent*, 100–01.

30. Grinnell, 109.

31. Hyde, *The Life of George Bent*, 102.

32. Grinnell, 112; Hyde, 102–03.

33. Monnett, *The Battle of Beecher Island*, 46–47; Grinnell, 205, 276; Hyde, 336.

34. Monnett, 47, 150.

Chapter 11

1. Peck, "Recollections," 493; E. Long, "Journals," July 4.

2. Lowe, *Five Years a Dragoon*, 199.

3. Chalfant, *Cheyennes*, 128–30.

4. Lowe, 199–200.

5. Peck, 492.

6. E. Long, May 30; Arnold, *Jeff Davis's Own*, 223.

7. Scott, *Memoirs*, 159.

8. Chalfant, 226.

9. Finerty, *Warpath*, 117; Robinson, ed., *Diaries*, vol. 1, 325.

10. Stuart, *Papers*, July 30, 1857.

11. Lowe, 199; Chalfant, 128.

12. Schlissel, *Women's Diaries*, 49, 106, 153, 223.

13. Peck, 494; Chalfant, 132–35; Lowe, 201–02.

14. Lowe, 202–03.

15. Peck, 494.

16. *Alexandria (Virginia) Gazette*, July 13, 1857, p. 2, and July 14, 1857, p. 2.

17. Chalfant, 143; Stuart, *Papers*, diary entries for July 17–21.

18. Chalfant, 141, 143–44.

19. Ibid., 152–53.

20. Peck, 494; Chalfant, 152–53; Scott, 150, Stuart, *Papers*, diary entry for July 24.

21. Chalfant, 157.

22. Scott, 153; E. Long, July 28.

23. Chalfant, 180–81; Grinnell, *Fighting Cheyennes*, 117.

24. E. Long, July 29.

25. Peck, 495.

26. Seabrook, "Expedition of Col. E.V. Sumner," 311.

27. Grinnell, 117; Peck, 496; E. Long, July 29.

28. Peck, 496.

29. Ibid., 497.

30. Ibid.

31. Grinnell, 112.

32. Cooke, *The 1862 U.S. Cavalry Tactics*, 53, 56.

33. Hyde, *The Life of George Bent*, 103.

34. E. Long, July 29.

35. Peck, 497–98.

36. E. Long, July 29; Chalfant, 195–97.

37. Stuart, *Papers*, July 30.

38. Ibid.

39 Grinnell, 115; Peck, 498.

40. Peck, 498.

41. Chalfant, 197–98.

42. Roy, "Un Quebecois Dans L'Armee Des Etats-Unis," 13, translation by author.

43. Peck, 498–99.

44. Chalfant, 202–03.

45. Stuart, *Papers*, July 30.

46. McAulay, *Civil War Pistols*, 15; Greener, *The Gun and Its Development*, 524; Chapel, *U.S. Martial and Semi-Martial Single-Shot Pistols*, 236.

47. Peck, 499.

48. Ibid., 500–01.

49. Ibid., 502.

50. Bandel, *Frontier Life in the Army*, 180.

51. Stuart, *Papers*.

52. Peck, 503–04.

53. McConnell, *Remember Reno*, 24–29; Roland, *Albert Sidney Johnston*, 185–214.

54. Peck, 504–07.

55. *New York Tribune*, December 14 and 19, 1857.

56. Hughes, *General William J. Hardee*, 60n40; Roland, 211.

Chapter 12

1. Roland, *Albert Sidney Johnston*, 188–89; McConnell, *Remember Reno*, 24–27.

2. Hafer, *Relations with the Indians of the Plains*, 142–43.

3. Hafer, 146–47.

4. Ibid., 192–93.

5. Ibid., 195–98.

6. Ibid., 199–200.
7. Ibid., 205–06.
8. Ibid., 245–46.
9. Ibid., 249–54.
10. Ibid., 257–58.
11. Ibid., 260–61.
12. Paraphrased from Shakespeare, *Richard III*, act 1, scene 1.
13. Hafer, 269, 277–79.

Chapter 13

1. Dell, *Lincoln and the War Democrats,* 70n18, 109, 384.
2. Edwin Vose Sumner, *Papers*, December 17, 1860, Onondaga Historical Association, Syracuse, NY.
3. De Borchgrave, *Villard,* 134; Teall, *Papers*, December 7, 1862.
4. Donald, *Lincoln,* 273, 277–78; Elliott, *Winfield Scott,* 694–95; Holzer and Symonds, eds., *New York Times Complete Civil War,* 59, 63; Howard, *Autobiography,* vol. 1, 180–81.
5. Mrs. Sara Sumner Teall, "Recollections of Mr. Lincoln's First Inauguration," March 4, 1913, Onondaga Historical Association, Syracuse, NY, 1915, 76–81.
6. *O.R.,* s. 1, vol. 50, part 1, 455.
7. Roland, *Albert Sidney Johnston,* 249; *O.R.,* s. 1, vol. 50, part 1, 471; G.T. Edwards, "Holding the Far West for the Union: the Army in 1861," 313; Robert U. Johnson, ed., *Battles and Leaders,* vol. 1, 599.
8. Roland, 241–42; *O.R.,* s. 1, vol. 50, part 1, 433.
9. Chandler, "The Velvet Glove," 35; Goldman, "Southern Sympathy in Southern California, 1860–1865," 577.
10. Chandler, 36.
11. *O.R.,* s. 1, vol. 50, part 1, 434, 444, 463; Tate, *Iron Eyelids,* xiv, 46, 49; R. Ball, *Springfield Armory,* 60. Marion V. Armstrong Jr. gives the number at 67,673 (Armstrong, *Unfurl Those Colors!* 38).
12. G.T. Edwards, 308; Roland, 241–42.
13. G.T. Edwards, 313.
14. Roland, 249; *O.R.,* s. 1, vol. 50, part 1, 463–64; Johnson and Buel, eds., *Battles and Leaders,* vol. 1, 540–41.
15. Johnson and Buel, vol. 1, 541; *O.R.,* s. 1, vol. 50, part 1, 666.
16. *O.R.,* s. 1, vol. 50, part 1, 471–02, 506.
17. Ibid., 474.
18. Dell, *War Democrats,* 198; Jordan, *Winfield Scott Hancock,* 24; Tucker, *Hancock the Superb,* 50.
19. *O.R.,* s. 1, vol. 50, part 1, 664–65.
20. Ibid., 487–88, 496.
21. Ibid., 481–82, 493–94, 501, 664.

22. G.T. Edwards, 321; Johnson and Buel, vol. 2, 103–04; *Syracuse Standard,* July 15 and 16, 1856, and April 30, 1873.
23. *O.R.,* s. 1, vol. 50, part 1, 614–15.
24. Ibid., 512, 593 94, 643.
25. Ibid., 605, 610, 620.
26. Ibid., 621.
27. Ibid., 607–09.
28. Ibid., 643, 645.
29. Ibid., 666–68.
30. Examples of the concerns of these residents who felt insecure and abandoned by their government can be found in the *O.R.,* s. 1, vol. 50, part 1, 658, 665–66.
31. *O.R.,* s. 1, vol. 9, 594.
32. G.T. Edwards, 323; *O.R.,* s. 1, vol. 50, part 1, 598–99, 603, 614–15.
33. *Sacramento Union.*

Chapter 14

1. Sparks, ed., *Inside Lincoln's Army,* 29; Sears, *The Civil War Papers of George B. McClellan,* 136; Nevins, *A Diary of Battle,* 84.
2. Howard, *Autobiography,* vol. 1, 181, 190–91.
3. *O.R.,* s. 1, vol. 5, 720; Howard, *Autobiography,* vol. 1, 194.
4. Walker, *History of the Second Army Corps,* 3–5.
5. Webb, *The Peninsula,* 13–14.
6. Ibid., 23 note.
7. Ibid., 27.
8. Ibid., 32–34.
9. Goss, *Recollections of a Private,* 29.
10. Ibid., 34, 35, 37.
11. Ibid., 38.
12. De Trobriand, *Four Years with the Army of the Potomac,* 190–91; Johnson and Buel, eds., *Battles and Leaders,* vol. 2, 201.
13. Wolseley, "An English View," 36.
14. Walker, *History,* 15–16; Johnson and Buel, vol. 2, 194.
15. Webb, 66, 68.
16. Webb, 69–71; Walker, *History,* 16, Stine, *History of the Army of the Potomac,* 49–52.
17. Nevins, *A Diary of Battle,* 58.
18. Goss, *Recollections of a Private,* 38–39.
19. Webb, 73–74; Nevins, *A Diary of Battle,* 57n; Broadwater, *The Battle of Fair Oaks,* 65.
20. Webb, 74–76.
21. Kearny, *General Philip Kearny,* 208, 217.
22. Crumb and Dhalle, *No Middle Ground,* 32–34.
23. *O.R.,* s. 1, vol. 11, part 1, 520–22; De Trobriand, *Four Years,* 191–93.
24. De Trobriand, 191–93.
25. Ibid., 195.
26. De Trobriand, 198–99; Styple, ed., *Our*

Noble Blood, 50–53; *O.R.,* s. 1, vol. 11, part 1, 464–68.

27. Webb, 77.

28. Walker, *History of the Second Army Corps,* 17; *O.R.,* s. 1, vol. 11, part 1, 533; Webb, 194.

29. Jordan, *Winfield Scott Hancock,* 93–94; Tucker, *Hancock the Superb,* 82–83.

30. Jordan, 44–45; Freeman, *Lee's Lieutenants,* vol. 1, 188–89; Kearny, *General Philip Kearny,* 211–12.

31. Longstreet, *From Manassas to Appomattox,* 77–78.

32. *O.R.,* s. 1, vol. 11, part 1, 538, 547–48.

33. Ibid., 451–52.

34. De Trobriand, 201.

35. De Trobriand, 202; Sears, *The Civil War Papers of George B. McClellan,* 256.

36. De Trobriand,, 210.

37. Sears, *Civil War Papers,* 254–58.

38. Webb, 73–74, 81, 83.

39. *O.R.,* s. 1, vol. 11, part 1, 452.

40. Ibid., 451, 453.

41. Ibid., 547–48.

42. Ibid., 464.

43. Ibid., 464–69.

44. Ibid.

45. Ibid, 468.

46. U.S. Congress Joint Committee on the Conduct of the War, *Army of the Potomac,* vol. 1, 577; Tap, *Over Lincoln's Shoulder,* 2.

47. U.S. Congress Joint Committee on the Conduct of the War, *Army of the Potomac,* vol. 1, 361–62.

48. Ibid., 19.

49. *O.R.,* s. 1, vol. 11, part 1, 450.

50. *O.R.,* s. 1, vol. 11, part 1, 452; Webb, 72.

51. Gibbon, *Personal Recollections of the Civil War,* 21.

52. Powell, *The Fifth Army Corps,* 25–26.

53. Sears, *George B. McClellan,* 44–45; Rafuse, *McClellan's War,* 61–62.

54. Walker, *History,* 10–11.

Chapter 15

1. Webb, *The Peninsula,,* 83; Johnson and Buel, eds., *Battles and Leaders,* vol. 2, 220; Davis et al., *Atlas,* plate xvii.

2. Johnson and Buel, vol. 2, 211.

3. Walker, *History,* 20.

4. Duane, *Manual for Engineer Troops,* 14.

5. Malles, *Bridge Building in Wartime,* 69; Goss, *Recollections of a Private,* 48.

6. Howard, *Autobiography,* vol. 1, 228–29.

7. Howard, *Autobiography,* vol. 1, 230–35; Webb, 100–110.

8. Bruce, *The Twentieth Regiment of Massachusetts Volunteer Infantry 1861–1865,* 92–94; Howard, *Autobiography,* vol. 1, 235–39.

9. Howard, *Autobiography,* vol. 1, 236–37.

10. Ibid., 237.

11. Bruce, *The Twentieth Regiment,* 94–95.

12. *O.R.,* s. 1, vol. 11, part 1, 808, 801–02, 804–05.

13. Howard, *Autobiography,* 237–38.

14. *O.R.,* s. 1, vol. 11, part 1, 75.

15. *O.R.,* s. 1, vol. 11, part 1, 794.

16. Ibid., 763–64.

17. *O.R.,* s. 1, vol. 11, part 1, 879; Bates, *History of Pennsylvania Volunteers,* vol. 1, 954.

18. *O.R.,* s. 1, vol. 11, part 1, 903.

19. Ibid., 881.

20. Ibid., 904.

21. French et al., *Instruction for Field Artillery,* 12; Gibbon, *The Artillerist's Manual,* 147; Benton, *Ordnance and Gunnery,* 82; Crary, *Dear Belle,* 176.

22. *O.R.,* s. 1, vol. 11, part 1, 884.

23. Ibid., 886.

24. Ibid., 881.

25. Walker, *History,* 35–37.

26. Ibid.

27. Bruce, 97–98.

28. Ibid.

29. *O.R.,* s. 1, vol. 11, part 1, 805; Bates, vol. 2, 1203–04; *Harper's New Monthly Magazine* 25 (July 1862): 261.

30. *O.R.,* s. 1, vol. 11, part 1, 810.

31. Laas, *Wartime Washington,* 155.

32. Govan and Livingwood, *A Different Valor,* 156; Alexander, *Military Memoirs,* 87.

33. Bruce, 102–03; Webb, 118–19.

34. Dowdey and Manarin, eds., *The Wartime Papers of R.E. Lee,* 184–85; Rafuse, *McClellan's War,* 270.

35. Bates, vol. 1, 539–40.

36. Kreiser, "7 Days That Made Robert E. Lee an Icon," 50–55; N.M. Curtis, *From Bull Run to Chancellorsville,* 132–34.

37. Walker, *History,* 54; Davis et al., *Atlas,* plate XVII.

38. *O.R.,* s. 1, vol. 11, part 2, 388; McCall, *Letters from the Frontiers,* xxvi–xxvii, Goss, 57–58; Webb, 135.

39. Crumb and Dhalle, *No Middle Ground,* 73–77.

40. Goss, 60–61.

41. Crumb and Dhalle, 78.

42. Webb, 137–39; Walker, *History,* 22.

43. *O.R.,* s. 1, vol. 11, part 2, 50–51; Cullen, *The Peninsula Campaign 1862,* 135–36, 142–43.

44. R. Cleaver, "Blunting the Confederate Onslaught," 24.

45. Freeman, *R.E. Lee,* vol. 2, 201; McCall, xxvii.

46. *O.R.,* s. 1, vol. 11, part 2, 49–52.

47. Johnson and Buel, eds., *Battles and Leaders,* vol. 2, 416–17; Alexander, *Military Memoirs,* 123, 161–63.

48. *O.R.*, s. 1, vol. 51, part 1, 716.
49. Oates, *A Woman of Valor*, 102.
50. Welcher, *The Union Army, 1861–1865*, 315; Hennessy, *Return to Bull Run*, 240.
51. *O.R.*, s. 1, vol. 19, part 2, 381.
52. A.L. Long, *Memoirs of Robert E. Lee*, 542–43.

Chapter 16

1. A.L. Long, *Memoirs of Robert E. Lee*, 516–17.
2. Armstrong, *Unfurl Those Colors!*, 145.
3. *O.R.*, s. 1, vol. 19, part 1, 275; vol. 51, part 1, 839; Sears, *Landscape Turned Red*, 240; Johnson and Buel, eds., *Battles and Leaders*, vol. 2, 631, 635; Wise, *The Long Arm of Lee*, 284–85; Gary Gallagher, ed., *Fighting for the Confederacy*, 500–01; Parrott, *Ranges of Parrott Guns*, 12–13, 24.
4. Armstrong, *Unfurl Those Colors!*, 158–59.
5. *O.R.*, s. 1, vol. 19, part 1, 30; Armstrong, "A Failure of Command?" 74.
6. Rafuse, *McClellan's War*, 310.
7. Rafuse, 308–10.
8. Armstrong, *Unfurl Those Colors!*, 165.
9. Harsh, *Taken at the Flood*, 272–73; Armstrong, "A Failure of Command?" 75–76.
10. Sears, *George B. McClellan*, 305; Murfin, *The Gleam of Bayonets*, 277.
11. Johnson and Buel, eds., *Battles and Leaders*, vol. 2, 598; Bundy, *The Nature of Sacrifice*, 223–24; Armstrong, *Unfurl Those Colors!*, 160.
12. Harsh, *Taken at the Flood*, 385, 396; Rafuse, 309.
13. Armstrong, *Unfurl Those Colors!*, 167.
14. Stine, *History of the Army of the Potomac*, 209–10; Johnson and Buel, vol. 2, 639.
15. Nosworthy, *The Bloody Crucible of Courage*, 228, 401.
16. A. Williams, *From the Cannon's Mouth*, 131.
17. Ibid., 135.
18. Woodworth, *Leadership and Command*, 83, 115–16.
19. Sears, *George B. McClellan*, 309–10.
20. *O.R.*, s. 1, vol. 19, part 1, 476–77.
21. A. Williams, 135.
22. United States Congress Joint Committee on the Conduct of the War, *Army of the Potomac*, vol. 1, "Report of the Joint Committee on the Conduct of the War," 368.
23. S.S. Sumner, "The Antietam Campaign," 10.
24. Woodworth, *Leadership and Command*, 84; Johnson and Buel, vol. 2, 598; Armstrong, *Unfurl Those Colors!*, 171–72.

25. Johnson and Buel, vol. 2, 640–42; Harsh, *Taken at the Flood*, 377.
26. Woodworth, *Leadership and Command*, 85–86; Harsh, *Taken at the Flood*, 386; Johnson and Buel, vol. 2, 640, 643; Alexander, *Military Memoirs*, 256–58.
27. General French's report, *O.R.*, s. 1, vol. 19, part 1, 323–24.
28. Harsh, *Taken at the Flood*, 406–07.
29. The best artillery shot Longstreet witnessed up to the time of Antietam was at Yorktown. "There a Federal officer came out in front of our lines," Longstreet wrote. The Yankee sat at a small table, evidently preparing to make a map. A Confederate officer sighted a gun and dropped a shell onto the table killing the officer (*Battles and Leaders*, vol. 2, 671).
30. Johnson and Buel, vol. 2, 671; Freeman, *R.E. Lee*, vol. 2, 391–92.
31. Gibbon, *Recollections*, 87–89, Gibbon, *Adventures on the Western Frontier*, 5, 15.
32. Gibbon, 83, 89; Sears, *Landscape Turned Red*, 221–22.
33. Johnson and Anderson, *Artillery Hell*, 54.
34. Armstrong, *Unfurl Those Colors!* 180; Wert, "Disaster in the West Woods," 38.
35. Woodworth, *Leadership and Command*, 90.
36. *O.R.*, s. 1, vol. 19, part 1, 321–13; Ellis, *Sharpshooters*, 43; Bilby, "Small Arms at Antietam," 55; Yee, *Sharpshooters*, 190.
37. *O.R.*, s. 1, vol. 19, part 1, 311; Wert, 35.
38. *O.R.*, s. 1, vol. 19, part 1, 316.
39. *O.R.*, s. 1, vol. 19, part 1, 316; Harsh, *Taken at the Flood*, 391–92.
40. *O.R.*, s. 1, vol. 19, part 1, 313.
41. Marion V. Armstrong, Jr., and a Parks Service Ranger both told this author of a letter in the National Archives from General Sumner to his wife following the battle. He said he was hoarse from shouting for several days. Interview on the Antietam Battlefield, July 27 and 28, 2012.
42. Bates, *History of Pennsylvania Volunteers*, vol. 2, 701, 794, 831.
43. Howard, *Autobiography*, vol. 1, 296–97.
44. Woodworth, *Leadership and Command*, 97; Sears, *Landscape Turned Red*, 251.
45. Rafuse, 317.
46. Sully, *No Tears for the General*, 154–55.
47. Armstrong, *Unfurl Those Colors!* 190.
48. Emerson, *Life and Letters of Charles Russell Lowell*, 410; Walker, *History*, 120. Confederate artilleryman Edward Porter Alexander in his book *Military Memoirs of a Confederate* (pp. 257–59) explained the tactical difficulty of Sedgwick's division's formation when it was hit on its left flank by General Lafayette McLaws: "When troops are in masses, only the outside

men can fire. The outside men are few." Alexander went on to explain that the mass was weak for both the offense and defense "until it can deploy into lines from which every individual can fire free to the front.... It has rarely happened," Alexander continued, "that heavier losses have been incurred more rapidly. Sedgwick himself was wounded, with Dana, one of his brigadiers, and the losses of his division were 2210." However, in the attack McLaws pushed his assault too far. Union artillery punished his men severely. Of the 2,883 men who went into action 1,103 became casualties.

49. Johnson and Buel, vol. 2, 598; Palfrey, *The Antietam and Fredericksburg*, 90; Walker, *History*, 120.

50. Crary, *Dear Belle*, 157; *O.R.*, s. 1, vol. 19, part 1, 309–10.

51. Rafuse, 317.

52. *O.R.*, s. 1, vol. 19, part 1, 279, 407.

53. Harsh, *Taken at the Flood*, 413–14; S.S. Sumner, "The Antietam Campaign"; McCaul, *The Mechanical Fuze*, 72–73.

54. Sparks, *Inside Lincoln's Army*, 146, 151.

55. Sears, *George B. McClellan*, 309.

56. Johnson and Buel, 637–39; *O.R.*, s. 1, vol. 19, part 1, 66; part 2, 348–49; Cleaves, *Meade of Gettysburg*, 79.

57. Woodworth, *Leadership and Command*, 116–18; Harsh, *Taken at the Flood*, 387.

58. Goss, *Recollections of a Private*, 106.

59. Alexander, 251.

60. Johnson and Buel, vol. 2, 643.

61. Bundy, *The Nature of Sacrifice*, 245–46.

62. Palfrey, *The Antietam and Fredericksburg*, 88; Walker, *History*, 102; Woodworth, *Leadership and Command*, 114.

63. Bruce, *The Twentieth Regiment*, 167–68.

64. Sears, *Landscape Turned Red*, 239–40, 244–45; Sears, *McClellan*, 309–10, 313.

65. Nevins, *A Diary of Battle*, 112, 113; Catton, *This Hallowed Ground*, 166–67; Wert, "Disaster in the West Woods."

66. Krick, "The Army of Northern Virginia in September 1862," 53.

67. Greene, "I Fought the Battle Splendidly," 70.

68. Johnson and Buel, vol. 2, 643.

69. Harsh, *Taken at the Flood*, 386–87.

Chapter 17

1. Teall, *Papers*, November 7, 1862.

2. Woodworth, *Leadership and Command*, 143–44.

3. Marvel, *Burnside*, 165–67; Johnson and Buel, eds., *Battles and Leaders*, vol. 3, 107; Alexander, *Military Memoirs*, 285; N.M. Curtis, *From Bull Run to Chancellorsville*, 222–23.

4. Nevins, *A Diary of Battle*, 131–32.

5. *O.R.*, s. 1, vol. 21, 85–86.

6. A.L. Long, *Memoirs of Robert E. Lee*, 233–34.

7. Freeman, *R.E. Lee*, vol. 2, 434.

8. Teall, *Papers*, November 21, 1862.

9. Sparks, *Inside Lincoln's Army*, 179–80.

10. *O.R.*, s. 1, vol. 21, 103.

11. Marvel, *Burnside*, 169–70.

12. Crumb and Dhalle, *No Middle Ground*, 92.

13. O'Reilly, *The Fredericksburg Campaign*, 24.

14. Johnson and Buel, vol. 3, 107–09.

15. Teall, *Papers*, November 25, 1862.

16. Marvel, *Burnside*, 171–72; Jordan, *Winfield Scott Hancock*, 61; O'Reilly, *The Fredericksburg Campaign*, 53–54.

17. Teall, *Papers*, December 10, 1862.

18. Marvel, *Burnside*, 172; Meade, *Life and Letters*, vol. 1, 351.

19. De Borchgrave, *Villard*, 207.

20. Malles, ed., *Bridge Building*, 108; O'Reilly, *The Fredericksburg Campaign*, 57–58.

21. Malles, ed., *Bridge Building*, 109; Oates, *Woman of Valor*, 109–10.

22. Oates, *Woman of Valor*, 109–10.

23. Marvel, *Burnside*, 175.

24. Tate, "The Delicate and Dangerous Work of Placing Pontoon Bridges," 8; Marvel, *Burnside*, 176.

25. Crumb and Dhalle, 91.

26. Alexander, 291–92; Sparks, 187.

27. O'Reilly, *The Fredericksburg Campaign*, 294–95; Crary, *Dear Belle*, 176.

28. Allan, *Stonewall Jackson, Robert E. Lee and the Army of Northern Virginia*, 470.

29. Marvel, *Burnside*, 179–80; O'Reilly, *The Fredericksburg Campaign*, 119–126; Sparks, 189.

30. Priest, *Captain James Wren's Diary*, 94–95.

31. Marvel, *Burnside*, 189; O'Reilly, *The Fredericksburg Campaign*, 273–75.

32. Crumb and Dhalle, 95–96.

33. Teall, *Papers*, December 13, 1862.

34. Scott, ed., *Memoirs*, 404, 406.

35. Gibbon, *Recollections*, 104–05.

36. O'Reilly, *The Fredericksburg Campaign*, 443–47; Stine, *History of the Army of the Potomac*, 285–87.

37. O'Reilly, *The Fredericksburg Campaign*, 458–59.

38. Ford, *A Cycle of Adams Letters, 1861–1865*, 250.

39. Laas, *Wartime Washington*, 236.

40. O'Reilly, *The Fredericksburg Campaign*, 472; Teall, *Papers*, January 8, February 3, 1863.

41. O'Reilly, *The Fredericksburg Campaign*, 491; *O.R.*, s. 1, vol. 21, 1005.

42. Crumb and Dhalle, *No Middle Ground*, 108.

43. Winslow, *General John Sedgwick*, 59–60.

Epilogue

1. *Syracuse Journal*, December 10, 1880; *Syracuse Courier*, December 11, 1880.

2. Phister, *Statistical Record of the Armies of the United States*, 193–97.

3. *New York Times*, August 25, 1912.

4. *New York Times*, March 7, 1932, and July 27, 1937.

5. Altshuler, *Cavalry Yellow and Infantry Blue*, 324.

6. Heller and Stofft, eds., *America's First Battles, 1776–1965*, 132.

Bibliography

Primary and Secondary Sources

Abert, James William. *Expedition to the Southwest: An 1845 Reconnaissance of Colorado, New Mexico, Texas and Oklahoma.* Lincoln: University of Nebraska Press, 1999.

Alexander, Edward P. *Military Memoirs of a Confederate: A Critical Narrative.* New York: Charles Scribner's Sons, 1907.

Allan, William. *Stonewall Jackson, Robert E. Lee, and the Army of Northern Virginia, 1862.* New York: Da Capo, 1995.

Altshuler, Constance W. *Cavalry Yellow and Infantry Blue: Army Officers in Arizona Between 1851 and 1886.* Tucson: Arizona Historical Society, 1991.

Appleton, William Sumner. *Record of the Descendants of William Sumner of Dorchester, Mass., 1636.* Boston: David Clapp and Son, 1879.

Armstrong, Marion V., Jr. "A Failure of Command? A Reassessment of the Generalship of Edwin V. Sumner and the Federal II Corps at the Battle of Antietam." In *Leadership and Command in the American Civil War*, ed. Steven E. Woodworth, pp. 75–76. Campbell, CA: Savas Woodbury, 1996.

_____. *Unfurl Those Colors! McClellan, Sumner, and the Second Army Corps in the Antietam Campaign.* Tuscaloosa: University of Alabama Press, 2008.

Arnold, James R. *Jeff Davis's Own: Cavalry, Comanches, and the Battle for the Texas Frontier.* Edison, NJ: Castle Books, 2007.

Ball, Durwood. "Scapegoat? Colonel Edwin V. Sumner and the Topeka Dispersal." *Kansas History: A Journal of the Central Plains* 33 (Autumn 2010): 164–83.

Ball, Robert W.D. *Springfield Armory Shoulder Weapons 1795–1968.* Norfolk, VA: ATB, Landmark Specialty Publications, 1997.

Bandel, Eugene. *Frontier Life in the Army, 1854–1861.* Philadelphia: Porcupine, 1974.

Bates, Samuel P. *History of Pennsylvania Volunteers 1861–5.* 5 vols. Harrisburg: State Printers, 1869.

Bauer, K. Jack. *The Mexican War, 1846–1848.* Lincoln: University of Nebraska Press, 1974; reprint, 1992.

Beach, Edward L. *The United States Navy: 200 Years.* New York: Henry Holt, 1986.

Benét, Stephen V. *A Collection of Annual Reports and Other Important Papers, Relating to the Ordnance Department, Taken from the Records of the Office of the Chief of Ordnance, from Public Documents and from Other Sources.* Vol. 1, 1812 to 1844; vol.

2, 1845 to 1860; vols. 3–4, 1860 to 1889. Washington, D.C.: Government Printing Office, 1878–1890.

Benton, James G. *A Course of Instruction in Ordnance and Gunnery.* New York: D. Van Nostrand, 1862; reprint, Thomas Publications, n.d.

Bilby, Joseph G. "Small Arms at Antietam." *The American Rifleman* 160 (July 2012): 51–55.

Birkhimer, William E. *Historical Sketches of the Organization, Administration, Matériel and Tactics of the Artillery, United States Army.* New York: Greenwood, 1968; reprint of 1884 original.

Blanchard, Paula. *Margaret Fuller: From Transcendentalism to Revolution.* Reading, MA: Addison-Wesley, 1987.

Boatner, Mark M., III. *Encyclopedia of the American Revolution.* Mechanicsburg, PA: Stackpole, 1994.

Borneman, Walter R. *Polk: The Man Who Transformed the Presidency and America.* New York: Random House, 2009.

Broadwater, Robert P. *The Battle of Fair Oaks: Turning Point of McClellan's Peninsula Campaign.* Jefferson, NC: McFarland, 2011.

Bruce, George A. *The Twentieth Regiment of Massachusetts Volunteer Infantry 1861–1865.* Boston: Houghton Mifflin, 1906; reprint Butternut and Blue, 1988.

Bundy, Carol. *The Nature of Sacrifice: A Biography of Charles Russell Lowell, Jr., 1835–1864.* New York: Farrar, Straus and Giroux, 2005.

Butler, David F. *United States Firearms: The First Century, 1776–1875.* New York: Winchester, 1971.

"Carlisle Papers." Vols. 1828–1838 and 1838–1857. Archives of Carlisle Barracks, Red Book, Box 6, Folder 20.

Catton, Bruce. *This Hallowed Ground: The Story of the Union Side of the Civil War.* Garden City, NY: Doubleday, 1956.

Chalfant, William Y. *Cheyennes and Horse Soldiers: The 1857 Expedition and the Battle of Solomon's Fork.* Norman: University of Oklahoma Press, 2002.

Chandler, Robert J. "The Velvet Glove: The Army During the Secession Crisis in California, 1860–1861." *Journal of the West* 20 (October 1981): 35–42.

Chapel, Charles E. *U.S. Martial and Semi-Martial Single-Shot Pistols.* New York: Coward-McCann, 1962.

Cleaver, Anne Hoffman, and E. Jeffrey Stann, eds. *Voyage to the Southern Ocean.* Annapolis: Naval Institute Press, 1988.

Cleaver, Randy. "Blunting the Confederate Onslaught: The Pennsylvania Reserves." *Hallowed Ground* 13, no. 2 (Summer 2012): 24.

Cleaves, Freeman. *Meade of Gettysburg.* Dayton, OH: Morningside Bookshop, 1980.

Coit, Margaret L. *John C. Calhoun: American Portrait.* Boston: Houghton Mifflin, 1950; reprint, University of South Carolina Press, 1991.

Cooke, Philip St. George. *The 1862 U.S. Cavalry Tactics.* Mechanicsburg, PA: Stackpole, 2004.

_____. Autographed letter. Facsimile in author's possession.

Crary, Catherine, ed. *Dear Belle: Letters from a Cadet and Officer to His Sweetheart.* Middletown, CT: Wesleyan University Press, 1965.

Cress, Lawrence D., ed. *Dispatches from the Mexican War by George Wilkins Kendall.* Norman: University of Oklahoma Press, 1999.

Crist, Lynda L., Mary S. Dix, and Richard E. Beringer, eds. *The Papers of Jefferson Davis.* Vol. 6, *1856–1860.* Baton Rouge: Louisiana University Press, 1989.

Crumb, Herb S., and Katherine Dhalle. *The Eleventh Corps Artillery at Gettysburg: The Papers of Major Thomas Ward Osborn.* Hamilton, NE: Edmonston, 1991.

_____, and _____. *No Middle Ground: Thomas Ward Osborn's Letters from the Field (1862–1864).* Hamilton, NY: Edmonston, 1993.

Cullen, Joseph P. *The Peninsula Campaign 1862: McClellan and Lee Struggle for Richmond.* New York: Bonanza, 1973.

Curtis, George W., ed. *Correspondence of John Sedgwick, Major-General.* N.p: DeVine, 1902.

Curtis, Newton M. *From Bull Run to Chancellorsville: The Story of the Sixteenth New York Infantry Together with Personal Reminiscences.* New York: G.P. Putnam's Sons, 1906.

Custer, George A. *My Life on the Plains.* Lincoln: University of Nebraska Press, Bison Books, 1972.

Davis, George B., Leslie J. Perry, and Joseph W. Kirkley, eds. *Atlas to Accompany the Official Records of the Union and Confederate Armies.* Washington: Government Printing Office, 1891–1895; reprint, New York: Thomas Yoseloff, 1958.

Davis, William C. *Jefferson Davis: The Man and His Hour.* New York: HarperCollins, 1991.

Dawson, Joseph C., III. *Doniphan's Epic March: The First Missouri Volunteers in the Mexican War.* Lawrence: University Press of Kansas, 1999.

De Borchgrave, Alexandra Villard, and John Cullen. *Villard: The Life and Times of an American Titan.* New York: Nan A. Talese, 2001.

De Trobriand, Régis. *Four Years with the Army of the Potomac.* Boston: Ticknor, 1889.

Dell, Christopher. *Lincoln and the War Democrats: The Grand Erosion of Conservative Tradition.* Rutherford, NJ: Farleigh Dickinson University Press, 1975.

Dodge, Richard I. *The Plains of North America and Their Inhabitants.* Wayne R. Kime, editor. Newark: University of Delaware Press, 1989.

Donald, David H. *Charles Sumner and the Coming of the Civil War.* New York: Fawcett Columbine, 1960.

_____. *Lincoln.* New York: Simon & Schuster, 1995.

Dowdey, Clifford, and Louis H. Manarin, eds. *The Wartime Papers of R.E. Lee.* New York: Bramhall House, 1961.

Duane, James C. *Manual for Engineer Troops.* Reprint. New York: Van Nostrand, 1862.

Eckert, Edward K. *In War and Peace: An American Military Anthology.* Belmont, CA: Wadsworth, 1990.

_____, and Nicholas J. Amato, eds. *Ten Years in the Saddle: The Memoir of William Woods Averell, 1851–1862.* San Rafael, CA: Presidio, 1978.

Edwards, G. Thomas. "Holding the Far West for the Union: The Army in 1861." *Civil War History,* December 1968, 313.

Edwards, William B. *Civil War Guns: The Complete Story of Federal and Confederate Small Arms: Design, Manufacture, Identification, Procurement, Issue, Employment, Effectiveness, and Postwar Disposal.* Mechanicsburg, PA: Stackpole, 1962.

Eisenhower, John S.D. *Agent of Destiny: The Life and Times of General Winfield Scott.* New York: Free Press, 1997.

_____. *So Far from God: The U.S. War with Mexico, 1846–1848.* New York: Random House, 1989.

Ellicott, C.J., and Samuel J. Andrews. "The Chronology, Topography, and Archaeology of the Life of Christ." *The North American Review* 97 (July 1863): 74–102.

Elliott, Charles W. *Winfield Scott: The Soldier and the Man.* Reprint. Cranbury, NJ: Scholar's Bookshelf, 1937.

Ellis, Alden C., Jr. *The Massachusetts Andrew Sharpshooters.* Jefferson, NC: McFarland, 2012.

Elting, John R. *Amateurs to Arms: A Military History of the War of 1812.* Chapel Hill, NC: Algonquin, 1991.

Emerson, Edward W. *Life and Letters of Charles Russell Lowell.* Boston: Houghton, Mifflin, 1907.

Etcheson, Nicole. *Bleeding Kansas: Contested Liberty in the Civil War Era.* Lawrence: University of Kansas Press, 2004.

Faulk, Odie B. *Crimson Desert: Indian Wars of the American Southwest.* New York: Oxford University Press, 1974.

Fehrenbach, T.R. *Comanches: The Destruction of a People.* New York: Da Capo, 1994.

Field, Maunsell B. *Memories of Many Men and Some Women.* Onondaga County [New York] Historical Society, 1875.

Finerty, John F. *Warpath and Bivouac: The Big Horn and Yellowstone Expedition.* Lincoln: University of Nebraska Press, 1966.

Fleek, Sherman L. "The Mormon Battalion." *On Point, the Journal of Army History* 17 (Fall 2011): 21–25.

Ford, Worthington C. *A Cycle of Adams Letters, 1861–1865.* Boston: Houghton, Mifflin; 1920; New York: Kraus Reprint, 1969.

Freeman, Douglas S. *Lee's Lieutenants: A Study in Command.* 3 vols. New York: Charles Scribner's Sons, 1944.

_____. *R.E. Lee: A Biography.* 4 vols. New York: Charles Scribner's Sons, 1941.

French, William H., William F. Barry, Henry J. Hunt, and the United States War Department. *Instruction for Field Artillery.* New York: Greenwood Press, 1968 (reprint of 1861 edition).

Gallagher, Gary W., ed. *Fighting for the Confederacy: The Personal Recollections of General Edward Porter Alexander.* Chapel Hill: University of North Carolina Press, 1989.

Gallagher, Kenneth S., and Robert L. Pigeon, eds. *Infantry Regiments of the United States Army.* New York: Military Press, 1986.

Ganoe, William A. *The History of the United States Army.* Ashton, MD: Eric Lundberg, 1964.

Gibbon, John. *Adventures on the Western Frontier.* Bloomington: Indiana University Press, 1994.

_____. *The Artillerist's Manual.* Dayton, OH: Morningside, 1991 (reprint of 1859 edition).

_____. *Personal Recollections of the Civil War.* Dayton, OH: Morningside, 1978 (reprint of 1928 edition).

Gluckman, Arcadi. *United States Muskets, Rifles and Carbines.* Buffalo, NY: Ulbrich, 1948.

Goldman, Henry H. "Southern Sympathy in Southern California, 1860–1865." *Journal of the West* 4 (October 1965): 577–586.

Goodwin, Doris Kearns. *Team of Rivals: The Political Genius of Abraham Lincoln.* New York: Simon Schuster, 2005.

Goss, Warren Lee. *Recollections of a Private: A Story of the Army of the Potomac.* New York: Thomas Y. Crowell, 1890; reprint, Time-Life Books, 1984.

Govan, Gilbert, and James Livingwood. *Joseph E. Johnston, C.S.A.: A Different Valor.* New York: Smithmark, 1995 (reprint of 1956 edition).

Greene, A. Wilson. "'I Fought the Battle Splendidly': George B. McClellan and the Maryland Campaign." In *Antietam: Essays on the 1862 Maryland Campaign,* ed. Gary W. Gallagher, pp. 56–83. Kent, OH: Kent State University Press, 1989.

Greener, W.W. *The Gun and Its Development.* 9th ed. New York: Bonanza, 1910.

Greiner, John. "Private Letters of a Government Official in the Southwest." *Journal of American History* 4 (1909): 542–53.

Grinnell, George Bird. *The Fighting Cheyennes.* North Dighton, MA: JG Press, 1995.

Hafer, LeRoy R., and Ann W. Hafer. *Relations with the Indians of the Plains.* Glendale, CA: Arthur H. Clark, 1959.

Hagan, Kenneth J., and William R. Roberts, eds. *Against All Enemies: Interpretations of American Military History from Colonial Times to the Present.* New York: Greenwood, 1986.

Hale, Richard W., Jr. *Milton Academy 1798–1948.* Milton, MA: Milton Academy, 1948.

Hamlin, Percy G. *The Making of a Soldier: Letters of General R.S. Ewell.* Richmond: Whittet and Shepperson, 1935.

Harsh, Joseph L. *Taken at the Flood: Robert E. Lee and Confederate Strategy in the Maryland Campaign of 1862.* Kent, OH: Kent State University Press, 1999.

Hart, Albert Bushnell. *Salmon P. Chase.* New York: Chelsea House, 1980 (reprint of 1899 edition).

Hebard, Grace R., and E.A. Brininstool. *The Bozeman Trail.* Vol. 2. Lincoln: University of Nebraska Press, 1990.

Heitman, Francis B. *Historical Register and Dictionary of the U.S. Army, from Its Organization, September 29, 1789, to March 2, 1903.* 2 vols. Washington: Government Printing office, 1903; reprint, Olde Soldier Books, 1988.

Heller, Charles E., and William A. Stofft, eds. *America's First Battles, 1776–1965.* Lawrence: University of Kansas Press, 1986.

Hennessy, John J. *Return to Bull Run: The Campaign and Battle of Second Manassas.* New York: Simon & Schuster, 1993.

Herr, John, and Edward S. Wallace. *The Story of the U.S. Cavalry 1775–1942.* New York: Bonanza, 1984.

Holmes, Kenneth L. *Covered Wagon Women: Diaries and Letters from the Western Trails, 1851.* Vol. 3. Lincoln: University of Nebraska Press, 1984.

Holt, Michael F. *Franklin Pierce.* The American Presidents Series. New York: Henry Holt, 2010.

Holzer, Harold, and Craig L. Symonds, eds. *The New York Times Complete Civil War, 1861–1865.* New York: Black Dog and Leventhal, 2010.

Howard, Oliver O. *Autobiography of Oliver Otis Howard, Major General United States Army.* 2 vols. Freeport, NY: Books for Libraries, 1971.

Hughes, Nathaniel C., Jr. *General William J. Hardee: Old Reliable.* Baton Rouge: Louisiana State University Press, 1992.

Hutton, Paul A. *Soldiers West: Biographies from the Military Frontier.* Lincoln: University of Nebraska Press, 1987.

Hyde, George E. *Life of George Bent: Written from His Letters.* Norman: University of Oklahoma Press, 1968.

Johnson, Curt, and Richard C. Anderson, Jr. *Artillery Hell: The Employment of Artillery at Antietam.* College Station: Texas A&M University Press, 1995.

Johnson, Paul E. *The Early American Republic, 1784–1829.* New York: Oxford University Press, 2007.

Johnson, Robert U., and Clarence C. Buel, eds. *Battles and Leaders of the Civil War.* 4 vols. New York: Century, 1884–87.

Johnson, Timothy D. *A Gallant Little Army: The Mexico City Campaign.* Lawrence: University of Kansas Press, 2007.

Jordan, David M. *Winfield Scott Hancock: A Soldier's Life.* Bloomington: Indiana University Press, 1988.

Kane, Elisha Kent. *Arctic Explorations: The Second Grinnell Expedition in Search of Sir John Franklin 1853, 54, 55.* Chicago: R.R. Donnelley and Sons, 1996.

Kearny, Thomas. *General Philip Kearny: Battle Soldier of Five Wars.* New York: G.P. Putnam's Sons, 1937.

Kreiser, Christine M. "7 Days that Made Robert E. Lee an Icon." *America's Civil War* 25 (May 2012): 50–55.

Krick, Robert K. "The Army of Northern Virginia in September 1862: Its Circumstances, Its Opportunities, and Why It Should Not Have Been at Sharpsburg." In *Antietam: Essays on the 1862 Maryland Campaign,* ed. Gary W. Gallagher, pp. 56–83. Kent, OH: Kent State University Press, 1989.

Laas, Virginia J. *Wartime Washington: The Civil War Letters of Elizabeth Blair Lee.* Chicago: University of Illinois Press, 1991.

Lee, Fitzhugh. *General Lee.* Greenwich, CT: Fawcett, 1964.

Livingston, Phil, and Ed Roberts. *War Horse: Mounting the Cavalry with America's Finest Horses.* Albany, TX: Bright Sky, 2003.

Long, A.L. *Memoirs of Robert E. Lee: His Military and Personal History Embracing a Large Amount of Information hitherto Unpublished.* New York: J.M. Stoddart, 1886.

Long, Eli. "Journals of the Cheyenne Expedition of 1857, Monday May 18, 1857 through Monday, Sept. 14, 1857." U.S Army Military History Institute, Carlisle, PA.

Long, William W. *A Biography of Major General Edwin Vose Sumner, U.S.A., 1797–1863.* Ann Arbor, MI: University Microfilms, 1971.

Longfellow, Henry W. *The Letters of Henry Wadsworth Longfellow.* 6 vols. Ed. Andrew Hilen. Cambridge, MA: The Belknap Press of the Harvard University Press, 1972.

Longstreet, James. *From Manassas to Appomattox: Memoirs of the Civil War in America.* Millwood, NY: Kraus Reprint, 1976.

Lowe, Percival G. *Five Years a Dragoon ('49 to '54) and Other Adventures on the Great Plains.* Norman: University of Oklahoma Press, 1991.

Malles, Ed, ed. *Bridge Building in Wartime: Colonel Wesley Brainerd's Memoir of the 50th New York Volunteer Engineers.* Knoxville, TN: University of Tennessee Press, 1997.

Marvel, William. *Burnside.* Chapel Hill: University of North Carolina Press, 1991.

Maury, Dabney H. *Recollections of a Virginian in the Mexican, Indian and Civil War.* 1894.

McAulay, John D. *Civil War Pistols.* Lincoln, RI: Andrew Mowbray, 1992.

McCaffrey, James M., ed. *"Surrounded by Dangers of All Kinds": The Mexican War Letters of Lieutenant Theodore Laidley.* Denton: University of North Texas Press, 1997.

McCall, George A. *Letters from the Frontiers.* Gainesville: University Press of Florida, 1974.

McCaul, Edward B., Jr. *The Mechanical Fuze and the Advance of Artillery in the Civil War.* Jefferson, NC: McFarland, 2010.

McConnell, William F. *Remember Reno: A Biography of Major General Jesse Lee Reno.* Shippensburg, PA: White Mane, 1996.

McLaughlin, Andrew C. *Lewis Cass.* American Statesmen Series. New York: Chelsea House, 1980 (reprint of 1899 edition).

Meade, George G. *The Life and Letters of General George Gordon Meade.* 2 vols. New York: Charles Scribner's Sons, 1913.

Merk, Frederick. *Manifest Destiny and Mission in American History.* Cambridge: Harvard University Press, 1995 (reprint of 1963 edition).

Meyer, Howard N., ed. *The Magnificent Activist: The Writings of Thomas Wentworth Higginson.* Da Capo, 2000.

Miller, Robert R., ed. *The Mexican War Journal and Letters of Ralph W. Kirkham.* College Station: Texas A&M University Press, 1991.

Miller, William J. "I Only Wait for the River: McClellan and His Engineers on the Chickahominy." In *The Richmond Campaign of 1862: The Peninsula and the Seven Days,* ed. Gary W. Gallagher, pp. 44–65. Chapel Hill: University of North Carolina Press, 2000.

Monnett, John H. *The Battle of Beecher Island and the Indian War of 1867–1869.* Niwot: University Press of Colorado, 1992.

Morris, John D. *Sword of the Border: Major General Jacob Jennings Brown 1775–1828.* Kent, OH: Kent State University Press, 2000.

Mullis, Tony R. "The Dispersal of the Topeka Legislature: A Look at Command and Control (C2) During Bleeding Kansas." *Kansas History: A Journal of the Central Plains* 27 (Spring–Summer 2004): 62–75.

Murfin, James V. *The Gleam of Bayonets: The Battle of Antietam and the Maryland Campaign of 1862.* New York: Bonanza, 1965.

Nevins, Allan. *A Diary of Battle: The Personal Journals of Colonel Charles S. Wainwright, 1861–1865.* New York: Harcourt, Brace and World, 1962.

Nichols, Roy F. *Franklin Pierce: Young Hickory of the Granite Hills.* Philadelphia: University of Pennsylvania Press, 1958.

Niven, John. *John C. Calhoun and the Price of Union: A Biography.* Baton Rouge: Louisiana State University Press, 1988.

_____. *Salmon P. Chase: A Biography.* New York: Oxford University Press, 1995.

Nosworthy, Brent. *The Bloody Crucible of Courage: Fighting Methods and Combat Experience of the Civil War.* New York: Carroll and Graf, 2003.

Oates, Stephen B. *To Purge This Land with Blood: A Biography of John Brown.* Amherst, MA: University of Amherst Press, 1984.

_____. *A Woman of Valor: Clara Barton and the Civil War.* New York: Macmillan, 1994.

O'Reilly, Francis A. *The Fredericksburg Campaign: Winter War on the Rappahannock.* Baton Rouge: Louisiana State University Press, 2003.

Palfrey, Francis W. *The Antietam and Fredericksburg.* New York: C. Scribner's Sons, 1882.

Parrott, R.P. *Ranges of Parrott Guns, and Notes for Practice.* New York: D. Van Nostrand, 1863; reprint Dean S. Thomas, 1986.

Patterson, Gerard A. *From Blue to Gray: The Life of Confederate General Cadmus M. Wilcox.* Mechanicsburg, PA: Stackpole, 2001.

Peck, Robert M. "Recollections of Early Times in Kansas Territory." *Collection of the Kansas State Historical Society* 16 (1923–1925): 484–507.

Pfanz, Donald C. *Richard S. Ewell: A Soldier's Life.* Chapel Hill: University of North Carolina Press, 1998.

Philbrick, Nathaniel. *Sea of Glory.* New York: Viking, 2003.

Phipps, Michael, and John S. Peterson. *"The Devil's To Pay": Gen. John Buford, USA.* Gettysburg, PA: Farnsworth Military Impressions, 1995.

Phister, Frederick. *Statistical Record of the Armies of the United States.* New York: Jack Brussel, n.d.

Powell, William H. *The Fifth Army Corps (Army of the Potomac).* Dayton, OH: Morningside Bookshop, 1984 (reprint of 1895 edition).

Priest, John M. *Captain James Wren's Diary from New Bern to Fredericksburg.* Shippensburg, PA: White Mane, 1990.

Rafuse, Ethan S. *McClellan's War.* Bloomington: Indiana University Press, 2005.

Remini, Robert V. *At the Edge of the Precipice: Henry Clay and the Compromise that Saved the Union.* New York: Basic Books, 2010.

_____. *Henry Clay: Statesman for the Union.* New York: W.W. Norton, 1991.

Rhea, Gordon C. *The Battles for Spotsylvania Court House and the Road to Yellow Tavern May 7–12, 1864.* Baton Rouge: Louisiana State University Press, 1997.

Robinson, Charles M., ed. *The Diaries of John Gregory Bourke.* Vol. 1, *November 20, 1872–July 28, 1876.* Denton: University of North Texas Press, 2003.

Roland, Charles P. *Albert Sidney Johnston: Soldier of Three Republics.* Lexington: University Press of Kentucky, 2001.

Roy, Eugene. "Un Quebecois Dans L'Armee Des Etats-Unis." *Saguenayensia* 35 (July 1993): 3–20.

Russell, Carl P. *Firearms, Traps and Tools of the Mountain Man.* New York: Alfred A. Knopf, 1967.

Schaff, Morris. *The Spirit of Old West Point, 1858–1862.* Boston: Houghton, Mifflin, 1907.

Schlesinger, Arthur M., Jr. *The Age of Jackson.* Boston: Little, Brown, 1945.

Schlissel, Lillian. *Women's Diaries of the Western Journey.* New York: Schocken, 1982.

Scott, Robert G., ed. *The Memoirs, Journals, and Civil War Letters of Orlando B. Willcox.* Kent, OH: Kent State University Press, 1999.

Seabrook, S.L. "Expedition of Col. E.V. Sumner against the Cheyenne Indians, 1857." *Kansas Historical Collection,* 1923–1925, 16 (1925): 306–315.

Sears, Stephen W. *George B. McClellan: The Young Napoleon.* New York: Ticknor and Fields, 1988.

_____. *Landscape Turned Red: The Battle of Antietam.* New York: Ticknor and Field, 1983.

_____, ed. *The Civil War Papers of George B. McClellan: Selected Correspondence 1860–1865.* New York: Ticknor and Fields, 1989.

Secretaries of War Reports. In *Message from the President of the United States to the Two Houses of Congress at the Commencement of the_____-Congress.* Twenty-Sixth Congress, both sessions, Twenty-Seventh Congress, all sessions.

Semmes, Raphael. *Memoirs of Service Afloat.* Secaucus, NJ: Blue and Gray Press, 1987.

Sparks, David S., ed. *Inside Lincoln's Army: The Diary of General Marsena Rudolph Patrick, Provost Marshal General, Army of the Potomac.* New York: Thomas Yoseloff, 1964.

Spiller, Roger J., Joseph G. Dawson, III, and T. Harry Williams, eds. *Dictionary of American Military Biography.* 3 vols. Westport, CT: Greenwood, 1984.

Stampp, Kenneth M. *America in 1857: A Nation on the Brink.* New York: Oxford University Press, 1990.

Stanley, Francis L.C. *E.V. Sumner: Major-General United States Army, 1797–1863.* Borger, TX: Jim Hess, 1968.

Stine, J.H. *History of the Army of the Potomac.* Washington: Gibson Bros., 1893.

Stockbridge, V.D. *Digest of U.S. Patents Relating to Breech Loading and Magazine Small Arms, 1836–1873.* Washington: 1874; reprint, N. Flayderman, 1963.

Storrow, Samuel A. "The North-West in 1817." In *Report and Collections of the State Historical Society of Wisconsin,* vol. 6, ed. Lyman C. Draper and Reuben G. Thwaites, pp. 169–81. Madison: Wisconsin State Historical Society, 1872.

Stuart, James Ewell Brown. *Papers, 1850–1908.* Mss 1ST 923c2. Virginia Historical Society. Richmond, Virginia.

Styple, William B., ed. *Our Noble Blood: The Civil War Letters of Major-General Régis de Trobriand.* Kearny, NJ: Belle Grove, 1997.

Sully, Langdon. *No Tears for the General.* Palo Alto, CA: American West Publishing, 1974.

Sumner, Edwin Vose. Papers. Onondaga Historical Association, Syracuse New York.

Sumner, Samuel S. "The Antietam Campaign." *Papers of the Military Historical Society of Massachusetts,* vol. 14, *1918,* pp. 5–18.

Tap, Bruce. *Over Lincoln's Shoulder: The Committee on the Conduct of the War.* Lawrence: University Press of Kansas, 1998.

Tate, Thomas K. "The Delicate and Dangerous Work of Placing Pontoon Bridges Fall to the Corps of Engineers." *America's Civil War* 6 (May 1993): 8.

_____. *From Under Iron Eyelids: The Biography of James Henry Burton, Armorer to Three Nations.* Bloomington, IN: AuthorHouse, 2005.

_____, ed. *Col. Frank Huger, C.S.A.: The Civil War Letters of a Confederate Artillery Officer.* Jefferson, NC: McFarland, 2011.

Taylor, Emerson G. *Gouverneur Kemble Warren: Life and Letters of an American Soldier.* Boston: Houghton Mifflin, 1932; reprint 1988.

Teall, William W. Teall. *Papers, 1862–1864.* V-K-@, Box 1 folder 1–4. Accession Number 554. Tennessee State Library and Archives.

Tousey, Thomas G. *Military History of Carlisle and Carlisle Barracks.* Richmond, VA: Dietz, 1939.

Trafzer, Clifford E. "Politicos and Navajos." *Journal of the West* 13 (October 1974): 3–16.

Tucker, Glenn. *Hancock the Superb.* Dayton, OH: Morningside Bookshop, 1980.

United States Congress Joint Committee on the Conduct of the War. *Army of the Potomac.* 2 volumes. Millwood, NY: Kraus Reprint, 1977.

United States War Department. *Atlas to Accompany the Official Records of the Union and Confederate Armies*. Washington, D.C.: Government Printing Office, 1891–1895. Reprint, New York: Thomas Yoseloff, 1958.

_____. *War of the Rebellion: A Compilation of the Official Records of the Union and Confederate Armies*. Washington, D.C.: The Government Printing Office, 1888. Cited in text as O.R.

Utley, Robert M. *Frontiersmen in Blue: The United States Army and the Indians, 1848–1865*. Lincoln: University of Nebraska Press, 1967.

Villard, Oswald G. *John Brown: A Biography Fifty Years After*. Boston: Houghton Mifflin, 1910.

Vose, Ellen, ed. *Robert Vose and His Descendants*. Stroughton, MA: private printing, 1932.

Wade, Mason, ed. *The Journals of Francis Parkman*. 2 vols. New York: Harper and Brothers, 1947.

Walker, Francis A. *History of the Second Army Corps in the Army of the Potomac*. Gaithersburg, MD: Butternut, 1985 (reprint of 1887 edition).

Warren, L.P.D. "A History of Officer Procurement and the Development of the Officer Corps." Unpublished monograph, 1947. Department of the Army, Center of Military History.

Webb, Alexander S. *The Peninsula: McClellan's Campaign of 1862*. New York: Charles Scribner's Sons, 1881.

Weigley, Russell F. *History of the United States Army*. Bloomington: Indiana University Press, 1984.

Welcher, Frank J. *The Union Army, 1861–1865: Organization and Operations*. Vol. 1: *The Eastern Theater*. Bloomington: Indiana University Press, 1989.

Wells, Gideon. *Diary of Gideon Wells*. 3 vols. Boston: Houghton Mifflin, 1911.

Wert, Jeffery D. "Disaster in the West Woods." *Civil War Times* (October 2002): 32–40.

Wetherington, Ronald K. "Cantonment Burgwin." *New Mexico Historical Review* 81 (October 2006): 391–411.

Wheeler, Joe. *Abraham Lincoln: A Man of Faith and Courage*. New York: Howard, 2008.

Wilcox, Cadmus M. *History of the Mexican War*. Washington, D.C.: Church News, 1892.

Wilentz, Sean, and Johnathan H. Earle, eds. *Major Problems in the Early Republic, 1787–1848*. Boston: Houghton Mifflin, 2008.

Wilkes, Charles. *Autobiography of Rear Admiral Charles Wilkes, U.S. Navy 1798–1877*. Washington: Naval History Division, 1978.

Williams, Alpheus, General. *From the Cannon's Mouth*. Lincoln: University of Nebraska Press, 1995.

Williams, Frances L. *Matthew Fontaine Maury: Scientist of the Sea*. New Brunswick: Rutgers University Press, 1963.

Williams, T. Harry. *The History of American Wars from 1745 to 1918*. Baton Rouge: Louisiana State University Press, 1981.

Winslow, Richard E. III. *General John Sedgwick: The Story of a Union Corps Commander*. Novato, CA: Presidio, 1982.

Wise, Jennings C. *The Long Arm of Lee*. 2 vols. Lincoln: University of Nebraska Press, 1991.

Wolseley, Garnet J. "An English View of the Civil War, II." *North American Review* 149 (July 1889).

Woodward, C. Vann, ed. *Mary Chestnut's Civil War*. New Haven: Yale University Press, 1981.

Woodworth, Steven E. *Manifest Destinies*. New York: Alfred Knopf, 2010.

_____, ed. *Leadership and Command in the American Civil War*. Campbell, CA: Savas Woodbury, 1996.

Wooster, Robert. *The Military and United States Indian Policy 1865–1903.* Lincoln: University of Nebraska Press, 1988.

Yee, Gary. *Sharpshooters 1750–1900: The Men, Their Guns, Their Story.* Broadmore, CA: 2009.

Zuver, Paul E. *A Short History of Carlisle Barracks.* 1934. Collection of the United States Army Military History Institute, Carlisle, PA.

Newspapers and Periodicals

Alexandria Gazette, Alexandria, VA.

Augusta Chronicle, Augusta, GA.

Barre Gazette, Barre, MA.

Charleston Courier, Charleston, SC.

Cincinnati Enquirer, Cincinnati, OH.

Cleveland Plain Dealer, Cleveland, OH.

Daily National Intelligencer, Washington, D.C.

Farmer's Cabinet, Amherst, NH.

Harper's New Monthly Magazine.

International Magazine of Literature, Arts and Science, The.

Morning Oregonian, Portland, OR.

New London Democrat, New London, CT.

New York Herald, New York, NY.

Newport Mercury, Newport, RI.

North American Review, The.

Onondaga Standard, Syracuse, NY.

Philadelphia Inquirer, Philadelphia, PA.

Providence Evening Press, Providence, RI.

Richmond Whig, Richmond, VA.

Scientific American.

Syracuse *Courier, Daily Journal, Journal, and Standard*, Syracuse, NY.

Index

223